£6.95.

To be

The Thirties: Fiction, Poetry, Drama

Edited by

WARREN FRENCH

SECOND EDITION, REVISED

everett/edwards,inc.

post office box 1060 / deland, florida 32720

Library of Congress Cataloging in Publication Data

French, Warren G.   1922-
  The thirties.

  Bibliography: p.
  Includes index.
    1. American literature—20th century—History and criticism—Addresses, essays, lectures. I. Title.
PS221.F68 1976   810'.9'0052   75-45270
ISBN 0-912112-08-5

In appreciation,
we respectfully
dedicate to

CLARENCE GOHDES

this survey
of the writings
of the decade
during which he
began his long and
discerning editorial
services to
American literature

Contents

The Thirties: Fiction, Poetry, Drama

General Introduction

"A cold coming we had of it." T. S. Eliot's Magi is describing the wintry trip to the Christ-child's manger, but the remark might well have been made by anyone looking back on the perilous passage through the Thirties.

The beginning and end of few decades can be fixed with such doleful precision. On October 24, 1929, the bottom dropped out of the stock market, ending the "get-rich-quick" dreams of millions and plunging this nation and the world into a decade of economic depression, political turbulence, and social panacea-seeking. Only a few weeks short of ten years later, on September 3, 1939, Hitler unleashed his *blitzkrieg* on Poland, ending the years of temporizing and restoring financial prosperity at the expense of holocaust.

Most people would like to forget the major events of the 30s, recall wistfully instead Glenn Miller and Mae West, Amos 'n Andy and Fala. Few like to be reminded that the trademarks of the era were the breadline, the apple stand, the WPA shovel, the siege of Madrid, the scrapped treaty. For Americans there were small rewards: evenings with Astaire and Rogers, Nelson Eddy and Jeannette MacDonald for a quarter; the old *Saturday Evening Post* for a nickel and the new *Life* for a dime; Sally Rand at the Century of Progress; the vision of a brave new world inside the Perisphere at the New York World's Fair. Many lacked, however, even the small price of escape. It was a dark time.

Yet like many times of travail, it produced a triumphant literature. Far from being disillusioned by economic and political catastro-

1

phe, writers were galvanized into action. They, after all, had experienced their disillusionment earlier. They had not been taken in by the sham glories of the twenties; Eliot, Fitzgerald, O'Neill had tried to penetrate the armor of our complacency. The depression years were for them, in fact, a kind of unsought vindication. Poetry fared worst. The teens and twenties had been years of extraordinary advance, and most young writers during the 30s remained too much under the influence of Eliot's *The Waste Land* to find their own voices in the actual waste land the world had become. Attempts, too, to press poets into the uncongenial defense of ideologies choked their song.

The drama and novel, however, flourished as rarely before. Eugene O'Neill had liberated the American stage from the melodramatic clichés of the nineteenth century without, like Eliot, overwhelming the initiative of his successors. Drama, furthermore, could serve with vivid effectiveness the purposes of timely propaganda. The novel proved the ideal vehicle for recording and attempting to structure the chaotic flux of the cheerless years. Writers and readers alike had time for contemplation that they were to lack in the next frenetic decade.

This book is an unsystematic introduction to the generally exciting American literature of a generally depressing decade. Rather than attempt to chronicle with pedantic thoroughness the principal literary productions of the 30s, we have brought together a series of short, we hope insightful, essays to stir the memories of those who lived through the decade and kindle the interest of those who did not experience it and are just beginning to discover its literature. Our approach is that of an enthusiastic guest at a rich banquet, darting from dish to dish to sample what entices him rather than that of a dieting ascetic taking an inventory of the groaning board.

The collection has also, quite unintentionally, developed into a kind of "sampler" of varieties of critical essays. Although the contributors had free rein to shape their own essays, their temperaments inevitably led them to considerations of differing breadth and intensity. Looking over the finished collection, one finds that it serves to show the surprisingly diversified possibilities of a seemingly restricted form—the short, tightly organized critical essay.

The contributions run from Kingsley Widmer's staccato exploration of all Nathanael West's increasingly highly regarded novels to Sheldon Grebstein's intensive focussing upon one short work as representative of Hemingway's accomplishments in the 30s. Donald

Sheehan explores in detail in his essay on Wallace Stevens one significant quarrel between poetic theorists; whereas David Pugh takes us on a tour of a whole anthology of the nearly forgotten writings of the "proletarians." Gene Ruoff sums up with a conciseness one would not have thought possible the history of the emergence of the influential "New Criticism," while Frederick J. Hoffmann puts into a wholly new light the stereotyped image of Henry Miller. William Freedman produces a truly enlightening "appreciation" in his celebration of Henry Roth; on the other hand, the editor attempts to stir up controversy with an outrageous thesis about Faulkner's relation to a tradition.

Since the essays provide a diversity of not only matter but manner, we think they will have many uses. We have tried to make the book not only profitable, but enjoyable for the general reader; we also hope, however, that we have produced a collection that can prove especially stimulating in college honors courses, American studies programs, and as a basis for adult study courses. We will have succeeded in our purpose if we in any measure help destroy the artificial barrier between literary study and pleasure reading.

What may distinguish this collection from those often assembled by various hands is that it is the work of friends. All of the contributors were either chosen by the editor on the basis of his admiration for their work or suggested by other contributors. This relationship between the essayists has not, however, resulted in any sameness of tone or viewpoint. The only common denominator of the essays is an informality and briskness that we hope will give the book the sound of a conversation between friends rather than a series of readings in an overheated lecture hall. This is no conclave of experts seeking to "one-up" each other, but a kind of "after-class" gabfest to try to arouse the interest of others in a literature that we have found enjoyable and rewarding.

WARREN FRENCH

Introduction to the Second Edition

All of the essays included in this book have been specially commissioned and have not appeared in print elsewhere in their present form. Gerald Rabkin's essay on the Federal Theatre Project is based on a chapter in his *Drama and Commitment: Politics in the American Theatre of the Thirties* (Indiana University Press, 1964), and Blyden Jackson's "Richard Wright in a Moment of Truth" has been condensed and revised from his article of the same title in *Southern Literary Journal,* Spring, 1971, pages 3-17.

While the other essays have not been changed, the Selected Bibliography has been completely rewritten and brought up to date, with a section added by the editor on the literature relating to the Spanish Civil War.

W. F.

The Thirties — Fiction

Fiction comes first, for this was a great age of the novel. Perhaps only in the 1890s have so many American novelists of enduring stature produced major works during the same decade.

Five groups of writers can be distinguished. Those who had begun to write before World War I did not produce new work that met the challenge of the depression years or matched the accomplishments of the younger men. Dreiser failed to follow up *An American Tragedy* (1925) with any fiction of significance, and devoted the decade to polemics. Willa Cather's novels after *Death Comes for the Archbishop* (1927) are increasingly remote from contemporary concerns. Ellen Glasgow's major novels of the 30s, *The Sheltered Life* and *Vein of Iron,* belong to cycles of earlier work. Gertrude Stein devoted the 30s to autobiography and drama; *Ida,* the only work she describes in the subtitle as a novel, did not appear until 1941. Upton Sinclair took on a variety of targets during the 30s — prohibition, the steel and automobile industries, the Spanish rebels — but failed to generate the excitement he had three decades earlier with *The Jungle.* He was not to discover the magic appeal of the social-minded superman Lanny Budd until 1940. We include no separate discussions of the work of any of these writers during the 30s.

The group that revolutionized American fiction in the turbulent days immediately after World War I also lost its impetus. It is ironic that Sinclair Lewis, after winning the Nobel Prize in 1930, produced no more novels that might have entitled him to consideration for such an honor. *It Can't Happen Here* (1935) still has historical

5

interest as a fictional warning against the forces of fascism then spreading like a fatal virus throughout the nation as well as the world, but it suffers from the same stereotyped characters, thin invention and gross style that cause *Ann Vickers* (1933), *Work of Art* (1934) and *The Prodigal Parents* (1938) to be numbered among Lewis's least regarded productions.

Sherwood Anderson—who many forget survived the decade— published several novels—*Beyond Desire* (1932) and *Kit Brandon* (1936)—but they have found few champions. James Branch Cabell (who had been writing since early in the century, but won widespread attention with *Jurgen* in 1919) continued to produce as prolifically as Lewis; but his brittle allegorical comedies had little appeal for a depression audience, although Edmund Wilson in an essay collected in *The Bit Between My Teeth* pleads eloquently for a rediscovery of the *Smirt-Smith-Smire* trilogy, which he calls "the most opalescent" of dream comedies. Carl Van Vechten published no novels after 1930.

We thus pass over Lewis, Anderson, Cabell to begin our detailed analysis with the earliest established group to make a memorable contribution to the literature of the 30s — the writers of "the lost generation," who had been most largely responsible for the distinctive style and tone of the fiction of the 20s. Even of these only John Dos Passos can be said to have reached the peak of his career in the 30s. While some readers still prefer his *Manhattan Transfer* (1925), his most impressive work remains the three volumes constituting *U. S. A.* (*The 42nd. Parallel, 1919, The Big Money*), which appeared between 1930 and 1936. Our book begins with Eleanor Widmer's analysis of some of the principal achievements and shortcomings of what is at least in terms of its scope and virtuosity a contender for the mythical title of "the great American novel."

Perhaps the soundest thing to say is that the two novelists who have come to symbolize the "lost generation" for Americans — Hemingway and Fitzgerald — seemed, too, to be suffering from the malaise that afflicted Lewis, but rallied as the decade ended: Hemingway to produce his longest and often most admired work, *For Whom the Bell Tolls;* Fitzgerald to leave behind after his "crack-up" a work that can stand with Kafka's *The Trial* and *The Castle* as one of the few great novel fragments, *The Last Tycoon*. Sheldon Grebstein reports on the decade during which Hemingway distressed readers with the novel *To Have and Have Not* (1935) and the play *The Fifth Column* (1938); Jonas Spatz illuminates the relationship between the early and late phases of Fitzgerald's work in the evolution of the novelist's treatment of the "capitalist fable."

What seems unquestionably the major body of American fiction produced during the 30s is the work of three men who published their first major novels in the year that the depression began — Thomas Wolfe, John Steinbeck, and William Faulkner. Wolfe's great first novel, *Look Homeward, Angel,* appeared only a week before the Wall Street crash, and the torrent of words that he produced before his untimely death in 1938 is probably the most graphic and revealing account of a sensitive individual's response to the period that we are likely to possess; certainly no writer was a more cherished spokesman for the adolescents and college undergraduates. The pattern that Richard Walser traces of Wolfe's changing responses to the times very likely reflects the movement from self-centered indifference to social involvement that many young Americans made during the period.

If Wolfe wrote the fictional history of the individual American in the 30s, Steinbeck performed the same task for America's "groupman" during these difficult years. Many writers attempted to portray the impact of the depression upon vast groups of Americans; but we are beginning to recognize that Steinbeck's distinction was his refusal to commit himself to any particular ideology of right or left that might have frustrated his desire, like Doc Burton's in *In Dubious Battle,* "to be able to look at the whole thing." Pascal Covici, Jr., whose father was Steinbeck's editor and defender through the novelist's most productive years, appropriately concentrates on Steinbeck's attempt to avoid the thicket of abstract issues and concentrate on the growth of human "awareness" and its attempts to articulate itself.

Although he has come to be recognized as the outstanding novelist of the period—probably of the first half of this century—William Faulkner held himself sternly aloof from the transient convulsions of the depression years, spent most of the period script-writing in Hollywood. Although some of his finest novels and short stories like *Light in August* and "Dry September" castigate obliquely the rising menace of fascism, Faulkner's work has been properly valued for its timeless rather than its timely qualities. Since these qualities have already been studied in detail in a long, seemingly endless procession of books, the editor has chosen to avoid traveling once again familiar paths and to concentrate on a controversial structural problem that may provide one clue to the genesis of Faulkner's distinguished creations.

The greatest number of essays in this collection concern—quite properly—the fifth group, those "children of the depression" who began to publish during the 30s. "Tough, ironic, hard-boiled" probably best describe the work of the "hard knocks" generation. James T. Farrell, whose *The Young Manhood of Studs Lonigan* was acclaimed as a triumph of naturalism in 1934, is generally regarded as the spokesman for this group; but his work has already been extensively examined by Edgar M. Branch and others, so that we felt it appropriate to focus attention on one of the other "hard-boiled" writers, who have often languished in Farrell's shadow. David Madden, who is readying a collection of essays on the group, might have chosen John O'Hara, Nelson Algren, or Homer McCoy (*They Shoot Horses, Don't They?*), but he singles out for re-evaluation as one of the most perennially interesting of the group, James M. Cain, whose *The Postman Always Rings Twice* (1934) was along with Erskine Caldwell's *God's Little Acre* (1933), one of the most scandalous successes of the early depression years.

Even more scandalous were Henry Miller's two rambling fantasies of Bohemian sexual prowess, *Tropic of Cancer* (1934) and *Tropic of Capricorn* (1939), which until early in the 1960's were available in the author's native land only in the treasured paperbacked editions smuggled in from France, Mexico or China. Although Miller became a center of controversy once again when his daring publisher fought a number of legal battles to prevent the suppression of the first American editions of the *Tropics*, he has mellowed in recent years into the garrulous defender and patron saint of the Beat Generation. In his essay about the *avant-garde* of the threadbare 30s, the distinguished scholar Frederick J. Hoffman, who has made his own critical survey of most of the works this section discusses in his *The Modern Novel in America* (1951), reminds us that Miller was once a young man himself.

If Miller was the John the Baptist of the Beats, the advance man for the even more influential post-war existentialist movement was the United States' first major Negro novelist, Richard Wright. Although best known for *Native Son* (1940), Wright had contributed to the literature of the 30s the powerful short stories in *Uncle Tom's Children* (1938) and *Lawd Today*, which—although not published until 1963—was written at the height of the depression and presents one of the most powerful and objective descriptions in our fiction of the plight of the confused and irresponsible ordinary man caught in the frightening and inescapable realities of the depression. Clifford Hand explores the powerful effort that Wright made through his work and his life to encourage others to shape their own lives creatively.

Because of his concern with this individual creative effort Wright is remembered today, whereas most of the "proletarian novelists," with whom he was once identified, have been forgotten. Their undoing is best summarized in Frederick Hoffman's observation in *The Modern Novel in America* that their novels "relied upon the speciously real and the dogmatically convincing for their effect; but only a very few of their authors survived the passing of that kind of reality and conviction." Once, however, these fiery young radicals flourished, and in their heyday their typical productions were assembled in Granville Hicks' anthology, *Proletarian Literature in the United States.* It is hard to believe that the good, gray critic of the *Saturday Review* once sponsored a movement that included Albert Halper, Albert Maltz, Edward Dahlberg, Josephine Herbst, Jack Conroy, and Meyer Levin. To recapture something of the vanished days of Michael Gold (*Jews Without Money,* 1930) and his cohorts, David Pugh takes us on a tour of the world that Hicks anthologized and explores the motives of those who created it.

The reputation of the proletarian novelists has declined sharply since the 30s; but the stock of other writers—little noticed at the time—has risen. Few writers of the 30s have benefitted as much from the re-examination of their works as Nathanael West, in whose four books are found the seeds of the recently popular "black humor." Because of West's growing importance, his great influence on recent novelists, and his comparative neglect—despite an increasing number of studies recently, one of our most detailed essays is Kingsley Widmer's survey and evaluation of West's brief career not as delineator of the depression, but prophet of the absurd world that lay unguessed beyond it.

Even less known than West during the 30s and for many years afterward was Henry Roth, whose story of a boy growing up on New York's East Side, *Call It Sleep*, found its admirers only in the 1960's. Although three decades old, the novel remains a "new" enough work not yet to have been as firmly placed among the writings of the 30s as most works discussed in this collection. The case of Henry Roth is still open, and William Freedman—who became increasingly enchanted with the novel as he worked on his essay— argues it enthusiastically. Because *Call It Sleep* both appeals to those to whom it recalls the 30s and introduces to a lost world those who never knew it, it reminds us more forcefully than any other single work that the literature of the 30s is both a subject for nostalgia and a living force whose merits have not been completely assessed. Freedman reminds us that great novels are ultimately about individuals, not periods, not issues; he thus provides a fitting "open end" to our rapid survey.

Other novelists might, perhaps should have been represented. The selection has been arbitrary, governed largely by the affections of the contributors. J. P. Marquand's probings of New England life, *The Late George Apley* (1937) and *Wickford Point* (1939), might provide the basis for another survey that should also include James Gould Cozzens' early work, Christopher Morley's sentimental satire of Philadelphia society, *Kitty Foyle,* and James Thurber's *My Life and Hard Times* (1933), ostensibly a collection of comic sketches, but really an episodic novel about man's ability to bounce back from the ravages of the plagues that beset him. Daniel Fuchs' Williamsburg trilogy might be studied along with the works of West and Henry Roth.

Erskine Caldwell, whose earthy works enjoyed their greatest vogue during and immediately after World War II, has been mentioned only in passing, although his *Tobacco Road* and *Journeyman* created almost as much sensation as *God's Little Acre.* Some novelists highly regarded during the 30s, like T. S. Stribling, Louis Bromfield and Pearl Buck (all of whose novels have essentially what Frederick Hoffman calls "a documentary bias") appear no longer of general interest; but there will always be a small but responsive audience for George Santayana's *The Last Puritan* (1935), which stands like a giant isolated boulder in the turbulent stream of the period.

No account of fiction in the 30s could close without at least a passing nod to the two mammoth works that would probably have been the first to leap into the minds of most readers upon mention of the word "novel": Hervey Allen's *Anthony Adverse* (1933) and Margaret Mitchell's *Gone with the Wind* (1936). Scorned by most critics, these behemoths provided what most readers wanted during the 30s—prolonged escape into a more colorful, romantic world than the shabby one about them. We will not really understand how fiction works upon its readers and how the 30s affected individuals until we learn something of the secret of the success of the "big" novels of the period.

WARREN FRENCH

The Lost Girls of U.S.A.:
Dos Passos' 30s Movie

by Eleanor Widmer

John Dos Passos' ambitious trilogy, *U.S.A.*, begins in 1900 and ends with the execution of Sacco and Vanzetti in 1928, but in its social analysis, its strident criticism, its unrelenting delineation of the dispossessed from the monied and the powerless from the powerful, it both anticipates and characterizes the "protest" awareness of the 30s in which it was completed. In both its harsh lines and functional exaggerations, *U.S.A.* now seems to many the repulsively fascinating culmination of the "Thirties Moderne" in literature. Yet, as with much of the history of the 30s, it is more an end than a beginning, part of an insistent past—literary naturalism, embittered traditional American individualism, and, even, the 19th century heroine.

Surely, few of Dos Passos' contemporaries embraced either his vision or design. Himself a youthful exile and world traveller, he chose nothing less than to write of the whole American experience during the first three decades of the 20th century. A patrician by birth and education, he gave his allegiance to Wobblies, Vags and political hostages. Intrinsically disillusioned, he nevertheless carried on his heartbreaking love affair with America through 1800 pages and via four varied techniques in an effort to exorcise his despair over his country.

11

U. S. A. has enormous vitality and range and the modes of presenting the material are cinematically visual and energetic. It is properly toned by The Newsreel, with its headlines, flashes of song and rhetoric, bombast and cliché, which serves as a dissonant, ironic chorus to actual events. The Camera Eye, shyly autobiographical, provides impressionistic sketches of the author from his belated arrival at these shores through his labors for the doomed anarchists. The several dozen biographical sketches, dealing with such diverse, though undeniably American temperaments as Eugene Debs, J. P. Morgan, Frank Lloyd Wright, Thorstein Veblen, Rudolph Valentino and Isadora Duncan, are written in a hard edged, swift prose rarely excelled in the Dos Passos canon. Interspersed and alternated with these other three techniques are the narratives of a dozen major characters whose personal histories reflect the changes and discrepancies in American mores.

No writer of this century better provides us with a sense of place and the harsh, dogged rhythms of travelling and physical mobility than does Dos Passos in *U.S.A.* The whole country appears on the move, with everyone in it shuttling from state to state, from city to city, in a restless, compulsive urge to reify the diversity and sameness of America. Beginning with the initial volume, *The 42nd Parallel,* and the first character, Fainy, we witness a migration that commences in early childhood and ceases presumably at death. Fainy is lowly born in Middletown, Connecticut, spends his bleak childhood in Chicago, takes a job with the sleazy Doc Bingham selling religious tracts and pornographic books throughout the eastern seaboard, rides freights with his socialist pal to Duluth and Winnepeg, gets rolled in Seattle, meets his bride-to-be in San Francisco, helps put out a newspaper for the Wobblies in Goldfield, Nevada, marries and settles in San Diego, leaves his wife for the Mexican revolution via Yuma, El Paso, Juarez, Mexico City, and when last we see him in Vera Cruz, debating whether to stay in Mexico or return to the States, it is with the expectancy that his unfolding remains intertwined with a specific place, either an exotic or common town that symbolizes his destiny.

So strong is Dos Passos in the naming of cities that, with Charlie Anderson, the poor mechanic who begins his "success story" in *The 42nd Parallel* but whose defeat as a financier epitomizes *The Big Money,* whole pages are devoted to parallel identification of places with character and narrative development. Charley drifts from the Twin Cities to Tampico, joins the war, becomes a flyer in Europe, makes a financial fortune in New York, ruins himself in Detroit, and drunkenly engineers his fatal car accident in Miami. No one in *U.S.A* dies in the place he was born, as illustrated poignantly by the Sicilian Sacco and Vanzetti who are hanged in Charlestown, Mass. The magic of place thus becomes the magic—whether for good or evil—of the person or the event, and the contradictions of a burgeoning yet brutal America hypostatizes itself in the mobility of each of the characters.

The strength of *U.S.A.*, therefore, resides in the intertwining of historical events with life histories and specific places, and in conveying with bludgeoning strokes the fatalities of aspiration when confronted with America's naive and curious ability to crush the anonymous and render useless the significant. Nobody escapes unscathed. "It's the system, the goddamn lousy system," says Fainy's Uncle Tim at the beginning of *The 42nd Parallel.* And two volumes later, Mary French, the ardent socialist of *The Big Money,* closes the trilogy narrative with the words, "It's the waste. . . ."

But what lies between this "system" and the "waste"? Doomed men, defeated men, the poor alienated from the wealthy, the powerful from themselves, all caught in a restless, mobile quest, if not for self-identification then for the definition of their country. The city, the small town, the freight cars, the freight ships, the airplanes, the automobiles, are as much the subject of the trilogy as the individual characters. And indeed, Dos Passos' technique of naturalism, with its eye for endless, dispassionate detail, catches America's aggressive materialism enormously well. It is only when coping with his characters that Dos Passos breaks down, for unlike places and concrete objects, people are not brought to life by the mere naming of their parts, and neither logistic mastery, nor the frantic juggling from one locale to another, nor the evocation of sight and smell, can save his characters from their stereotyped conceptions and a basically external and mechanical psychology of response.

Robert Gorham Davis has suggested that Dos Passos was strongly influenced by the montage experiments of early film makers, but it would be a moot point to debate whether American films of the late 20's and early 30's influenced Dos Passos or vice versa. His men are hard drinkers, fast drivers, easy and guileless lovers. Hopping in and out of bed creates no more difficulty than hopping from freight car to limousine; no one suffers a forethought, let alone an afterpang, and regret, remorse, guilt, are relegated to too much bad whiskey or acquiring an unwanted "dose." Admittedly, the zealous application of naturalism denies the premises of more introspective techniques, but in *U.S.A.* the characters are not only stuck with "the smell of cabbages and babies" but with an almost cinematic caricature of their personalities.

J. Ward Morehouse, with his prematurely grey hair and equally shiny aspirations, early molds himself into an expensive Pierce Arrow, and no gesture or act, whether in relation to women or patriotism, violates his rich man's stance; when he has a heart attack he presumably fibrillates dollar bills. Or, take Joey Williams, the seaman, with his crude yearnings and bad luck, who goes from "stinking crate to stinking crate," from forged papers to cuckolding wife, accepting his sordid wanderings and inability to rise over them with the forebearance of a movie lackey. Charley Anderson, of course, with his rags-to-riches stunt, drinks himself to death with the lines and bravado of the early James Cagney, "They thought they had me out on my ass, but I fooled 'em . . . this passin' out's not like sleep, it's like . . . something phoney."

Nor do the intellectuals and labor leaders escape the stigma of the stereotype: invariably they wear glasses, have bad skin, are undernourished in body and quirkishly devoted to ideals. They crawl in and out of gloomy caves, exchanging meeting halls for jails and jails for filthy lodgings with the grim fatalism of John Garfield decrying himself as one of Saturday's children. Defeated, both by the "system" and the "waste," the radicals of *U. S. A.* march by with their rubrics conveniently writ large, lest they be overlooked or misidentified. Naturalism, in Dos Passos' hands, thus becomes the instrument of almost rigid cliché.

Nowhere is the undercutting of character for naturalistic effect more in evidence than in the heroines of *U.S.A.*, those sad victims of female biology. Purportedly dealing with the "new woman" and the influence of World War I and its aftermath on what roughly used to be talked of as "female emancipation," Dos Passos nevertheless handles women with a gentility closely akin to Edwardianism and defeats them by stock situations, lugubrious determinism, and his particular brand of social consciousness *cum* caricature.

In this non-gorgeous, naturalistic bestiary, the most easily disposed of are the extremely wealthy to whom Dos Passos lends neither patience nor authenticity. The two wealthy wives of J. Ward Morehouse veer toward aristocratic idiocy, the first, Annabelle, by her indiscriminate licentiousness, the second, Gertrude, by quickly retiring behind the veil of "female trouble" after the birth of her second child. This malady causes Gertrude to withdraw almost entirely from Morehouse; despite her salmon colored dressing gown and her occasional threats to withhold her money from her husband's public relations interests, she moves like a quickly forgotten shadow out of Morehouse's life.

Dos Passos takes curious delight in the ruse of after-birth illness, for not content to apply it to Gertrude Morehouse, he consigns this exact malady to Gladys Wheatley, the wealthy woman who marries Charley Anderson. No sooner does she bear her second child than Gladys propels Charley into a separate bedroom, and soon into a separate domicile. A carry-over from the 19th century novel, where a dreaded female indisposition eradicated women in droves (most blatantly in Dickens), it becomes an anti-naturalistic device in *U.S.A.,* a creaking *modus vivendi* for disposing of extraneous female characters.

Except for the millionaire's daughters who hide behind their locked bedroom doors, the heroines of *U.S.A.* share in the American Dream of pursuing their identities in cities far away from home, and in their desire "to do good" and to change and re-shape the world. Yet their modernity proves ironic, for their victimization stems from the oldest "system" and the most expected quarter of "waste"—men. Anne Elizabeth, also known as Daughter, one of the prominent heroines of *1919,* meets her downfall, in spite of some exotic trappings, in a manner similar to heroines of gaudy "penny dreadfuls." Born into a monied Texas family, Daughter persuades her father to allow her to study journalism in New York. Presently, she makes headlines by participating in a New Jersey strike, is rushed home to Texas, idles restlessly until she joins a missionary group in Europe. In Italy, she falls in love with Richard Savage, a sometime poet turned opportunist, and though a virgin, Daughter gives herself to him, stirred by his observation, " . . . Do you know what we are, Anne Elizabeth? we're the Romans of the Twentieth Century."

Roman or not, Daughter's first encounter impregnates her, for though Dos Passos may be a political radical he unimaginatively indulges in the standard, historical pitfall for women: illicit love equals pregnancy. While this affair takes place in Rome and Naples, the consequences are no different than for Hardy's milkmaids. Unmoved by Daughter's plight, her lover drops her, and bereft of solutions—illegitimacy does not appear an option for the Dos Passos heroine—Daughter compels a drunken friend to take her up in an airplane which inevitably crashes. The inevitability of defeat in *U.S.A.* is irking enough, but when combined with stock causes, such as an unwanted pregnancy, it moves away from its possibilities for tragedy into melodrama.

Though less dramatic in her defeat, the plight of Mary French of *The Big Money* illustrates Dos Passos' intrinsic design—the indifferent cruelty of men towards women and destiny towards the dedicated. Breaking with her clubwoman mother and identifying with her doctor father who treats the impoverished, homely Mary French throws up her education at Vassar to become a social worker at Hull House. Dogged by bitter frustrations—her ardent efforts for the striking mill hands in Pittsburgh end in a sell-out by the union and the various good works to which she commits herself fail—Mary drifts into an affair with the hypocritical labor leader, George Barrow. Though Barrow prides his knowledge of contraceptives, Mary instantly becomes pregnant and chooses abortion. But her greatest involvements collapse simultaneously: Sacco and Vanzetti are executed despite the efforts of her committee, and Don Stevens, the "comrade" whom she loves and who scorns "bourgeois marriage," marries a co-worker in Russia. To these disasters Mary reacts characteristically—by preparing for a new relief committee and a mass protest rally in Madison Square Garden. Loveless, homeless, as much a replaceable part in the infernal machine of good causes as Ward Morehouse and Charley Anderson are in the machine of high finance, Mary neither questions nor struggles against her heavy-handed fate.

The background against which Mary French operates appears contemporary enough, and the free discussions of her affairs and abortion conveys a deceptively revolutionary texture to *The Big Money,* but Mary French can no more exercise choice than the ill-used Marion Yule of Gissing's *New Grub Street,* or turn principled dedication to anything less savage than that encountered by Maggie Tulliver in Eliot's *Mill on the Floss.* Thus, Don Passos' thousand and one naturalistic details about Mary French can not truly modernize her fundamentally 19th century story.

This ambiguous modernity is re-enforced by the somewhat colorless figure of Janey Williams, the young secretary from Georgetown, who initially reads Arnold Bennett, shortens her skirts and considers herself an advanced bachelor girl, but who inexplicably settles into a dronish existence. No sooner does she become Morehouse's assistant than she relinquishes all thoughts except work, and by the time she reaches Paris during the war, she complains because Parisians sit around cafes and get nothing done. Slavishly devoted to every ridiculous detail of Morehouse's career, Janey Williams represents the Protestant work ethic in its most selfless and leveling form, a creed that sustained cottage industries and early industrialization a half century before.

Dos Passos fares somewhat better with his so-called artistic types, Eleanor Stoddard and her friend Eveline Hutchins, but only in the limited sense, that like the men of *U.S.A.*, they are not so much individuals as cinematic types. Of Eleanor Stoddard we are told, "When she was small, she hated everything." Driven by ambition, she becomes a successful interior decorator, first in Chicago, then in New York, and commences a lifetime, platonic relationship with Ward Morehouse. The archetypal frigid woman, Eleanor Stoddard invariably wears elegant grey dresses with pearls, presides over equally elegant apartments in both New York and Paris, and moves among the wealthy and powerful as if they provided the true patina to her otherwise grey existence. We see Eleanor presiding over endless teas, "her place . . . glittering with chandeliers and cutglass . . . her narrow face smooth and breakable as a piece of porcelain. . . ." When she finally decides to marry after the war, she selects a Russian prince, "the last word in the decorating business," and her soirées become dominated by "a houseful of Russian emigrees in tiaras."

The role of Eleanor Stoddard has appeared in dozens of the Thirties society movies, played by the cool Joan Fontaine or her earlier prototypes, the self-contained, highly motivated social climber whose esthetics are bound up with costly household trivia. We know Eleanor Stoddard only from the outside, by a series of visual tableaux in which we are conscious of the postures and the gestures that represent an illusory, rather than flesh-and-blood, woman.

Eveline Hutchins, on the other hand, though more genuine in her struggle for self-achievement, never manages to discover the hard core of her needs. Like most of the figures in *U.S.A.* she appears victimized by the fortuitous and incapable of coping with each minor defeat that finally compels her to suicide. A dabbler, Eveline starts and soon drops painting, interior decorating, socialism, war relief, free love. Never deeply in love, never out of love, she marries Paul Johnson because he makes her pregnant, returns to New York from Paris where she entertains the *au courant,* and goes from affair to affair in the same haphazard way that she attempts to produce stage plays or sponsor ballets. When her writer-lover of long standing leaves her, she takes an overdose of sleeping pills. Yet her romantic escape into death is no more surprising than her flirtations with art and the arty; neither she nor her commitments are serious, and her melodramatic end, on the very night when she has crowned her achievement as a hostess by entertaining a famous movie star, smacks of the historic cinema, the camera pulling away from the prone body as the party conversation dissolves in the still air.

Perhaps this is why the character of Margo Dowling, the orphan turned movie star is the most successful in the trilogy, for here conception and technique are united—the movie star plays herself, her screen image, and the personification of the American Dream simultaneously. Margo Dowling begins her career under the aegis of her stepmother's second husband who soon rapes her, elopes with a young entertainer from Havana who not only proves to be a homosexual but gives her syphilis, loses her baby, leaves her husband, resumes her career and becomes Charley Anderson's mistress—all before the age of twenty-one. The true whore-with-the-golden-heart, golden-headed Margo rarely complains, and when Charley's death leaves her penniless in Miami, she packs up her stepmother and with her foolish husband disguised as her chauffeur drives to the golden land, California. A chance meeting with her former photographer, now director, proves a double boon: he turns her both into a movie star and into his wife, encouraging her affair with her male co-star for its publicity value. Our last view of Margo is at Eveline Hutchin's party, accompanied by husband and lover, where it is already whispered that her high, reedy voice will cause her failure in "talkies."

Because of its stereotyped elements—the child orphan, the teenage-rape and marriage, the period of mistress before success—it would be possible to take this portrayal of Margo Dowling as satire, except that Dos Passos means it for real. Neither by temperament nor act does Margo ever behave selfishly; her generosity and ability to forgive are indicative of her easy going role. At the same time she is an American, and she believes in getting ahead and in the simple precepts of opportunity. She lives with Charley because he's rich, and marries the director, Margolies, because he's powerful. Vulnerable, corruptible, without standards or scruple, and because and in spite of these, dazzling, she symbolizes and becomes the U.S.A., the big money, the system and the waste of which Dos Passos despairs.

Since the very premise of movie stardom is the synthetic, since the very quality of the American Dream is its false bravura, we can accept in the portrayal of Margo Dowling what is indefensible in Eleanor Stoddard, the interior decorator, or Eveline Hutchins, the dilettante. Perhaps Dos Passos intended socialist Mary French as his outstanding heroine, for she is the last one of whom he wrote before his epilogue, "Vag." But for all her worthiness, Mary French does not have the glamour, the toughness, the resilience and the immorality of Margo Dowling, who is America.

The heroines, lost girls all, as well as the heroes of *U.S.A.* rest on 19th century types and naturalistic techniques which culminate in our standard cinematic images. Inadequately individualized and lacking complex and subtle development, the stereotypes nonetheless merge into a revealing vision of this country. The sordid patterns of defeat and the harsh cadences of the style, with their hyper-visuality of place, poeticize the U.S.A., providing us with an America as recognizable and painfully endearing as an old movie. The experience of reading *U.S.A.* represents just this poetic and cinematic image of America, and in this Don Passos does not fail.

Hemingway's Dark and Bloody Capital

by Sheldon Norman Grebstein

As even Hemingway's most loyal and admiring readers must confess, the 1930s were not, on the whole, the writer's best years. Quantitatively, they were among the most productive of his career, for during this decade Hemingway published his "encyclopedia of bullfighting" *Death in the Afternoon* (1932), a collection of short stories *Winner Take Nothing* (1933), a narrative account of his African big-game hunting expedition *Green Hills of Africa* (1935), the novel *To Have and Have Not* (1937), and a play "The Fifth Column," which was first printed in the collected edition of Hemingway's stories, *The Fifth Column and the First Forty-nine Stories* (1938). The same volume also reprinted four stories which had appeared earlier in periodicals: "The Capital of the World," "Old Man at the Bridge," "The Short Happy Life of Francis Macomber," and "The Snows of Kilimanjaro." In addition to all this Hemingway was at different intervals engaged in journalistic writings, in the early and mid-30s contributing frequent articles to *Esquire,* later in the decade reporting the Spanish Civil War for the North American Newspaper Alliance.

But despite this productivity and despite Hemingway's admirable efforts on behalf of the Spanish Loyalists, which included raising $40,000 on his personal notes for the purchase of ambulances, one nevertheless tends to respond to his work during this period and to the personality so often and so patently a part of it with disappointment at the work and distaste for the man. In too much of this writing, especially *Death in the Afternoon, Green Hills of Africa,* and the *Esquire* essays, Hemingway strutted, postured, and pontificated, maintaining that the *corrida de toros,* the hunting of African game, and deep-sea fishing were consummate human activities, and that as a writer who had already served time for democracy he could do damned well as he pleased.

We must grant, at least in principle, that the writer's choice of material is entirely his own, as we must also grant that the work just mentioned is hardly a total loss. *Death in the Afternoon* is still probably the best book in English about bullfighting, and *Green Hills of Africa* is often informative and entertaining; both, moreover, embody some superbly written passages as well as some exceedingly comic ones. Together with the *Esquire* pieces they also provide a number of valuable insights into Hemingway's literary opinions, worldview, and writing process. Yet whatever the value of these works to *aficionados,* hunters, fishermen, and professional students of Hemingway, we must conclude that they are not art and that they fall far short of the literary gains Hemingway had made in the 20s. We are too often compelled to agree with this seemingly facetious bit of dialogue between Hemingway and his hilariously sober and candid Old Lady in *Death in the Afternoon:*

> *Old lady:* You know I like you less and less the more I know you.
> Madame, it is always a mistake to know an author.

* * *

With this notation of Hemingway's failure in the large works written during the 30s, a failure which includes *To Have and Have Not* (although it is a more serious and interesting failure than the others), we can now attend to his successes and be more profitably instructed by them. If Hemingway was often bad in his longer works, he was perhaps better than ever in his shorter ones. *Winner Take Nothing* contained at least four stories equal to anything he had written: "A Clean, Well-Lighted Place," "A Way You'll Never Be," "The Gambler, the Nun, and the Radio," and "Fathers and Sons." Furthermore, in 1936 Hemingway drew once again upon his experience of Spain and Africa, on this occasion with enormous advantage, to write three stories, "The Snows of Kilimanjaro," "The Short Happy Life of Francis Macomber," and "The Capital of the World," the first two of which are generally acknowledged to be masterpieces. The third of these, "The Capital of the World," is not a masterpiece, but it is a very good story nonetheless. Because it has been virtually ignored by critics (in contrast, "Snows" and "Macomber" have provoked a great deal of commentary), and because it is in tòne, substance, and technique a microcosm of much of Hemingway's writing of the 30s, I will devote the remainder of this essay to a critical analysis of it and also attempt to demonstrate how it is characteristic of Hemingway's career during this period. "Let those who want to save the world," Hemingway said at the end of *Death in the Afternoon*, "if you can get to see it clear and as a whole. Then any part you make will represent the whole if it's made truly." The story is one of those representative parts, truly made.

The fundamental theme of "The Capital of the World" is among the most basic and frequent in Hemingway's stories: the initiation of an innocent into the bitterness of life through suffering. In this case there are, however, significant differences. The hero is not Nick Adams, whose wounds eventually heal and who becomes stronger at the broken places. He is the Spanish boy Paco, one of the very good, very brave, and very gentle people whom the world kills because they cannot be broken. The cause of Paco's death is his excess of courage and illusion. Indeed, so filled with illusion is Paco, who aspires simultaneously to hold a steady job and to be a revolutionary, a good Catholic, and a matador, that he completely lacks the prudence, caution, and restraint necessary for survival. In a sense Paco and his manner of death are ironic reminders of the Swede of Stephen Crane's story "The Blue Hotel," likewise a victim of excessive courage and illusion, or delusion, and likewise the victim of a knife thrust. In the Crane story—and we recall that Crane was one of Hemingway's literary ancestors—the Swede's body, ironically described as "this citadel of virtue, wisdom, and power," "was pierced as easily as if it had been a melon." In the Hemingway story the knife enters Paco "as easily as into a wineskin." Note, also, that in *Green Hills of Africa* Hemingway calls "The Blue Hotel" Crane's best story. While other comparisons could be made between these stories, I do not want to push the matter too far. My point is simply that in the graphic image of the death of the protagonist in each story we have the sense, shared by both Crane and Hemingway, of the transiency of life and the terrible consequences of self-deception.

Paco's rare qualities of innocence, goodness, and courage are played off against the cynicism, fear, degradation, commoness, and aggression of the other characters in the story: the three failed matadors, one of them a coward; the surly dishwasher Enrique, confessedly fearful of the bull's horns, who is the instrument of Paco's death; the arrogant and dissipated picador; the violently anarchical waiter who would destroy all who oppose his politics; the somewhat soiled priests who drink too much; and Paco's very ordinary sisters. All of these survive as if because of their imperfections. Even the sort of man Paco aspires to be, although without perceiving the true character of his idol, the matador who has become afraid after once feeling the bull's horn in his groin, stays alive by dint of his cowardice. None of these characters is made attractive and only Paco is portrayed with Hemingway's compassion, yet at the story's conclusion, and such is its thematic irony, the others are living and Paco is not.

In still another sense "The Capital of the World" is an amplification and dramatization of what Hemingway had rendered discursively in *Death in the Afternoon.* That is, Paco's story illustrates the ethos of a country, Spain, where the bullfight was given such importance because it demanded the ultimate display of *pundonor,* in Hemingway's definition "honor, probity, courage, self-respect and pride in one word." I believe that Hemingway's love for Spain, a love greater and more permanent than for any country but his own, grew so deep because he found its national ethos to be much like his own, formed in war and in the hunt. Paco's death occurs at the end of a terribly brief apprenticeship, different only in detail from the hundreds of deaths which Hemingway tells us occurred in Spain each year in the provincial towns staging their own informal town-square bullfights (*capeas*), when local men and youths faced the bull under the most hazardous conditions. *Pundonor* was their motive, as it is in this story and in such other Hemingway stories of the 30s as "The Undefeated," as it is among Robert Jordan's prime motives in *For Whom the Bell Tolls,* and as it is also the source of Santiago's heroism in *The Old Man and the Sea:* " 'I told the boy I was a strong old man,' he said. 'Now is when I must prove it.' " To take the matter to its limits, I think it probable that *Pundonor* was so vital to Hemingway himself that when he no longer felt able to meet his own self-imposed standards of conduct, he could not bear to live. In his suicide we have the paradox of the simultaneous fulfilment and betrayal of *pundonor*. "The Capital of the World" conveys the identical paradox.

Thematically, then, this story advances the mordant conclusion that to be brave, good, and innocent is to be unfit for life, a conclusion whose somber tone is echoed everywhere in Hemingway's work of the period, notably in the consistently hard-bitten stories of *Winner Take Nothing* (the title is itself evidence), and a conclusion whose specific content is given voice in *Death in the Afternoon*. As Hemingway describes the intricacies of the bullfight in that book, and as he discusses the personal and professional traits of the various toreros, it becomes manifest that one avoids the horns of the bull not by courage alone but by craft and cunning as well. To be still more emphatic, courage without craft is a great danger to any who possesses it. In the Hemingway canon the absence of craft is an intolerable form of innocence. Paco's fatal error, once his courage has placed him in a situation where the bull's horns are to be duplicated by the sharp, heavy knives Enrique has tied to the chair, is merely to place his left foot two inches out of position during the moment of Enrique's charge. In such a situation two inches measure the total length of a human life.

This matter of craft, trenchantly documented by Paco's death, is perhaps the one consistent and profound affirmation in Hemingway's writing of the early and mid 30s. Even as he celebrated the joys of witnessing bullfights, killing kudu, and drinking good wine, as he deplored the state of the world and asserted the necessity of the artist's disengagement from it, and as he rather contemptuously surveyed the literary scene past and present, he was at the same time affirming the writer's fundamental obligation to his discipline and his art. He affirmed it both by direct statement in his discursive prose, and by symbol and dramatic action in his fiction. For example, in *Green Hills of Africa* Hemingway spoke of the extreme possibilities of style, of a "fourth and fifth dimension," which, if attained, "is more important than anything he [the writer] can do." This is a style "more difficult than poetry . . . a prose that has never been written." It is a style durable enough to last forever.

Furthermore, Hemingway's preoccupation with craft encompassed other than purely literary concerns. Among the reasons for Hemingway's fascination with the bullfight and with hunting was the high degree of expertise each sport demanded. As in "The Capital of the World," one who faced dangerous game without the requisite ability, discipline, and technical skill, risked annihilation. Thus in the writing of these years Hemingway's view of his art, and of art in general, became inextricably intertwined with the aesthetics of the bullfight, and with shooting well. In *Death in the Afternoon* he wrote: "I know no modern sculpture, except Brancusi's, that is in any way the equal of the sculpture of modern bullfighting." Note, too, a fact not commonly observed in "The Short Happy Life of Francis Macomber": Macomber's regeneration as a man, his achievement of *pundonor,* begins when he makes a number of excellent shots at buffalo, under not especially perilous circumstances. Expertness with a rifle (and there are, of course, sexual overtones here) is requisite to manhood.

But craft, to be completely valid, must be tested not merely in practice, private, and safety. In his fantasies Paco has already achieved the perfect performance with the bull. However, just as the writer undergoes his test in public, judged by the critics and the audience in his competition with all the great writers who have preceded him, with extinction his lot if he fails, and just as the hunter must finally prove his skill against the charging lion or buffalo, not small game or paper targets, so Paco must authenticate his craft before actual, not make-believe, horns — or, in this instance, knives. I am aware of no more violent and memorable symbolism for the exposure and punishment of inadequate craft than that advanced by this story: the severing of a vital artery and the quick, fatal loss of blood. This symbolic action is made so vivid as to be nearly unbearable, for Paco's mortal wound is in the region of the groin.

Although "The Capital of the World" is highly characteristic of Hemingway's fiction during this period in the grimness of its *weltanschauung* and the bleakness of its irony, reminiscent of such stories as "A Clean, Well-Lighted Place" and "A Natural History of the Dead," it differs from many of Hemingway's other stories in the obtrusive presence of its narrator. Unlike its exact contemporaries "The Snows of Kilimanjaro" and "The Short Happy Life of Francis Macomber," with their ambiguous endings which have proved so provocative to critics, Hemingway begins and concludes "The Capital of the World" in the editorializing manner of direct address which typifies *Death in the Afternoon.* Throughout the story Hemingway not only creates the characters and action, he also comments upon them. And, quite uncharacteristically, Hemingway ends the story not with a gesture or a passage of dialogue, but with a coda which seems to summarize its themes and point its ironic moral. After surveying the behavior of the other characters against whom Paco has been juxtaposed, and recording their vulgar or commonplace activities during the very moments of Paco's death, Hemingway writes:

> The boy Paco had never known about any of this nor about what all these people would be doing on the next day and on other days to come. He had no idea how they really lived nor how they ended. He did not even realize they ended. He died, as the Spanish phrase has it, full of illusions. He had not had time in his life to lose any of them, nor even, at the end, to complete an act of contrition.
>
> He had not even had time to be disappointed in the Garbo picture which disappointed all Madrid for a week.

It is perhaps because of the seeming finality of this coda and the apparent simplicity of the story's action and characters that critics, with the recent exception of Joseph DeFalco in *The Hero in Hemingway's Short Stories,* have paid so little heed to it.

We should by now, however, be aware that to accept a Hemingway story wholly on its literal level is a very dubious procedure. Despite the transparency of its narrative point of view and the straightforward declaration of its theme, "The Capital of the World" conceals a number of subtle ironies. Moreover, the story's ironic strategies support and intensify the irony of its substance.

The title itself constitutes the first of these ironies. When originally published in *Esquire* in June of 1936, the story was called "The Horns of the Bull," but by the time it appeared in Hemingway's collected stories in 1938, the title had been changed to "The Capital of the World." The original title is more narrowly limited to the thematic dimension I have already remarked, that of testing one's craft against real antagonists in an actual situation in combat. As Enrique mockingly tells Paco, "If it wasn't for fear every bootblack in Spain would be a bullfighter." The new title incorporates this dimension of the story but goes beyond it. In its most literal sense the capital of the world is Madrid, that is, the bullfighting capital of the world. As Hemingway informs us in *Death in the Afternoon,* a torero's triumphs in the provincial towns and bullrings are suspect. Only in Madrid, before the most sophisticated audiences and critics, and in combat with the finest fighting bulls, does a matador truly establish his courage, craft, and reputation. Paco, the country boy who has attained triumphs in the provinces of his imagination, must prove himself before the horns of the bull in Madrid. Madrid thus becomes a synecdoche, transforming the particular situation of the bullfight into the universal concept of the ultimate standard, the Moment of Truth.

But in a much different sense the revised title evokes meanings which have nothing at all to do with bullfights. In the time between the story's publication and its inclusion in the collected stories, Hemingway had been to Spain and had witnessed the savage fighting there in the months after the outbreak of civil war. This experience, and Hemingway's subsequent renunciation of his earlier proclaimed political isolationism, is reflected directly in his work in the rather hastily revised *To Have and Have Not,* which culminates in Harry Morgan's dying words: "No matter how a man alone ain't got no bloody f..............g chance." I believe Hemingway's renewed political commitment is also suggested in the revised title of this story. The *capital* of the world therefore takes on some of the meaning of Marx's *Das Kapital,* capital in the sense of *resources* (for this suggestion I am indebted to my colleague William Bysshe Stein). But Hemingway gives the term another ironic turn: the "capital" is less that of the Marxist definition, material resources, modes of production, goods, than it is human resources, man's moral, social, and emotional values.

From this perspective Madrid and its inhabitants comprise a dark and bloody capital. The beautiful youth Paco, who dies full of illusion, is, in the largest sense, Spanish illusion and idealism of the utopian variety, soon to be extinguished in the brutal conflict. In fact, by the time Hemingway gave his story its second title, the tide was already moving against his side, the side of democracy, and Hemingway probably knew it and foresaw the Loyalists' defeat while he continued to believe in their aims. Paco, typical of the brave, illusioned, and unpracticed youths who are always the first to die in battle, and symbolic of the pure idealism which is always despoiled in the arena of combat, is indeed the capital of a world now verging on bankruptcy. The other capital, the tired, cynical, cowardly, anarchistic, commonplace characters against whom Paco is ironically juxtaposed, is what remains. In their ages, which range from young to old, in their values, and in their occupations they represent a panorama of Spanish life in its middle and lower orders. Significantly, and as appropriate to their function as ironic contrast, these characters are not named, merely designated by vocation. We should remember, with regard to this matter of idealism, that when Hemingway created his hero in *For Whom the Bell Tolls* four years later, he made him, in contrast to Paco, an experienced and mature man hardened by war and aware of the corruption and cynicism of the cause he sustains. Robert Jordan is an idealist, but not a blind and naive idealist, who, unlike Paco, knows from the start that he will die.

As appropriate to the ironic possibilities of the story's title, Hemingway employs as his narrative technique one almost unique in his work, that of ironic montage, rapidly but smoothly shifting focus back and forth between the central action of Paco's combat with Enrique and the various peripheral actions of the other characters. The major ironic juxtaposition is that between Paco and the sexual humiliations of the attractive, stylish, but cowardly matador whom Paco emulates. The un-manning of Paco by Enrique's "horn" is ironically paralleled by the matador's rebuffs first by Paco's sister, later by a prostitute. Observe, also, that the interior monologue passage which recreates the matador's goring, whence originated his fear, is ironically paralleled by the stark narrative account of Paco's fatal accident. In both passages the real situation merges into and then abruptly out of ideality at the instant of the wound. All illusion of perfection is banished by the penetration of the horn. This, too, has symbolic implications which are widely pertinent.

Although I have not sufficient space to explore fully all the subtleties of Hemingway's technique in this story, ironic and otherwise, I must call attention to a few of its verbal ironies. One that resembles what in poetry is called "incremental repetition" occurs throughout the story but nowhere more effectively than in these phrases in the concluding paragraphs quoted above, whose strong, mounting sentence rhythms suggest a mood ironically in contrast with the message contained in the paragraphs:

> The boy Paco had never known . . .
> He had no idea how . . .
> He did not even realize . . .
> He had not had time . . .
> He had not even had time . . .

Their effect is augmented by the repetition of the word "disappointed" in the story's last sentence.

There is also a pervasive verbal irony in the story which operates as a type of "lowering," that is, utilizing a more lighthearted idiom

or manner of statement than appropriate to the situation. This juxtaposition of jocular, facetious, or casual address against a tragic action
is instrumental to the story's striking and peculiar tone. For example,
consider this contrast of voices and manners of Enrique and Paco,
immediately after Paco's wounding, as he attempts futilely to staunch
the fountain of blood from his body:

> "I came straight," said Enrique, crying. "All I wanted was
> to show the danger."
> "Don't worry," said Paco, his voice sounding far away.
> "But bring the doctor."

In some other context this kind of incongruous dialogue, between
the frantic (but unhurt) boy and the serene (but mortally wounded)
one with his "Don't worry . . . But bring the doctor" might even be
construed as comic. In this case, and because of the fact of the
wound, it serves to create the most bitter irony.

As I have tried to demonstrate, "The Capital of the World"
stands as salient evidence that Hemingway's writing of the 30s was
not without value and pertinence. It was not, by the standards of
those years, as topical as the writing of John Steinbeck or James T.
Farrell or John Dos Passos, whose work was explicitly social and
political and who were not distracted by bullfights and African
safaris. But topicality does not always make for durability. There is a
larger topicality, one pertinent to the human condition and only
passingly concerned with particular historical moments and social
conditions. The liberal and Marxist critics of the 30s, almost unani-
mous in their demand for the immediate sort of pertinence, tended
to forget there could be other, perhaps higher kinds. Some of them,
in their dismay at Hemingway's seemingly perverse display of his
literary independence, concluded that his career had reached a
dead end all the more regrettable because of the brilliance of his
beginnings. Others, like Max Eastman and Wyndham Lewis, took
the occasion to deride him—in part deservedly—for his stress on
masculinity and physical sensation at the expense of humanity and
intellect, at least as they defined these values.

We wonder now whether the critics who lamented or celebrated
the end of Hemingway's literary promise had read "The Snows of
Kilimanjaro," "The Short Happy Life of Francis Macomber," and
"The Capital of the World." As we have seen, and as the magnificent
For Whom the Bell Tolls was soon incontestably to reassert, the
Hemingway of the 30s had not yet reached the end of his resources.

Fitzgerald, Hollywood, and the Myth of Success

by Jonas Spatz

It is evident, as many have noted, that F. Scott Fitzgerald's best work is deeply indebted to the tradition of success literature in America and that in Hollywood he discovered a perfect vehicle for the expression of his own version of the capitalist myth. Particularly in *The Great Gatsby* and *The Last Tycoon,* Fitzgerald recognized that the figure of the solitary capitalist was crucial in the statement of his major theme: the relationship between past and present. The past of the three major novels is the world of the American dream— of frontier individualism, economic independence, and inspired democratic leadership. It is a younger and more romantic world, somehow simpler, more honest, and yet with "a grandeur unmatched in the present." Thus the sense of loss that unites all of Fitzgerald's fiction is not only individual; it is national and even universal. The New World, once the last outpost of hope, has been corrupted by the materialism of the industrial age.

But less apparent is the fact that as Fitzgerald matured, his attitude toward Hollywood and its relation to the American experience became increasingly complex. At first he saw in Hollywood the contemporary image of the New World, a vulgar reflection of the reduced stature of modern man. Finally he romanticized Hollywood's history, emphasizing in the contrast between the old and new tycoons

31

the gap between the old vision of the American dream and its present reality.

Similarly, Fitzgerald became more sympathetic toward the myth of success. At first he satirized America's economic history and lampooned its financial leaders. Later he romanticized the "grandeur" of the dream and its followers and shifted his attack to their descendants whose greed had all but buried the heroic vision. Thus each of his heroes is doomed to failure in a brutal world no longer "commensurate to his capacity for wonder." The central tragedy is not merely the death of a superior individual whose idealism is unsuited to his time but, more significantly, the loss of all idealism.

Fitzgerald's interest in Hollywood and the myth of success found its earliest expression in "The Diamond as Big as the Ritz." John T. Unger, a student in a fashionable prep school, is invited to a classmate's home "in the West." There he discovers that his friend's father, Braddock Washington, is the richest man in the world and that he owns a mountain which is really a diamond as large as the Ritz-Carlton Hotel. The rest of the story describes the infinite splendor of the estate, which could have been designed only by a Hollywood producer—the only man "used to playing with an unlimited amount of money, though he did tuck his napkin in his collar and couldn't read or write." The estate has been built entirely upon the selfishness and brutality of the pioneer Washingtons who found the mountain, exploited it, and killed trespassers to hide its existence. Braddock Washington is the epitome of the American tycoon and a prototype for many later Hollywood caricatures. He maintains his empire through slavery and violence, and in the ironic climax of the story, in order to protect his land from invasion, he attempts to bribe God to turn back the clock. Washington's madness, however, is only a logical extension of the Gospel of Wealth. The history of his family is the history of the American dream in the nineteenth century, and his complete disregard for human values is merely modern capitalism in action. The story is also a condemnation of the hollow luxury that money can buy, a reduction to absurdity of the dream of wealth and power. Washington's estate is like a colossal movie set, the ultimate in bourgeois vulgarity and an image of the American dream itself. At the end of the tale, the hero survives and learns that maturity means a disenchantment with material values. In this early story, Fitzgerald relates Hollywood to the tasteless luxury and the despotic power of the myth of success.

Fitzgerald's later work is a variation on this basic pattern. Both

The Great Gatsby and *The Last Tycoon* contain a kind of romantic triangle between the hero, his antagonist, and the image of the American dream. James Gatz and Monroe Stahr are two self-made men, the last of a breed of believers in individualism and unlimited economic freedom. Set against them are the cruel and hostile figures of Tom Buchanan and Pat Brady—symbols of the materialism and selfishness that have perverted these ideals. In each case, the prize is a combination of youth, romance, beauty, and wealth constituting the dream. In *Gatsby* this complex is embodied in the person of Daisy, without whom Gatsby's life was "material without being real." In *The Last Tycoon* the symbol is Hollywood, Stahr's empire, the vehicle of his intense hope.

Not until we have read through almost all of *The Great Gatsby* does it become apparent that the novel is a continuation of Fitzgerald's treatment of the capitalist myth. Gatsby's career is a parody of the Horatio Alger theme. His boyhood schedule, prescribing the balanced and sober life that Benjamin Franklin had cited as "the way to wealth," illustrates his early commitment to the dream of success. With unintentional insight, his father compares him to the notorious robber baron, James J. Hill ("He'd of helped build up the country.") Dedicated to his destiny, like some god, he "sprang from his Platonic conception of himself." And like an Alger hero, he strikes his luck first through the whim of a benefactor, the last of the "pioneer debauchees," and later, in a grotesque shift of fortune, in association with "the man who fixed the World Series." Sometime between that boyhood resolution and his rise to fortune the dream of wealth and beauty had been corrupted. Gatsby tells Nick a "Hollywood" tale of his past, vainly pretending that he has actually fulfilled his early expectations. Like the robber barons, he has become a parvenu, living in isolation, throwing wild and vulgar parties in an attempt to recapture his youthful idealism—that is, to meet Daisy again. In making her admit to Tom that she never loved him, Gatsby attempts to repeat the past, to recapture Daisy as she was, and to recover "some idea of himself perhaps that had gone into loving Daisy." But he fails to realize that his dream is "already behind him, somewhere back in that vast obscurity beyond the city," in the vanished paradise of the New World.

But there is a greater tragedy in the novel than either Gatsby's blindness or his lost virtue. Just as Gatsby's earlier associations represent the destruction of his innocence, Daisy becomes the symbol of the central irony of the novel: the expectation and disillusionment of the dream of success. Once she had embodied beauty and romance and his youthful desire. He returns to find only that "her voice is full of money." He discovers in her a shallow greed, reflecting his own failure to live up to his ideals. Although he desires her "beyond wealth," she chooses Tom Buchanan, "a hulking brute," a bigot, a defender of "art" and "civilization" against the colored peril. Tom's doctrine of racial superiority and his social irresponsibility suggest the Social Darwinism which, Fitzgerald believed, had already undermined the innocence of capitalism. Tom converts Daisy to his values, and her denial of Gatsby is America's refusal to honor its past. The prize is no longer worthy of the heroism of its empire builders. The new tycoons will reap the spoils of a stolen world.

This comparison of past and present is reinforced in sexual terms. Daisy was "the first nice girl" that Gatsby had met, but on his return he realizes that his battle with Tom is on sexual grounds, a test of masculinity that Gatsby must ultimately fail. Tom is unfaithful to Daisy, but their physical relationship has long ago erased the memory of her former experience with Gatsby. The loss of moral innocence in the novel is parallel to the loss of sexual innocence and the rejection of the conventions of romantic love.

Nick finally concludes that the novel's characters, all Midwesterners, had some deficiency which made them "subtly unadaptable to Eastern life." That is, as survivors of an agrarian past, they are unable to cope with urban society that is grinding American ideals under the heel of materialism. Thus on one level, the novel can be read as a capitalist fable with an unhappy ending. Yet Fitzgerald departs from the attitude of "The Diamond as Big as the Ritz," since he is essentially sympathetic to Gatsby, who, after all, belongs to the same race as Braddock Washington. Like Gatsby, capitalism has been a victim of its own success. For the first time Fitzgerald shares in its expectation and weeps at its defeat.

Seen in this somewhat restricted light, *The Great Gatsby* is a logical predecessor to *The Last Tycoon*. Apparently Fitzgerald intended to portray in more detail a hero of the same type as Gatsby. *The Last Tycoon* is more specific about the forces in modern America which threaten to destroy men like Gatsby and Monroe Stahr. It is a less symbolic, less suggestive novel, but it successfully combines the myth of success with the myth of Hollywood. Fitzgerald adapted the capitalist theme to a real economic situation and transferred to Hollywood all the symbolic overtones in Daisy's character.

In *The Last Tycoon,* Fitzgerald attempts to analyze the capitalist myth in terms of those who most believed in it and built an industry on it. Monroe Stahr represents the old Hollywood and the frontier phase in American history. He is the most complete of Fitzgerald's Horatio Alger heroes, yet unlike the classic nineteenth century tycoon, and like most Hollywood leaders, he is a Jew. We learn almost nothing about Stahr's youth, but the central features of the myth are present. Brought up on the streets of the Bronx with little education, he was a born leader, a "frail boy" walking "always at the head of the gang . . . occasionally throwing a command backward out of the corner of his mouth." Like Dreiser's Cowperwood he had wanted to be be chief clerk, "to know where everything was," but his ambition has made him much more than that. Fitzgerald, in his notes, describes Stahr as a "scrapper, one of the boys, a boy destined to succeed."

Stahr is a symbol of intelligence and authority. Despite his background, he possesses a natural creative genius that has carried him "through trackless wastes of perception into fields where very few men were able to follow him." Moreover, he has the judgment and character of the capitalist men of action and the glamorous energy of the pioneer "builder of empires." Like the Romans (and the Fords and Rockefellers), he is not only a creator but a ruler of creators, an adapter of men and things for his own purposes. Kathleen considers him more a king than any of the European monarchs she has met. He is the last of the "merchant princes."

Stahr, however, is not merely a symbol of power and wealth; he is the ideal capitalist. His artistic ability and, above all, his humanity make him the last of the individualists and a mourner for the golden age of capitalism. Stahr's compassion is his distinguishing characteristic. Like most brilliant men, "he had grown up dead cold," but resolved to learn "tolerance, kindness, forbearance, and even affection like lessons." As a paternalistic employer, he has inspired his employees to new heights of productivity and professional satisfaction. With a rare combination of idealism and practicality, he has resisted the pressures of economy and competition and has carried films "way up past the range and power of the theatre." Brimmer, the communist labor leader, fears his influence above all others because men like Stahr are the only heroic figures still capable of making capitalism attractive to the masses.

Yet Stahr's idealism is in the process of destroying him. Another cluster of images surrounding him suggests decay and death—the end of his reign. For some time before the novel opens, Stahr has been weakening physically; yet he works even harder, "ruling with a radiance that is almost moribund in its phosphorescence." Brimmer, at the climax of his debate with Stahr, realizes that the transferral of power is soon to come: " 'Is *this* all? This frail half-sick person holding up the whole thing?' " The atmosphere of death hangs over all that Stahr does, and it is not the least of Fitzgerald's achievements that we feel that the old Hollywood and an era in American history are dying with him.

Brimmer and Brady represent what will replace Stahr, who is caught in the widening split between the collective forces of Capital and Labor. Brimmer is a relatively sympathetic character, "a Spencer Tracy type," as Celia describes him. Although he is dedicated to Stahr's downfall, he regrets that history must make them enemies. Brady, a more important figure, is the composite image of "Wall Street," the enormous, depersonalized concentration of capital that is driving the individual out of the marketplace and transforming the adventure of frontier enterprise into a cynical pursuit of corporate control. Brady symbolizes this loss of identity; he never confronts us directly, even in the most climactic scenes. Schwartz senses him only as impending doom, one of the Furies pursuing him for having made a fatal slip on the financial tightrope of Hollywood. Even his daughter, Celia, finds it difficult to visualize him as person, except in the most general terms:

> What did father look like? I couldn't describe him except for once in New York when I met him where I didn't expect to! I was aware of a bulky, middle-aged man who looked a little ashamed of himself, and I wished he'd move on—and then I saw he was father.

His rise to power has been an accident, a trading on the talents of others. He has little knowledge of film production and hasn't learned much about "the feel of America." He is an exploiter rather than a creator, a "shrewd and lucky" manipulator who is not "a passable man."

The contrast between Stahr and Brady, as in *Gatsby,* is most clearly expressed in their approaches to sex. Stahr's affair with Kathleen, whatever its eventual fate, is highly romantic, emphasizing the dying values of both her European and his American tradition. Brady's materialism, however, emerges when Celia stumbles onto Birdie Peters in her father's office closet—a mistress "stuffed

. . . naked into a hole in the wall in the middle of a business day."

According to Fitzgerald's outline for the novel, Stahr and Brady were to destroy each other in a struggle for control of Hollywood and, symbolically, all of American industry. Stahr must lose his fight not only because individualism has been pushed into the past by the corporations and the labor unions but also because the prize he seeks no longer exists in its original form. Stahr's affair with Kathleen fails because he must compare her with the lost perfection of his dead wife. And just as Kathleen (who "doesn't fit in with the grandeur Stahr demands of life") is a less glamorous copy of the woman who shared Stahr's days of glory, modern Hollywood is a pale imitation of its heroic frontier days—no longer worthy of his effort. In Fitzgerald's later work, Hollywood represents the totality of past and present. It is the last memory of the epic age of capitalism, and its surrender to the forces of collectivism, both in management and labor, will inevitably bury the magnificence of the past in the mediocrity of the present.

The Last Tycoon is Fitzgerald's final version of the capitalist fable. Many critics have noted the real or imagined debt that this vision owes to Frederick Jackson Turner's interpretation of American history. An insistence on this dependence, however, presumes that Fitzgerald is attacking the Gospel of Wealth in an industrial age in the name of an earlier, agrarian America. Certainly he regrets the passing of individualism and the degradation of frontier democracy. But as we have seen, the dream of success permeates *The Great Gatsby* and *The Last Tycoon*. In these works, Fitzgerald attempts to reconcile the contradiction between the heroic ideal of individualism and the monster of greed and tyranny it must become. If he does not regret the passing of men like Carnegie and Rockefeller, he recognizes the immense scale on which they were reconstructing the New World. And he laments for a world which could turn Gatsby's daily schedule into a formula for achievement—"a lavish, romantic past that perhaps will not come again into our time." Hollywood, for all its vulgarity, contained the vitality of that past. The tragedy in *The Last Tycoon*, as in *The Great Gatsby*, depends as much on the intensity of the hero's hope as on the finality of its disillusionment.

The Transformation of
Thomas Wolfe

by Richard Walser

When *Look Homeward, Angel* was published on October 18, 1929, its author was only fifteen days into his thirtieth year. The book was a first novel, and tall Tom Wolfe, with his dark eyes shifting nervously from a small head perched incongruously upon broad, mountain-bred shoulders, looked very much like a fellow who might indeed have written a poetic work rhapsodic in its depiction of a young man's alternating agonies and joys. Later Wolfe remarked that his autobiographical hero Eugene Gant was "a kind of romantic self-justification." For the Eugene of *Look Homeward, Angel,* in any case, the world existed only within the sights and sounds and feelings of the sensitive youth. The novel revealed no social consciousness, nor, one suspects, did Wolfe have one. It is well if he did not, for the lyrical splendour of the book is chief among its admirable qualities.

Then, in the last two weeks of that same October, even as Wolfe was reveling in the glorious reviews that came to his attention and smarting with anger at the slightest unfavorable word about his creation, the mighty men of Wall Street looked on with unbelieving eyes as the stock market crashed about them. It was, of course, the beginning of the 30s. Yet there is no indication that Wolfe had any awareness of what had happened. At that time he was so involved in his own personality that the big events of the world—and certainly those of the business world—took place without his noticing or caring. During those autumn days he wrote to his friends, as would be expected, about the reception of *the* book. He complained about having to grade themes assigned his freshman students at New York University. "God! the torture of it!" he groaned. And even after the turning of the year, when a Guggenheim Fellowship and earnings from the book made it possible for him to leave the classroom, Wolfe thought only about plans for his next novel and his fifth trip to Europe. The world-wide crisis had not yet shaken his little personal world.

An initial emergence from his isolated shell can be noticed late in 1930, when Wolfe's large family in the South lost most of their money, their property, and their jobs. Before this, his reasonably affluent family had been, in the eyes of the financially shaky young man, a rock of security on which he could depend when in need. Now the situation was reversed. "Things must be in a terrible condition all over the country—everyone I know has suffered," he observed. From his account at the publisher he asked that $500 be sent his brother Fred for relieving conditions in the family. He seemed to glory in his mature, unexpected role as protector, and with a cheerfulness never to be abandoned he wrote his sister Mabel, "We will not be beaten because *we can not be beaten.*" This unrationalized optimism in the ability of his family and himself to pull through the rough days, he gradually extended to apply to all Americans everywhere.

The family dilemma did not, of course, take Wolfe's mind off the necessity of getting on with the next novel. Moving about Europe with his manuscripts and notebooks, he was incessantly seeking the form it would take. It was the form and outline that troubled him, for even before the publication of *Look Homeward, Angel,* he had rather hazily decided that the new novel would embody an American theme. In June, 1930, he confided to a friend: "I am writing a book so filled with the most unspeakable desire, longing, and love for my own country and ten thousand things in it, that I have to laugh at times to think what the Mencken crowd and all the other crowds are going to say about it." At another time he protested that he "could not sleep for thinking of the sights and sounds and colors, the whole intolerable memory of America, its violence, savagery, immensity, beauty, ugliness, and glory." And he believed he could fashion a novel from this material, for "no one," he declared to Maxwell Perkins, "has ever written a book about America—no one has ever put into it the things I know and the things everybody knows." For the next several years, through 1933, Wolfe tried to carry out his purpose. Returning from Europe, he settled in Brooklyn not only because it was cheap but because he would be let alone. He set to work.

The real test of a writer lies in his second book—or so the saying has it. Certainly Wolfe found it true. There he was in Brooklyn, turning out huge disconnected segments of manuscript, hoping they would fit an outline based on mythological figures, pursuing the youthful adventures of Eugene Gant, while all about him lay a vast numbed city struggling for life in the midst of the Great Depression. Was there not something wrong, something asunder in the way Wolfe had to deal, at the same time, with the romanticism of Eugene and the realism of misery and disaster? "I have felt much closer to people in the last two or three years," he wrote his sister Mabel, "than I ever did in my life before, and the misfortune and suffering everywhere around me has touched me more than it ever did before." Something asunder, yes perhaps, but something right and complete too, for out of suffering and pity can come love.

Of Time and the River (1935), which his work during these years eventually became, was not merely the further peregrinations of Eugene Gant, but a great gushing hymn of devotion to America and her heroic people. It is, though not the most respected of his novels, the one most characteristic of the Wolfe style and the Wolfe spirit. No longer confined within the closed circle of an adolescent hero, Wolfe has enlarged his scope "from personal self-consciousness," in the words of Richard S. Kennedy, "to include national consciousness as well." His method was poetic: the dithyrambic train journeys across the nighttime land, the paeans to youth and October and time, the rhythmic roll calls of battles and states and Indian tribes, and the unashamed love songs to America. ". . . It is a fabulous country; it is the one place where miracles not only happen, but where they happen all the time. . . ." These words come from a new and different Wolfe, moving slowly away from the world of Eugene Gant.

Of *Time and the River,* based roughly on Wolfe biography between 1920 and 1925, did not reflect—nor would it have been suitable that it should reflect—the disturbing political and sociological tendencies developing within the author while the novel was being written. It was enough that Wolfe was moving outside self to contain an entire nation. Yet as early as 1931 he was beginning to remark on the evils of over-production under a capitalistic system that condemned people to such poverty that they were unable to enjoy the rewards of their work. The old days were, he felt, gone for good. He wrote his mother, "You have lived through one kind of world; you may live to see the beginning of another one." Two years later he went down to Washington for the inauguration of President Franklin D. Roosevelt, whom he ardently supported. While condemning the ignorant businessmen—"a set of foolish little boys"—who were responsible for the mess America was in, Wolfe echoed the new President in a belief that all would come out all right. His flag of hope and certainty never drooped.

Wolfe's was a commonplace attitude, not yet strident nor philosophically synthesized. His feelings were deep, naturally, but he was no soap-box orator; rather, he was a gentle man whom only anger or blunt opposition could force into action. Opposition came from an unexpected direction, from his beloved mentor and editor Maxwell Perkins. In 1934 the two met regularly in the evenings to shape the novel for the printers and, after several hours of work at the Scribner office, walked across to the Chatham Hotel for a nightcap. There, tensions released, they discussed the issues all intellectuals discussed in mid 1934. "Max and I get together," Wolfe reported to a friend of Perkins', "and pound the table and shake our fists and argue about Communism. After the second round of drinks I make Trotsky look like a republican." Such a good-humored description is obviously one in which two friends are arguing their points of view for the sheer fun of it. It seems, even so, that the conservative New Englander was somewhat alarmed about his jovial, free-thinking North Carolina novelist. From London the next year, Wolfe laughingly wrote Perkins that he was contemplating a visit "to Russia in time for the May Day celebrations—this because I am now planning a monumental work in three volumes on The Success of Russian Communism, and following the example of some of my American colleagues, I figure I shall need at least a week in Russia to gather the necessary material."

But pleasantries like these were not without their serious side. If Wolfe over and over again disclaimed any sympathy with Communism, and certainly as it was practiced in Russia, he thought of himself, in his mature years, as a working man, the son of a stonecutter, and not a member of the well-to-do and privileged class, as doubtless he gradually came to look upon Perkins. At this point the difference in the two was not serious, nor were the witticisms hardened into solemn convictions till Wolfe's famous break with Scribner. The break, triggered by a minor financial matter, put Wolfe on the defensive; and among the flood of artistic irritabilities which he had kept dammed up so well, Wolfe recited with cold intensity the ideological separation of the two. He accused Perkins of trying to block his intellectual development, of seeking to restrain his political awareness, in short of wishing to keep him in a state of romantic innocence. His book, he began to feel, had been ruined. Perkins, who loved Wolfe, was shattered by the injustice of the accusations. Though Wolfe, too, was unhappy and dejected, he was, in late 1936, no longer the tall, slender young man, with dark childlike eyes, whom Perkins had first met eight years before.

An astute observer might have noted early literary steps in the progress of Wolfe's eventual transformation. In June, 1933, *Scribner's Magazine* had printed his story "Death—the Proud Brother," containing four episodes about the unrecognized, unimportant human beings who perish in the midst of a big unnoticing and uncaring city. In such a story Wolfe's self-centeredness was quietly diminishing. Here and elsewhere, as in " 'The Hollow Men' " of *You Can't Go Home Again,* we have Wolfe's Whitmanian tribute to the little, almost anonymous people of America whose only dignity is "the dignity of Death." Another step was the appearance in the *American Mercury* of May, 1934, of "Boom Town," in which he condemned American boosterism. America was a place where the fast dollar, the quick sell, was uppermost in the minds of those in high position; it was the place where life and human integrity were worthless goods in any transactions. If Wolfe's expression of these beliefs in fictional guise was less than political, it nevertheless foreshadowed the firmer convictions to come later.

A third step was "I Have a Thing To Tell You," a long piece on his brush with Nazism. In 1935, upon returning to his beloved Germany, he was delighted to find himself a celebrity there. The translation of *Look Homeward, Angel* had brought him fame in a foreign land. Wined and dined and honored, Wolfe had reached the pinnacle he had so energetically sought since college days. But there was an evil in the land, he sensed, an evil "curiously and inextricably woven." At that time, though he could not define the evil, he sensed that "we are all of us bound up and tainted by whatever guilt and evil there may be in this whole world"—a far cry from the adolescent persecution felt by Eugene Gant. In 1936, again in Germany, this time for the Olympic Games, Wolfe recognized the Nazi terror for what it was. Everywhere he went, there were restrictions and difficulties. Distrust, secrecy, evasion characterized his meetings with old friends as well as with new. Then on his way out of the country he witnessed the seizure of a little Jewish man at the Belgian border. This climactic incident turned him forever from "self-absorbed designs . . . outward toward the rich and life-giving soil of a new freedom in the wide world of all humanity." By now, even as he was writing "I Have a Thing To Tell You" about these experiences in Germany, he was so different from the Thomas Wolfe whose books had come from the famous house of Scribner that he felt he needed, among other things, a new publisher to signalize the change in himself and what he planned to write henceforth.

With the severance from Scribner all but accomplished—with Wolfe writing Perkins in January, 1937, that he would use his strength "for revolution—for the abolition of this vile and rotten system under which we live—for a better world, a better life," and disdaining a conservatism based on "fatalism" and a "determined resignation" that "life will never change"—he launched forth on the composition of "The Party at Jack's," which in an expanded version became Book II of *You Can't Go Home Again.* The story, far more than any other by Wolfe, belongs to the proletarian school of fiction of the 30s. Always careful to avoid a charge of Communism, he insisted that the piece was "certainly not at all Marxian, but it is representative of the way my life has come—after deep feeling, deep thinking, and deep living and all this experience— to take its way." The incident details an evening gathering, attended by wealthy and artistic New Yorkers, at a luxurious apartment on Park Avenue. After a vulgar entertainment using circus dolls, a fire starts in the basement of the apartment building. The guests escape down the staircase to safety, but two elevator men, trapped when the electricity is cut off, die of smoke. Throughout the story, Wolfe's social and proletarian intention is clear and simple: the unworthy rich survive, while the hard-working poor succumb. Now Wolfe was standing beside most of his fellow American novelists of the 30s.

"The Party at Jack's" and other pages in *You Can't Go Home Again* bring the reader to the optimistic Credo at the end of the novel, where Wolfe's transformation is complete. It was a transformation for which he had worked and of which he was well aware. Nine months before his death, he confessed proudly that his "vision of life" had changed. His original "intense and passionate concern with the design and purposes of . . . youth" was now replaced by "an intense and passionate concern with the designs and purposes of life." The change in him had been gradual but constant: from romanticism to realism, from self to all men, from uncertainty to assurance. While Wolfe did not always have the answers to difficult questions, and rarely was positive about ways and means, he was, during the 30s, when the people of his country were downcast and terrified, firm in his belief that America was "deathless, undiscovered, immortal, and must live."

John Steinbeck and the Language of Awareness

by Pascal Covici, Jr.

Wrote John Steinbeck in his daily "log" during the composition of *East of Eden* (1952), the book he then saw as a culmination of all that he had previously done: "Very few people ever mature. It is enough if they flower and reseed. . . . But sometimes . . . awareness takes place—not very often and always inexplainable. There are no words for it because there is no one ever to tell. This is a secret not kept a secret, but locked in wordlessness. The craft or art of writing is the clumsy attempt to find symbols for the wordlessness."

As one rereads the body of work that Steinbeck brought forth in the 30s, one finds his definition of the art of writing more useful than anything that his critics have said, and more relevant than the hesitant or scornful protests of those (including Steinbeck himself) who wondered why the Nobel Prize should have been awarded to him. The memorable characters of the early books linger in one's imagination primarily as they struggle toward various sorts of "awareness."

This is not to denigrate the full sensibility of the writer, the capacity to "make life" upon the page that is the decisive criterion for fiction as opposed to reportage. But if we grant Steinbeck the sheer talent for fiction that has surely never been an issue even

47

among his detractors, we come immediately to the question of the precise direction that his fiction can be seen to take. To limit the problem to the scope suggested by the title of this group of essays, let us try to identify the important and lasting concerns that order his fiction of the 30s.

The Pastures of Heaven (1932), *To a God Unknown* (1933), *Tortilla Flat* (1935), *In Dubious Battle* (1936), *Of Mice and Men* (1937), *The Long Valley* (1938), and *The Grapes of Wrath* (1939) comprise the fiction Steinbeck published in the 30s. Add to this the newspaper articles appearing in the San Francisco *News* in October of 1936, expanded and published as *Their Blood Is Strong* in 1938, and take into account both the biological philosophy, or philosophical biology, of *The Sea of Cortez* (1941) and the first published novel, *The Cup of Gold*, in 1929, and one begins to understand why Steinbeck's early reviewers and critics were at a loss as to how to approach his work.

Not only was there lots of it, but it seemed to be heading in too many, and too contradictory, directions at once to be forced into any viable critical frame. Yet even by the early 40s, certain recurring elements in his fiction had been identified and explored. A concern for common, human values, for warmth, love, and understanding, led to a view of Steinbeck the sentimentalist. The social relevance of some of his writing revealed him as a reformer. His tender evocation of the land itself, his celebration of its fertility and of his characters' concern for the bringing forth of life, implied an interest first called "primitive" and then seen as "mythic." His capacity to make both his characters and his country come alive was traced to his increasing mastery of vernacular as a counter-weight to the sonorous, almost mystical, rhythms of his frequently incantatory language. Finally, his explicit discussion, in *The Sea of Cortez*, of what he called "non-teleological thinking" confirmed what for many had been the primary motif of his fictional writing, his conception of man as a biological mechanism, purposeless as well as animal-like. The proponents of this view of Steinbeck found in the halfwitted Lennie (*Of Mice and Men*), the retarded Tularecito (*The Pastures of Heaven*), and the moronic Johnny Bear (*The Long Valley*)—the three most frequently cited—an obsession with human approximations of the animal. Others, equally struck by the pointed absence of didactic moralizing, saw in the stories and novels a pseudo-scientific concern to record without judging ("*is*-thinking" was to be a Steinbeck synonym for "non-teleological thinking"), to present specimens simply for the reader's contemplation.

These, and other, insights into Steinbeck's work are necessary and useful; they alert one to the many currents of feeling and implication that run through Steinbeck's books. One way of approaching the first full decade of this flow is to examine some of the people Steinbeck has created, to see what relationships he has established between character and structure, and to see how he has gone about "unlocking" the wordless secret by forging the language of awareness.

John Steinbeck in the 30s introduces his readers to his own imaginatively possessed territory of the Salinas Valley in California, and to the characters—also his own—that inhabit it in increasing variety and complexity. " 'Deep down it's mine, right to the center of the world,' " says Joseph Wayne of the land he has just bought at the start of *To a God Unknown.* Of the kinds of awareness that Steinbeck's stronger characters bring to their confrontation of life, this sense of an intimate and even overpowering connection between man and land becomes the most pervasive, the most elemental. Even unaware characters feel it, all unknowingly, so that Grandpa Joad, comic relief and all, is said to have died as soon as the Joad caravan leaves the Oklahoma farm where he had his roots, although Grandpa's body still breathes until long after. The rhythm of the seasons makes the texture of *The Grapes of Wrath;* that is, even that potentially simply "angry" book is as much a paean to the succeeding seasons and their effect upon the physical terrain as it is a compassionate presentation of the lives of oppressed Okies in California.

The land wildly blossoms in the springtime, quietly gestates during summer, yields its harvest in the fall, and then lies bare and dead during the winter, only to give birth once more. So, too, the lives of Steinbeck's people are presented not only as complex patterns of action and desire but also as variations on the simple pattern that Eliot's Ape-Neck Sweeney so tersely identified as "birth, copulation, and death." The imagery of sexuality in Steinbeck's books generally derives from the progression of the seasons itself, or from farming, which amounts to the same thing. The *paisanos* in *To a God Unknown* copulate ecstatically in response to a much-needed rain-fall; the inevitability of sexuality in *Grapes* is irresistible: "Might as well stop the fall from comin', and might as well stop the sap from movin' in the trees." And in the same integrated way, Ma comforts Rose of Sharon, pregnant in the midst of death,

50

with the assurance that " 'bearin' and dyin' is two pieces of the same thing.' " Jody's Red Pony, in the famous short novel, lives through its mother's death, and the emotions of the humans involved in both events are presented as inseparably "two pieces of the same thing."

But the awareness of nature and of nature's processes that Steinbeck's fiction engenders in a reader remains secondary, although poignant and vital. The people, the characters, even more than the soil, the rocks, and the trees (one cannot speak of Steinbeck's "landscape," for the word's connotations of superficiality belie the psychological weight that the author imparts to the natural environment of his stories), live in a reader's imagination not only because of what they do but because of what they feel, and because of their struggles to understand their own unique positions upon the earth. This uniqueness emerges as a function not so much of their psychological and spiritual identity as of their participation in the lives of other people and simultaneously in their own destinies. The Steinbeck protagonists repeatedly feel themselves to be somehow "different" from others, and the reader sees this difference as existing not only in their isolation—which they themselves see—but also in their oceanic sense of involvement with all humanity. Only as they become aware of this sense of community do they cease to feel so tortured, so alone, so painfully unique—yet it is this very sense of communion that, for the reader, sets them apart from the mass of men who feel readily enough their own self-important loneliness but who cannot break through the walls of narcissism that keep them from seeing themselves as specially important in the universe.

This seeming paradox, this state of feeling that combines lonely aloofness with a burgeoning sense of communal participation in the human race, Steinbeck implies as early as *The Cup of Gold* and articulates in *To a God Unknown*. Joseph Wayne, speaking to a giant oak as though to the spirit of his recently dead father, laments the calm acceptance with which he greets all events, laments the loneliness that this aloof imperviousness creates in him. " 'Thomas and Burton [his brothers] are allowed their likes and dislikes, only I am cut off. I am cut off. I can have neither good luck nor bad luck.' " And in the same address to the oak, Joseph explains why "luck" is irrelevant to him: " 'All things are one, and all a part of me.' " The feeling of the farmer for the land is here left far behind; Joseph speaks as both patriarch and savior, anticipating the more persuasive attitude that Jim Casey will pass on to Tom Joad in

Grapes, that " 'maybe all men got one big soul ever'body's a part
of.' " Only gradually does Joseph Wayne come to accept his own
approximation to this sense of participation, and even then, his
awareness—as that of the other "strong" character in the novel,
Rama, his sister-in-law—is that of a transcendental seeker rather
than of a man who has really accepted his humanity. Rama says
of him: " 'I tell you this man is not a man, unless he is all men.
. . . a repository for a little piece of each man's soul, and more than
that, a symbol of the earth's soul.' "

When Rama goes one step further than this, one sees that the
limitation that binds Joseph Wayne is Joseph's, written into him by
an author whose own awareness is not to be measured simply by his
character's. Joseph's wife dies, yet Joseph's concern is still, as always, primarily for the land and his connection to it. " 'You aren't
aware of persons, Joseph,' " says Rama, without horror but with
compassion; " 'only people. You can't see units, Joseph, only the
whole.' " Joseph wants, without quite knowing it, to be himself the
whole, the all, the giver and guardian of life. Searching for water
to save his thirsting cattle in a time of drought, he comes upon an
old man who sacrifices " 'every night some creature' " to the setting
sun. " 'This man has discovered a secret,' Joseph said to himself.
'He must tell me if he can.' " But neither the old man, nor anyone
else, can put the secret into words; it is the first avatar of that
awareness "locked in wordlessness" that flickers through all of
Steinbeck's work. The old man can say only, " 'I do this because
it makes me glad.' "

Unaware himself, but deeply in touch with the cycle of the
sun, the old man has found a peacefulness that, simple-minded and
even imbecilic, haunts Joseph for the rest of his life. The reader,
on the other hand, is not attracted to the old man's mystical nature-
worship whose ritual has no words. Too much is symbol, not enough
has been made human. The problem confronting Steinbeck here
at the start of his career—a problem that he solved and partially
solved in many books, but that returned to trouble him in such
unlike works as *The Moon Is Down* (1942) and *Burning Bright*
(1950)—is that of finding for his characters ways to reveal levels
of their experience and awareness that people do not naturally put
into words. Humans, as Steinbeck will explicitly emphasize in *East
of Eden* (1952), have consciousness, choice, and awareness as
animals do not. Yet people are also animals. How create a full
sense of the human without overstating it, and without belying the

ignorance and the reserve of the shy animal behind the articulate man? So at Joseph Wayne's wedding, the new father-in-law speaks as surely few, if any, men have ever spoken: " 'It's because you're stronger than I am that I hate you. Here I'm wanting to like you, and I can't because I'm a weak man.' " As Joseph points out, no weak man could bring himself to say what McGreggor has said— but then, neither could any sort of man at all. Not until Doc Burton and Jim Nolan of *In Dubious Battle* does Steinbeck find a way to present persuasively the insight and awareness of articulate, knowing people.

But meanwhile, *Tortilla Flat* provided a wonderful holiday from the problem, satisfying the expectations raised by the situation and by the characters. Because the people—Danny and his *paisano* friends—are presented as very simple people, their range of awareness is narrow without being unbelievable. The reader is satisfied, however, because these characters are fully aware of undercurrents of feeling and motivation, and their awareness emerges both realistically (that is, convincingly) and completely. Through dialogue, through perfect rendition of the spoken language, Steinbeck makes his reader believe in the world of petty chicanery, mildly corrupt poverty, loyalty, and unambitious gusto that is Tortilla Flat. The humor of the book lies primarily in the rationalizations that reveal the very awareness of motive that the characters pretend to hide. Pilon, deciding to steal Big Joe Portagee's pants, indulges in mental gymnastics that exemplify much of the book's flavor: "If, with one action, he could avenge Danny, discipline Big Joe, teach an ethical lesson, and get a little wine, who in the world could criticize him?" Big Joe has stolen Danny's blanket and must now learn how it feels to be robbed. Pilon will trade the pants for wine. Fooling no one, least of all himself or the reader, each character reasons in a similar fashion about such things as the gaps in Mrs. Morales's fence, through which chickens may be encouraged to slip, a bottle of wine that might endanger the health of a friend, or the rent, that, if paid, might corrupt a kind landlord.

The complex human qualities spotted through *The Pastures of Heaven* and *The Long Valley,* both written early in the decade despite the publication date of the latter, suggest that the joys of simplicity were always only a small part of the potential of this writer. Even *Of Mice and Men,* the first of Steinbeck's experiments in constructing a novel in as close to dramatic form as possible, allowed neither the preoccupation with direct presentation nor the limitations of the idiot, Lennie, one of the main characters, to hold the impact of the story to that of simplicity starkly rendered. The character of Slim—"His ear heard more than was said to him, and his slow speech had overtones not of thought, but of understanding beyond thought"—the only one who senses the reciprocity in the relationship between George and Lennie, continues the sequence of Steinbeck's isolated and aware men that Doc Burton in *In Dubious Battle* and Tom Joad in *The Grapes of Wrath* most successfully exemplify. This type brings into focus the major impact of Steinbeck's work in the 30s.

The social issue, of course, is relevant; surely it is no coincidence that *In Dubious Battle* concerns a strike of California fruit-pickers and that *The Grapes of Wrath* had its origins in *Their Blood Is Strong,* a series of articles Steinbeck did for the San Francisco *News* in 1936 and to which he added an "Epilogue" for publication in book form in April of 1938. The last sentence of this grim description of what California was doing to the Okies anticipates the vintage from the grapes of wrath: "Must the hunger become anger and the anger fury before anything will be done?" Certainly Steinbeck the man cared deeply about the immediate social issues of corporate tyranny and the material lot of migrant workers. But— without attempting to account for the motives of the man—the books themselves present with equal vividness the loneliness, the capacity for choice, and—in Tom Joad—the development of the character whose awareness evades complete articulation but infuses a felt quality into his life. The "sad-eyed" Doc Burton, detached observer, who says, " 'I simply want to see as much as I can, Mac, with the means that I have,' " believes not at all in the "cause," the strike of the workers, but in men: " 'I guess I just believe they're men, and not animals.' " Trying to understand what he calls " 'group man,' " his total isolation from the men around him finally drives him out into the night where, if not killed, he is at least lost to the men who need him. Jim Nolan's development from socially "useless" involvement with suffering people into a man with the capacity to "use" people for the purposes of the group counterpoints Doc's notion that " 'the end is never very different in its nature from the means.' "

Jim dies for his cause, illuminating in his death not only the mob-behavior of "group man" but also a human being's capacity to choose his destiny. Tom Joad, two years later, goes on from there, developing his sensitive awareness of people into involved responsibility. In both of these books, the structure follows the rhythms of social action and of seasonal change; the primary emotional counterpoint, however, is that between "group man," the organism that has a life independent of its members, and those individuals who have, or who struggle toward, awareness. Perhaps here is the invigorating paradox behind all of the books Steinbeck has written: on the one hand, the democratic assumption that all men are potentially of the psychological and social elect does battle—generally embodied in conflicts between characters—with the equally egalitarian sense that all men share a basic animalistic nature, more buried in some than in others but always to be found. On the other hand, the humanistic assumption that only some men can understand their dilemma, their situation, and by understanding it, affect it, becomes embodied in the characters who struggle to order with their minds the chaos of feeling and matter that they encounter. "Sometimes . . . awareness takes place." The achievement of John Steinbeck in the 30s was to present not only the land, with the people and the social forces that make life upon it so engrossing and sometimes so terrifying, but also the struggle of individuals toward that awareness that is "locked in wordlessness." His vocabularies, his structures, his stories, and his people might well be approached as strategies toward this high end.

William Faulkner and the Art of the Detective Story

by Warren French

Some pioneer Faulkner enthusiasts were dismayed to learn that the novelist whose merits they had been extolling had entered a contest conducted in 1946 by *Ellery Queen's Mystery Magazine* and carried off second prize with "An Error in Chemistry." There was really little occasion for surprise, for many of the best and most profound as well as the most trivial· of the works of the man who seems indisputably America's greatest novelist in the first half of the twentieth century are basically detective stories.

Despite its many enthusiasts, the detective story remains critically a despised genre. The objections to it have been summed up in Edmund Wilson's exasperated question—after a depressing encounter with several highly recommended mystery novels—"How can you care who committed a murder which has never really been made to take place, because the writer hasn't any ability of even the most ordinary kind to persuade you to see it or feel it?" ("Who Cares Who Killed Roger Ackroyd?", printed in 1945 and collected in *Classics and Commercials*).

This question can be asked even of those of Faulkner's works that undeniably belong to the mystery genre, *Intruder in the Dust* and the tales collected in *Knight's Gambit*. Although in the former work, the reader does care about the fate of the proud Negro Lucas

Beauchamp, the silly mystery of the rednecked twins and the invaded grave matter only as contrived obstacles to the efforts of an old woman and an adolescent boy to establish the Negro's innocence. The title of the book has often puzzled readers because of Faulkner's insistence on calling attention to the creaky vehicle rather than the poignant tenor of his story of inter-racial and intra-racial tensions in the South.

Although when Faulkner deliberately set out to write detective stories, he produced works that deserved Wilson's strictures, he had earlier—quite probably less consciously—employed the techniques of the detective story in some of his most powerful works. Perhaps the greatest detective story in American literature is *Absalom, Absalom!* That we do not think of this novel as a "detective story" shows only that because so many specimens of the genre have—as Wilson charges—been such wooden things, we tend to use the label pejoratively rather than descriptively. We might understand more about both Faulkner and the potential of the detective story if we regarded *Absalom, Absalom!* as evidence that the genre appears trivial and sub-literary only because it has attracted so many hack writers. "The gift for telling stories is uncommon, like other artistic gifts," Wilson goes on to point out in his essay. Faulkner happens to have possessed and at times employed the rare gift that those usually branded "mystery writers" conspicuously lack.

So many mostly trivial detective stories have been written that critics have leaped to the conclusion that there is some necessary limitation or deficiency about the genre itself instead of exploring the hypothesis that it is such a difficult thing to endow this kind of story with life that examples of genuine literary quality—although theoretically possible—are exceedingly rare.

The trouble goes back to the origin of detective fiction as a conscious genre in Poe's "Murders in the Rue Morgue." Poe takes great pains in launching his story to acknowledge what Edmund Wilson later points out, that "a true connoisseur of this fiction must be able to suspend the demands of his imagination and literary taste and take the thing as an intellectual problem." Poe's narrator comments that "the narrative which follows will appear to the reader somewhat in the light of a commentary upon the propositions" that "the analytical power should not be confounded with simple ingenuity; for while the analyst is necessarily ingenious, the ingenious man is often remarkably incapable of analysis."

Poe was, in short, not interested simply in working out a far-fetched solution to some gruesome murders; he was concerned with showing the mind of the analyst in operation. His work thus escapes the condemnation justly visited upon that of most of his successors who have concerned themselves more often with ingenuity than analysis—as is evident from Wilson's comment that Jacques Barzun "informs the non-expert that the detective novel is a kind of game."

It was not a game to Poe. "Murders in the Rue Morgue" is his effort to dramatize the superiority of the lonely, isolated analyst to the pompous, bumbling official; it is a dramatic translation of the sensitive artist's struggle with the insensitive world about him that not only launches a new genre but stands—often unnoticed—as one of the first manifestoes of the artist's alienation from modern society. The barrier to understanding Poe's work is that in it as in the work of many later writers the superficial gadgetry is so distracting that the undercurrents of meaning that could justify Poe's saying in his review of Hawthorne's *Twice-Told Tales* that "some of the finest tales are tales of ratiocination" are completely overlooked.

Nor was the detective story, as Edmund Wilson points out, entirely a game to Conan Doyle, who achieved in the Sherlock Holmes stories the success that eluded him in his more consciously serious works. The Holmes stories, Wilson argues, "are literature, not because of the conjuring tricks and the puzzles, not because of the lively melodrama, which they have in common with many other detective stories, but by virtue of imagination and style." They are, in Poe's words, "tales of ratiocination," not just meaningless intellectual puzzles.

Nor was the detective story a game to Faulkner, at least when he was writing *Absalom, Absalom!* This labyrinthine narrative culminating in the young detective's hysterical cry when challenged about his feelings toward his native South, *"I dont hate it! I dont hate it!"* is not simply the tale of a morbidly inquisitive youth's efforts to fathom what mysterious things have gone on in a decaying mansion; it is rather the story of the young man's effort to solve the mansion's mysteries in order to come to terms with his own heritage, not just as Southerner, but as man.

Absalom, Absalom! is, as even early critics noted, a tale twice told. The reader is acquainted first with the public history of the rise and fall of Thomas Sutpen and his clan; then he participates in Quentin Compson's reconstruction—with the aid of his Harvard roommate—of the actual sequence of events. Some critics have denounced this double narrative as unnecessarily complicated (on the assumption that the novelist is just "telling" a story instead of forcing the reader to participate in discovering the story); others, more sensitive to Faulkner's aims, have praised the masterful construction. Few have noticed, however, that the novel employs one of the most conventional techniques of detective fiction. In "Murders in the Rue Morgue," for example, about the first two-fifths of the story is devoted to an account of what is public knowledge about the killings; the remaining three-fifths describes Dupin's reconstruction of the actual sequence of events. The proportions are not much different in *Absalom, Absalom!* A little less than half the book is devoted to "collecting the evidence," this inquiry culminating in Rosa Coldfield's long account of her part in Thomas Sutpen's fall. A little more than half details Quentin and his roommate's imaginative reconstruction of the events, which makes them participants in past history to the point that "it was not two but four of them riding the two horses through the dark over the frozen December ruts of that Christmas Eve" when Charles Bon and Henry Sutpen make the trip that seals the family's fate.

Nor is *Absalom, Absalom!* the only example among Faulkner's early important works of the use of the technique of the detective story. The famous fourth part of "The Bear," describing Isaac McCaslin's anxious reading of his family's ledgers in search of the secret of his contaminated heritage, involves the reader in piecing together a puzzle; "A Rose for Emily," with its shocking final revelation, uses the techniques of the detective story to tantalize the reader along; *Light in August* is, among other things, a kind of parody of the "hardboiled" detective story, in which the possibility of solving the mystery of Joe Christmas's origin is lost because of the irrational violence of his pursuers. Most important of all, even in the work that Faulkner himself regarded most highly, *The Sound and the Fury,* the interior monologues of the three brothers of the decaying family provide the "evidence" that gains its significance from the disclosures at the end of the narrative that allow all the "clues" to fall into place.

The difference between *The Sound and the Fury* and *Absalom, Absalom!* and the hundreds of detective stories that appear and disappear each year is not one of kind, but of intensity—as Edmund Wilson put it—of the author's ability to allow the reader "to see it and feel it." Faulkner was not concerned—at least during his greatest creative period in the late twenties and early thirties—with constructing arid intellectual puzzles. He perceived that life was full of mysteries that profoundly affect man's welfare, and he set about solving these with the mind of a detective coupled—as it rarely is—with the emotions and linguistic gifts of a great tragic artist.

As a result of the publication of Faulkner's interviews late in his life at Nagano, West Point, and Charlottesville and especially as a result of the disclosure of the correspondence constituting *The Faulkner-Cowley File* (1966), we are beginning to learn something of the way Faulkner approached his art. The most significant information that has so far come to light is found in Faulkner's brief reply to Malcolm Cowley's query about some remarks on *Absalom, Absalom!* that Cowley had made in an essay. Cowley had written:

> With a little cleverness, the whole novel might be explained as a connected and logical allegory, but this, I think, would be going far beyond the author's intention. First of all he was writing a story, and one that affected him deeply, but he was also brooding over a social situation. More or less unconsciously, the incidents in the story came to represent the forces and elements in the social situation, since the mind naturally works in terms of symbols and parallels.

Faulkner replied:

> You are correct; I was first of all (I still think) telling what I thought was a good story, and I believed Quentin could do it better than I in this case. But I accept gratefully all your implications, even though I didn't carry them consciously and simultaneously in the writing of it. In principle I'd like to think I could have. But I don't believe it would have been necessary to carry them or even to have known their analogous derivation to have had them in the story (Malcolm Cowley, *The Faulkner-Cowley File*, copyright 1966, pp. 13, 15-16).

This interchange sheds as much light on Faulkner's "creative process" as any critic of sensibility needs. Faulkner was primarily concerned not with "messages," but with spotting "good stories" and working out the most effective ways of telling them ("Quentin could do it better than I in this case"). The difference between him and the ingenious hack is that, as Malcolm Cowley puts it, Faulkner was "also brooding over a social situation." The stories that attracted him, that seemed worth telling, dealt with man's tragic relationship to his social situation. Faulkner's explanation of his own method of working provides one of the clearest evidences we have of just what Henry James meant when he said in "The Art of Fiction," "No good novel will ever proceed from a superficial mind; that seems to me an axiom which, for the artist in fiction, will cover all needful moral ground."

The implications of James's famous dictum have often been missed because of confusion about what is superficial. Poe is again helpful. Ridiculing the "boasted *acumen,* of the government agents," Dupin tells the narrator of "Murders in the Rue Morgue," "They have fallen into the gross but common error of confounding the unusual with the abstruse." *Depth* is commonly confused with the ability to perceive obscure, cabalistic secrets rather than to perceive undistorted a natural sequence of events. The agent of the murders in Poe's story, though bizarre and freakish, is completely natural, no supernatural or surrealistic force has intervened in human affairs. The mind that is not superficial does not necessarily know anything that is above or beyond nature and inaccessible to the rational mind; rather it has the comprehensive knowledge of nature that eludes those who can't see the forest for the trees and cannot escape a self-imposed preoccupation with trivia.

All the conscious moral purpose in the world thus will not gift an individual with the power to see through the superficial flux of events to the basic patterns of experience if he lacks the intensity of vision to "strike through the mask." The artist, on the other hand, with this intensity need not be disturbed by a conscious moral purpose; he would indeed be likely to be hampered by it, as Faulkner was late in his career when he substituted intellectual mapmaking for the intense effort to reconstruct hidden reality in a work like *A Fable.*

Yet if he lacked conscious moral purpose, he was surely driven by the detective's desire to solve a case, although the "case" that concerned him was no isolated crime, but man's whole situation in the world. Although he argued to Cowley that it was "Quentin Compson, not Faulkner," who brooded over the social situation, he made in the letter two statements that suggest singular intensity of purpose. First he observed, "I am telling the same story over and over, which is myself and the world . . . I'm trying to say it all in one sentence, between one Cap and one period." Later he added, "Art is simpler than people think because there is so little to write about. All the moving things are eternal in man's history and have been written before . . . ."

So Faulkner himself lends credence to the theory that his two greatest novels are about the same thing and that his other early works are simply glosses upon them. The perception that drove him through his greatest creative period is the timeworn adage about pride preceding a fall; but Faulkner brought what often remains platitude vividly to life. *Absalom, Absalom!* records the gradual reconstruction of the full measure of the devastation caused by a man who as a boy had been affronted by being sent around to the back door of a tidewater plantation house by a "monkey nigger." Instead of learning charity from this experience that destroys his ignorant innocence of social caste systems, Thomas Sutpen determines to work himself into a position in which he can push other people around as he has been pushed around. His ambition transplants tidewater corruption to the once virgin wilderness. Faulkner's rueful observation is that when men do lose their "innocence" about the structure of society, they repeat instead of correcting others' mistakes.

Absalom, Absalom! is itself only a variation upon the theme of *The Sound and the Fury,* that seeming tangle of fragments that moves briskly and relentlessly toward Luster's exultant cry as he smashes Benjy Compson's precarious world of sense impressions by driving the wrong way around the courthouse square, "Les show dem niggers how quality does, Benjy."

What Faulkner shows in the whole novel is how the self-styled quality of the Bascoms and Compsons destroys the families' patrimonies and alienates the community. What indeed Faulkner shows in all his work is what the kind of "quality" represented in their own minds by Temple Drake and Gowan Stevens (*Sanctuary*), Joanna Burden and Percy Grimm (*Light in August*), even the backwoods Bundrens (*As I Lay Dying*) and the oppressed Negroes (*Go Down, Moses*) does to make a shambles of the world. Pride is the destroyer of the natural order. No wonder the aged Ike McCaslin laments in "Delta Autumn," "No wonder the ruined woods I used to know don't cry for retribution! . . . The people who have destroyed it will accomplish its revenge."

Only the handful like Lena Grove in *Light in August,* who do not know the meaning of pride and exult in the simple positive act of bringing forth life, are exempt from the curse that lies not just over the South, but the whole world that Faulkner has perceived. As single-mindedly as the detective in *Les Miserables,* Faulkner looked beyond the petty triumphs and tragedies of individuals to perceive that man as species destroys himself; and out of this knowledge, possessed but not articulated into a generalization, he shaped the great novels that attempted to share his vision with the world.

The singularity of Faulkner's gifts—as a detective concerned not with contrived puzzles or petty daily crimes but with the concealed wellsprings of human behavior—help explain his obscurity during the thirties, when his novels moved almost unnoticed from the press to the remainder bin.

Most critics and readers were too preoccupied then with the day-to-day struggle to survive to gaze with Faulkner's awesome detachment on the phenomena around them, seeking dramatic evidence of the recurrent patterns of behavior underlying these phenomena. Although many of Faulkner's novels have important period applications (*Sartoris* and *Sanctuary* depict the alienation of the "lost generation"; *Light in August* and *The Hamlet* mirror the rise of fascism), they have been properly most highly valued for their timeless, "mythic" qualities. It remained for a later generation to appreciate the significance of the stories that Faulkner had ferreted out in his own unassuming quest. It still remains to be seen whether another writer can make equally impressive use of the technique of the detective story; for although not even all of the detective stories that Faulkner devised were works of consequence, the time that he spent upon the genre is vindicated by the mastery of techniques that made possible the culminating statement in *Absalom, Absalom!* of the vision of the human condition that he had gained from his Mississippi experience.

James M. Cain and the Tough Guy Novelists of the 30s

by David Madden

The twenty-minute egg of the hard-boiled school is James M. Cain. In 1940, in a famous essay called "The Boys in the Back Room," Edmund Wilson called him a poet of "the tabloid murder." A man and a woman, in the typical Cain novel, set out on a dangerous adventure. The object? For the man: the woman. For the woman: money. And murder is inevitable. "I write of the wish that comes true," says Cain, "for some reason a terrifying concept, at least to my imagination."

This conception produced his first and finest novel, *The Postman Always Rings Twice* (1934). Frank Chambers and Cora Papadakis meet on page 5, make love on 15, plot to kill Cora's husband on 22, and when their wish comes true on 72, the screws tighten on what Cain calls "the love-rack." Wilson charged that this novel, with its "too-well-oiled action" and "movie foreshortenings," came close to being a parody of tough movies, but he concluded that "brilliant moments of insight redeemed the unconscious burlesque; and there is enough of the real poet in Cain—both in writing and in imagination—to make one hope for something better." Of his thirteen other novels, only *The Butterfly* (1947), Cain's favorite, approaches the excellence of his first.

In the 20s and 30s, Cain worked as a reporter on *The Baltimore Sun,* editor of *The Lorraine Cross* (a weekly for the Allied Expeditionary Forces), professor of journalism at St. John's College, and editorial writer for Walter Lippmann on *The New York World;* he wrote articles interpreting the American scene for *The Atlantic, The American Mercury, The Nation, The New Yorker, The Saturday Evening Post, Esquire,* and *Vanity Fair.* Gang wars, union strife, and individual crimes of passion must have encouraged him to view American history as a long panorama of violence. Like Hemingway, Cain sharpened his vision in the midst of events, as when he reported on labor violence from the coalfields of West Virginia. Showing the spirit, if not the influence, of friends such as Mencken and Sinclair Lewis, and William Bolitho and Alexander Woollcott, who also wrote for the *World,* Cain's essays were iconoclastic, satirical, and cynical. For his raw, raw material, a jabbing, slicing prose and a tough tone seemed appropriate.

In his essays and dialogues (collected in *Our Government,* 1930), Cain examined the clichés of the union boss, the politician, the preacher, the pedagogue, and the editorial writer. These clichés, he observed, often came out of the American's compulsion toward self-dramatization. The unheroic quality of democracy is obvious in such people as the "servists," whom he analyzed in an essay called "The Pathology of Service," the purpose of which was "to isolate the bacillus of Service." The disease originated in the appetite of dull people for drama. In "Pastorale," an early short story, the American's need for self-dramatization betrays a man into confessing murder. As a young man, Cain admired the pyrotechnics of power, preferring "cynics" of the past (Napoleon was his favorite) to America's colorless public men, who lacked heroic lustre.

One aspect of self-dramatization is the inside-dopester strain in American character. Many American writers, Hemingway, for instance, strive to speak with authority on the fine points of special subjects. As a former journalist, Cain exhibits in his novels this voraciousness for facts, and therein lies part of his appeal. With the audacity and bravura of the fact-armed amateur, the Cain hero triumphs over great obstacles (though only momentarily, for when the wish comes true, nothing helps—he falls off the end of the plank). In the historical novels especially—*Past All Dishonor* (1946) and *Mignon* (1963)—Cain's immersion in his minutely researched background causes a conflict of intention: historical accuracy is achieved at the expense of drama. But if *The Moth* (1948) collapses under a burden of inside dope, *The Butterfly* succeeds, though both were heavily researched on the scene (he worked as a coal miner in West Virginia) and in the record.

As Dillinger walked toward the woman in red, thus signaling his own execution in the streets, Clark Gable, on the screen of Chicago's Biograph Theater, was walking to the electric chair in *Manhattan Melodrama*. Popular culture expressed the spontaneity of violence in America, and the public was eager, even while condemning it as evil, to experience it vicariously. On this craving for blood the American detective story has long thrived. (Our first literary export, it was immediately domesticated by the English; ironically, in the figure of James Bond—a "cool" version of Mike Hammer—England has assimilated the characteristics of our myth of masculine exploits and exported to us our own bill of goods.) On a higher level of intention, proletarian fiction also contributed to the atmosphere of violence. That the American's appetite for violence is stronger than his pretension to the refinements of civilization is clearly evident in popular culture. Cain has studied, some say cynically exploited, this trait in American character.

During Cain's New York years, the theater projected the tough attitude: *The Hairy Ape, Front Page, The Petrified Forest, Waiting for Lefty, Winterset, Dead End*. Although he had little success with plays, Cain's adaptation of *The Postman* did fairly well on Broadway in 1936. From his friend Philip Goodman, the New York producer, he learned about dramatic tension and narrative technique. But his greatest teacher of writing was Vincent Lawrence, former playwright, hard drinker, free spender, typical American tough guy, who hammered out highly successful movie scripts.

Hung over in the 30s, the disillusionment of the roaring twenties produced a public skepticism that welcomed a cycle of gangster films. *Public Enemy, Little Caesar,* and *Scarface* set the style. If in fighting to triumph over the limitations of his environment the glamorous gangster always lost, he made for everyone a momentary show of toughness. Now readers of Cain, Horace McCoy, and Dashiell Hammett could mentally cast Garfield, Cagney, Robinson, Muni, and Bogart as the aggressive hero. Classic gangster films have been made from tough novels; and not only hard-boiled but "serious" writers have been influenced by the pace, characters, tone, and attitudes of action films. At home and abroad, the tough guy became *the* American image. With his fast car and tommy gun, he resembled the cowboy with his fast horse and six-shooter. But the cowboy, a folk hero of the romantic past, offered escape from the depression; the gangster mastered, if only for an hour, conditions to which the average American had succumbed. Robert Warshow in "The Gangster as Tragic Hero" saw these movies as unconscious protests against the sham optimism of a society in collapse. "The experience of the gangster *as an experience of art* is universal to Americans," expressing "that part of the American psyche which rejects the qualities and the demands of modern life, which rejects 'Americanism' itself." James Agee and Parker Tyler have discussed movies made from Cain's novels as projecting special images of American attitudes.

But though *The Postman, Double Indemnity,* and *Mildred Pierce* (1941) were enormously successful as movies adapted by other writers, Cain, who moved to Hollywood in 1932, himself failed as a scriptwriter. And those novels which he thought naturals for the movies were never bought. As Raymond Chandler once demonstrated for Billy Wilder, Cain's dialogue is written to the eye; actors couldn't recite the visually exciting right-hand margin. Writing for the ear as Cain couldn't, Chandler caught the spirit of the dialogue in *Double Indemnity.*

The best tough novels were written by some of the finest screenwriters, and in Dashiell Hammett's *The Maltese Falcon* (1929), Horace McCoy's *They Shoot Horses, Don't They?* (1935), Raymond Chandler's *The Big Sleep* (1939), and Cain's Glendale novels, one relatively neglected area of the American fictional landscape— California (Hollywood in particular)—was presented in images as authentic and expressive as those in the novels of Huxley, West, Shulberg, Fitzgerald, and Waugh. Like those writers, Cain is interested in the way the high hopes of the romantic and violent westward movement wound down on the Pacific shore.

In its special way, the tough guy vision scrutinizes one of the central themes in American literature: the fate of American land, character, and dream. (Dream-seeker Gatsby, appropriately enough, rose from the underworld.) Leaving out the subtle phases between, the tough novelists show the failure of the dream by a camera-cold recording of the nightmare. Without attempting psychological analysis, they create psychological myths. Popular fiction can tell us much about ordinary people in a way that "serious" fiction, because it is aimed at an intellectual, aesthetically inclined minority, cannot. And tough novels are social documents, verifiable not by statistics but by facts of human nature as expressed at a certain time in a way appropriate to the social and cultural climate of that time.

With a purity of vision unimpaired by ideology, the tough novel projects a surface picture of American violence in the 30s. Violence is always close to the surface in a civilization resolutely committed to goals which create conditions for it as a kind of by-product. "Their characters," wrote Raymond Chandler, "lived in a world gone wrong, a world in which, long before the atom bomb, civilization had created machinery for its own destruction, and was learning to use it with all the moronic delight of a gangster trying out his first machine gun." As a journalist, Cain observed the tough guy mystique, recorded it in newspaper and magazine articles and editorials, then transformed it into myth in stories, plays, and novels.

Though Cain never deals directly with society's ills, his manner of dramatizing facets of American experience provides insights (expressionistically exaggerated perhaps) into the American dream turned nightmare, the all American boy turned tough guy. While they share the immediate realization of a common wish, Cora and Frank in *The Postman Always Rings Twice* each have another dream that persists mockingly in the background. Cora came to Hollywood from a small town in Iowa bemused by the dream most girls of the 30s cherished: to become a movie star. She failed, and Nick Papadakis rescued her from a hash house. But basically her values are middle-class, and above all she wants respectability, even if murder is the prerequisite. An anachronism in the age of technology, though he has a certain skill as a garage mechanic, Frank Chambers desires to be always on the move, compelled by something of the spirit of the open road that Whitman celebrated. For a moment, but only for a moment, he shares this romantic, idyllic vision with Cora. After the failure of their first attempt to murder Nick, they set out together for a life of wandering—like Charlie Chaplin, the tramp; and Paulette Goddard, the girl next door turned vagabond; abjuring modern times, striking out upon the open road, unfettered, into the sunset. Thus, in the criminal affair of these lovers, these deliberate outsiders, the two central dreams of the American experience—unrestrained mobility and respectable sedentariness—and two views of the American landscape—the open road and the mortgaged house—collide. As the dreams finally betray them, they begin, ironically, to turn on each other, for basically what Frank wants is Cora, the sexual dynamo, and what Cora wants is an instrument to be used in gaining her ends: money and respectability; and though she may convince herself that the right man, instead of a fat foreigner, is a necessary part of her aspirations, *this* man would soon wake up in the wrong dream.

Bemused by violence, Americans like to feel out, Cain says, all the nuances of the cliché "There but for the grace of God go I." To involve the reader more intimately in the social communion with violence, ritualized by mass media reportage, Cain deals with characters just removed from the gangster and private eye milieu. The death of a man like Frank releases the reader from the guilt of having identified with the character's wishes.

Cain claims that "the world's great literature is populated by thorough-going heels." Most of his own novels describe "life among the heels and the harpies." Though doomed by his faults, none whines about his punishment; on the eve of his execution, Frank Chambers refuses to shift responsibility for his actions to a hostile society. Cain admires the clear, hard, cold mind, and thrusts his characters into actions in which their daring and know-how enable them to meet any challenge. His typical hero is an "educated roughneck": a meat packing executive, an insurance agent, a bank executive, an engineer. But even his boxers, farmers, and mechanics prove adroit. These men crave praise and are sometimes immobilized, momentarily, by condemnation.

But Cain's men aren't afraid to be afraid; they weep or vomit when the sex is out of reach or the violence goes wrong. In "Tribute to a Hero," an early essay for *The Mercury,* he recalls a reluctant football hero at Washington College, where Cain's father was president. The boy displayed a combination of guts and cowardice that is seen in most Cain heroes and becomes a dangerous effeminacy in Howard Sharp, the hard-boiled opera singer of *Serenade* (1939). In conventional masculine traits, his women are often stronger than his men. Mildred Pierce is a banal American housewife who imagines herself noble as she exploits men, half-consciously, to gain her end—money. Cain's characters have been called crude, amoral, and uncomplicated. It is true that the dialectics of self-deception in which they become ensnarled are often only potentially profound, but he is primarily a master of the manipulation of surface action; the captive reader forgets that the characters—beyond the stark tensions of their predicament—are often not fully drawn.

Lust, pride, money, murder (and other forms of violence), food, religion—these are the simple raw materials of Cain's novels. Sex is deliberately implied when not directly expressed; as the characters lunge "rapidly from motive to act," the terrific pace of the narrative and the dialogue, with their climaxes, is sexual. Pursued in an atmosphere of evil, inseparable from violence, sex has an aura of the unnatural. Murder and money make the sex possible. Few writers permeate their characters' consciousnesses so thoroughly with the smell, the hot reaching anticipation, the grubby feel of money. The reader shares the urgency of the single-minded struggle for money and sex. The characters refer to their perfunctory and animalistic love-making as "holy"; love and murder produce a sham religious mystique. Cain has been accused of obscenity. That he seldom describes the sex act in detail and never uses four-letter words suggests his skill in creating the illusion of full description. "Criticism in this country," he has cause to remark, "is incorrigibly moralistic."

Tough optimism is clearly expressed in all of Cain's writing. At times he is cynical and satirical, but the American brand of masculine romanticism is also active, and occasionally even sentimentality intrudes. In Cain's world, chance, luck, coincidence, gamble and counter-gamble, risk, audacity, and the ability to improvise upon the given serve his characters, but usually end in defeating them. While he is capable of creating finely drawn moral dilemmas, as in *Mignon,* he is primarily interested in the *action* produced by them and their impact on character rather than in elaborating upon facets of the abstract issues.

But Cain is not all melodrama and disaster. Some of his novels are comedies, and none is without humor, wit, and even lyricism. Music is at the heart of three and is an element in most of the other novels. His mother was a singer; Cain himself worked hard at a music career but gave it up for lack of talent; his fourth wife, Florence McBeth, who died in 1966, sang opera in Chicago.

In the "pure novel" tradition of Flaubert and Gide, Joseph Hergesheimer aspired to "write a novel as compact and deadly as an automatic," and Georges Simenon has said, "I want to carve my novel in a piece of wood." Cain *has*—twice: *The Postman* and *The Butterfly.* Narrative, action, rhythm, character, and style, unencumbered by philosophy, are primary elements in a novel which, generated by pace, should move in a brief exposure toward the pure condition of abstract art and unprogrammatic music. Neither an instrument of instruction nor a medium of information, the pure novel is concerned only with its own drama. In Cain's use of "the love-rack," we view two people only in terms of the experience, which raises and answers its own questions and refers to nothing extraneous. Out of "a morbid fear of boring" the reader, Cain "needles a story at the least hint of a letdown," striving for a "rising coefficient of intensity," because he believes that "the worst offense of narrative . . . is tepidity, and in my work, God willing, you will never find it." He asks, "What is a 'popular' novelist? . . . The aim of art is to cast a spell on the beholder; it has no other aim." Casting a spell in sixteen languages, *The Postman* has had a vigorous 32 year sale.

A conscious technican of the "pure novel," Cain develops a theatrical and cinematic pace that is phenomenal in his best work. "You may not like *Serenade*," said William Rose Benét, "but I defy you to lay it down." Though the neat phrases sometimes falter into embarrassing cuteness, Cain manages to infuse virtually every moment with apparent urgency. As his simple dialogue progresses from point to point, it sustains subtle undercurrents. While stock devices sometimes mar his work, they are often used effectively as absurd helps or hindrances to the character who strives to score against "the way things are."

Even in Cain's essays, an aggressive, almost arrogant, but commanding "I" is in control. The first person works best for his deliberate transformation of the clichés of everyday speech. "Many of life's most moving things are banal. . . . I try, in using a cliché, to set it up so perhaps it gains its own awkward, pathetic eloquence." The third person often lures Cain into literary clichés, as in his short stories for *Liberty* in the 30s.

As a force in the tough school, Cain contributed to the revolutionary re-structuring of much of European fiction in the 30s and 40s. American literature first made a strong impact on the world through the tough novel; European literary historians stress this phenomenon. Objective and dispassionate, the tough writers dispensed with the Jamesean analysis of the psychological inner life and made character delineation subordinate to expressive action. Deeply pessimistic, they denied the validity of established institutions and attitudes by showing the futility of the wish come true, and by refusing to judge violent behavior in an absurd world. Cain was received on a level with Hemingway and Faulkner. Americans were too steeped in tough fiction to see *The Postman's* originality as the French did. According to Germaine Brée, that novel was the model for Camus' *The Stranger*. A close comparison of the two novels reveals not only a resemblance between Frank Chambers and Meursault, but an astonishing structural similarity as well. The first half of Camus' novel is in the coldly objective style of *The Postman;* in the second half, Camus enunciates a view of life that is only implicit in Cain.

In 1942, Cain said he wanted "to tell tales of a little wider implication." He continues at 75—most durable of the "tough" novelists—to promise a novel of greater depth and significance. While W. M. Frohock and other historians of American literature deplore his exploitation of violence and sex, few fail to note Cain's influence. Cain has said, "I don't lack for at least as much recognition as I deserve." But how much *does* he deserve? With that question, embracing the whole tough guy school, readers are reopening an important chapter in American literature.

Henry Miller, Defender
of the Marginal Life

by Frederick J. Hoffman

The convention that most people believe is that, a few weeks after the "Wall Street Crash" of October, 1929, boatloads of Americans returned from Europe, leaving the streets and the bars of Paris empty. There is another cliché: that when the young men and women reached stateside, they turned into serious workers, abandoned the cause of "l'art pur," and were never heard from again. Neither of these statements is correct, although expatriation was rather changed in the 1930s. There were fewer writers, artists and loafers in the Paris area. To the degree that the phenomena of expatriation had had economic causes, the number of expatriates diminished in that decade; but there were those who, for one reason and for another, either stuck it out in Paris or were moved to come for the first time.

This is not an argument for the invariable conjunction of Paris and the *avant garde*, though there have been times when the two seemed indispensable to each other. It is simply my point that the leftist point of reference (John Reed Clubs and magazines, the strike novel, proletarian manifestoes, the "grand tour" to Moscow, to see the future happening, etc.) is not invariably the proper one to use. While he did (in *Owl's Clover*, 1936) engage in debate with leftist ideologies, Wallace Stevens continued his poetic development along the lines of the 1920s, and it was a quite unideological search for a conjunction of the imagination with reality. If Eliot's career in the 1930's was dominated by anything, it was the quite unMarxist moral heroism of the Anglican Church and the quite conservative efforts to "define" society (in the sense of *limiting* it and thus enabling him to comprehend it). Faulkner's "time of genius" occurred from 1929 to 1942; yet almost none of his writings can be said to be relevant to a doctrinaire reading or interpretation. In other words, I maintain that there was a continuity of 1910s, 1920s, and 1930s in our culture and there is a sufficient mass of evidence to substantiate a claim of non-political *"avant-garde"* literary activity.

* * *

Henry Miller is perhaps an important case in point. He is also a strange phenomenon in modern literature. Born with the generation of Faulkner and even Eliot (Miller first saw the light of day on Manhattan island in 1891), he nevertheless did not become known as a writer until 1934, when he was 43 years old. He seemed to have leaped over the 1920s and part of the 1910s, to become established in the 1930s as a rallying point and a center of contention.

Let us look at the record of his life. His youth was spent in the Williamsburg and the Bushwick sections of Brooklyn. While others of his generation were at Harvard or in "the Village," Miller worked in clerical jobs and (from 1920-1924) as messenger employment manager for the Western Union (the "Cosmodemonic Telegraph Company" of *Sexus,* 1949); when most of these others came back from Europe, Miller was just beginning his pilgrimage abroad. Two wives and one child after his start as a man and a writer, he was in Europe (in 1928-1929) to see what he had missed thus far; and he returned (alone) the next year, to spend the next decade (except for a brief period in New York, in 1934) in or near Paris.

What kind of world was Miller's Paris? Surely there were many differences from James's, from Joyce's, and from Pound's. He spent several months in Dijon as teaching assistant in a *lycée;* from the experience came some fine descriptions of the mustard capital of the world. But the time in Paris is the most important. For a while he lived a hand-to-mouth existence (the record is in *The Tropic of Cancer,* 1934), just managing to stay one step ahead of the twin monsters of hunger and anonymity. Then he found work, and a room, both thanks to Alfred Perlès; and, once his roots were struck, he managed to stay long enough to become the center of an active group of writers, most of whose genius was not recognized until 1950 or later. Not that it was not published until then, but rather that it was either banned in the United States (as was Miller's) or insufficiently noticed until after World War II. Miller was not a coterie leader, as Pound had been in the years 1914 through 1930, but did manage to acquaint himself with a number of people and to make them glad for his praise and his encouragement.

Anaïs Nin was one of these, and the volume of his letters to her, ably edited by Gunther Stuhlmann (1965), testifies again and again to his enthusiasms, his kindness and concern, and his wish to shout both of them into fame in the shortest possible time. The friendship with Miss Nin began in Paris in the fall of 1931. Penniless and often quite beside himself from cold and hunger, he nevertheless was elated over his "escape" from Brooklyn and the "air-conditioned nightmare" of the United States. Miss Nin provided the right open door to a sophisticated world. Miller scarcely ever relented in his indictment of American culture.

Though he was subsequently, in his cross-country tour (1940-1941), to be amazed and even exhilarated by the vastness of the country, and especially by certain breath-taking passages of it, he was mistrustful of the people, and on the defensive about his position as expatriate, "rebel-buffoon," "apocalyptic comedian," what have you (the last two of these are Kingsley Widmer's phrases, taken from his *Henry Miller* [1963]). More explicitly, he loved what he discovered to be the freedom of the Gallic spirit, the sense (as he saw it) of concern with the arts, the absence of Puritan restraints. Though there were smug bourgeoisie in France (after all, the word was itself French) and he sometimes saw them for what they were, his Gallomania went quite far, and it included a general affection for those of his contemporaries who chose to remain "in exile" also. He shared their enthusiasms, and tried to communicate his own to them. For example, Miss Nin's first book was an appreciation of D. H. Lawrence (published by Edward W. Titus in Paris in 1932); having read it in MS and acclaimed it, Miller thereafter plunged into an ambitious work on his own, called *The World of Lawrence*. It was never published as such, though parts of it subsequently appeared, in *Sunday After the War* (1944).

In short, Miller was anxious to raise his enthusiasm for friends to the level of his being the equivalent of *Salon* leader, in the 1930's version of that phrase. What Gunther Stuhlmann calls "the new 'internationalists' without an Internationale" included Miss Nin, Perlès (who in 1956 published *My Friend Henry Miller,* an "intimate biography"), Michael Fraenkel (with whom he engaged in a long series of disquisitions called rather loosely *Hamlet* and first published in London in 1939), Walter Lowenfels, Hilaire Hiler, the Hungarian photographer Brassai, the German painter Hans Reichel, and the British novelist Lawrence Durrell. Some of these never achieved eminence; for others it was postponed. But they were a fairly congenial group of "internationalists," in part at least kept together by Miller's sense of the importance of artists and writers as a group, perhaps otherwise isolated in the wide world but unified in their recognition and appreciation of each other.

Henry Miller was pre-eminently a great letter writer. There were times when, as in the case of the *Hamlet* series, he could produce what he called a "pompous monologue" (see Widmer, p. 56), really much too pretentious to retain the warmth and charm of the correspondents, except occasionally. The letters to Miss Nin and those to Lawrence Durrell (a selection of the latter was edited by George Wickes and published in 1963), however, are frequently surcharged with Miller's personal charm; he often gave freely of himself, and even when he was blowing his own horn most loudly, he allowed his correspondent to hear himself think. In her *Diary* (only the 1931-1934 segment has so far been published, also edited by Gunther Stuhlmann), Anaïs Nin speaks of Miller as "a mythical animal." "I enjoy the power of his writing," she continues, "the ugly, destructive, fearless cathartic strength." But she does touch a tender, a sensitive spot when she writes: "He is a gentle savage, who lives directed entirely by his whims, moods, his rhythms, and does not notice others' moods or needs." But the record is there, of shared interests and tastes, of mutual services and sacrifices.

For a short while, Miller even had his "little magazine." The *Booster,* originally a tourist magazine in Paris, became something else again under the editorship of the "Villa Seurat" group, Miller, Perlès, Durrell, and others. From April to Christmas of 1938, its last months, it was more appropriately called *Delta,* and the large advertisements disappeared from its pages, and all of the editors searched for sustaining subscriptions and angels.

* * *

If there is any point in considering Henry Miller as an *avant-garde* personality, then we must establish his position, his stance, the point of view from which he judged life and art. First of all, he was a satirist-critic of the middle-class life in his native country. In this he was scarcely original, though some of his satirical commentary had a characteristic stamp. The shorter pieces (such as those in *The Cosmologic Eye*, 1945, and *Remember to Remember*, 1947) are sometimes memorable, and especially these: "Max," in the former (pp. 14-49); and, in the latter, "Astrological Fricassee" (pp. 217-73). There are important passages also in *Black Spring* (1936), *The Tropic of Capricorn* (1939), and of course *The Air-Conditioned Nightmare* (1945). Mainly the points are: that the majority of men are obtuse and dull, greedy and opportunistic: that they lack the sensitivity of the artist and the clown (a special version of the secular Jesus Christ, with which Miller occasionally associated himself); that, being such, they fail to take advantage of the genuine opportunities available to them, to realize themselves; that they spoil both nature and man (neon lights and the Grand Canyon, etc.). As the meditative man of Big Sur, California, in the years 1946-1960, Miller slowly worked some of these attitudes out of his system, though his conception of the artist as clown, of what Kingsley Widmer, in chapter one of his study, calls "The Apocalyptic Comedian" remained consistently there through most of his career. After all, he has become a well-fed man through the eventual release of his books from the oblivion of their being confined to Europe, the Orient, and on sailors' shelves on the way to and from these continents.

The characteristic that most distinguishes his denunciations of his country and his class is exuberance, or vitality. He not only believes in the necessary bifurcation of middle-class humanity into artist and non-artist; he has, for most of his life at least, acted out his separation from the stolid citizen, by remaining dependent upon his own resources, by loudly proclaiming his difference, and by noisily assisting and sponsoring others whom he considered equally fortunate in being equally isolated. In other words, in his satirical position he had "a flair," a manner of speaking, a way of assuming the responsibilities of the stand he took. At least in the Paris years of the 1930s, he was busy doing two things: staying "on the margin" and writing thousands of pages describing and defending that marginal life.

One of the freedoms he defended was, of course, sexual freedom. Or, rather, he fought quite innocently for sexual frankness in literature. This battle was a continuation of what had been going on in the second and third decades of the century. That it was no stranger in the nineteenth century is testified to in Steven Marcus's book, *The Other Victorians* (1966). There are certain basic differences, however, from the bohemian 1920s and the class which Marcus discusses. For one thing, Miller not only assumes that it is a healthy (and a healthful) thing to free the unconscious from the several Freudian traps provided for it by a Puritan society for centuries. He regards the discussion of sexual relations, entirely free of the taboos and hesitancies of middle-class society, as a natural and indispensable part of the life that literature copes and deals with. To exclude sex from literature is to deprive it of a necessary ingredient. To provide sex with a special and excluding vocabulary is to give the sexual relationship a set of nuances which distort.

So Henry Miller is frank about these matters in a new way. He is much too candid about them to call his literature pornographic. Yet there is also something strangely limited in his descriptions of the sexual affairs he and his friends had. The peculiarities come from three sources: one of these is his acceptance of naturalism in his portrayal of the act itself. The result is that there are no Laurentian embellishments. Compared with the sexual scenes of the two *Tropics* and the *Rosy Crucifixion* trilogy, the meetings of Lady Chatterley and Mellors, her gardener lover, are romantic, idyllic, and sentimental. Miller's attitude toward sex is, secondly, that of an individualist. Kingsley Widmer argues, perhaps too strenuously but not without cause, for Miller's being in the nineteenth century American tradition of Thoreau, Emerson and Whitman. Quoting from *The Black Spring,* Widmer describes Miller as "waiting on a Nietzschean mountain top for the new revelation," and meanwhile wishing "to contemplate 'a lone individual,' a man without name or country, a man whom I respect because he has absolutely nothing in common with you—MYSELF!" (p. 51)

There are two other characteristics of Miller's view of life, and, correspondingly, of his "style." In the first of these, there is a strong element in his work of the apocalyptic, of the frantically prophetic. He aims to push the human experience to a fourth and even to a fifth dimension. In those of his books which we must call novels because they are, though loosely, narratives, the vibrations of the physical experience move to one of two extremes: the abjectly and even despondently negative polarity of what Wallace Stevens calls "the malady of the quotidian," and the wildly exhilarating positive polarity of transcendent implication. Just how this latter act of transcendence is managed it is often difficult to comprehend, except that, as he nears it, his style thickens even though the plot doesn't; it becomes rich and luxuriant, rich in superlatives of language, punctuation, and apostrophe. It is sex on a grand scale and in a gawdy scene; from being "Henry Miller" (The "I" of these narratives is a "Henry Miller" as a subject of the Henry Miller as an author), undressed, ready and a bit ludicrous, he becomes a Gargantuan Henry who sits at a feast of the pleasures of the physical animal.

Finally, this hyperbole of attitude-taking has, within it, the grains of the absurd. Miller is like Lawrence often in being almost entirely humorless about himself and about his sexual prowess. When he rescues himself from these strangely vacuous situations, we can appreciate the absurdities and the ambiguities of the "combat with the sun" (Wallace Stevens's words again). Kingsley Widmer's approach to Miller is probably unnecessarily restrictive, though it is pertinent here. For one thing, one notices in this connection a didactic purpose, what Widmer calls the buffoonish role "of substituting writing for life." Just how profound this observation is, I do not know; I do know, however, that there is something of this spirit in Miller's writing, implicit in his attempts to elevate (or to escalate?) human experience to a surreal level (he once thought of himself as a surrealist, though it is doubtful that he could dissociate his own sentimentality from the movement). The writer who gives all to, as well as sacrifices all for, his art is, in many respects, a buffoon-hero. The effect of the writing is at once half-profound and half-comical; that is, it enlists our sentimentality and our wit at the same time.

In this role of artist-hero who has somehow taken over command of experience by means of writing about it (in the sense that writing about it becomes a new way of experiencing it), Henry Miller has become an elder-hero of the beatniks. Just where he belongs in the hierarchical game of who-preceded-whom, or the *einflüss* ploy, it is for the moment a bit difficult to say. He is the artist-hero for a later generation in being altogether frank, non-allusive (except in the explosive sense of "these are the books I read last week"), non-erudite, frankly physical, and quite shameless in the matter of trying out influences for size. In this sense, Rimbaud became Miller's "kind of man" (See *The Time of the Assassins*, 1956), as Buddhism was Kerouac's "kind of religion."

Some of this position-taking is ridiculous, though there is always an element of lonely grandeur in it (the man living at Big Sur, his books banned, etc.). When Miller is aware too that it is ridiculous, the laugh can be quite ingratiating. In this respect, one comes upon in his formless, even endless autobiographical narratives, moments of exquisite nonsense, of pure absurdity, which are nevertheless preserved from being worthless by the fact that they contain their own normative conditioners. Henry Miller is a curious example of the American genius waiting for a bus: the man who can spend one day in awesome stillness contemplating his navel, *becoming* a part of the being that is the eternally present time, and will on the next day pace furiously up and down the narrow corridor of the here and the now. He is often not at all profound when he thinks he is or wishes he were; he is often quite strikingly witty when he is least pretentious. And he has, in the meanwhile, proved I think, quite convincingly) what a man of the 1930s can contribute who is quite entirely unideological—in fact, often, not even logical. In this sense, he is of the *"avant-garde"* of the 1930s. The special forms of deprivation of that decade do not lead to "documents," but rather to a heroism of the ordinary.

Richard Wright in a Moment of Truth

by Blyden Jackson

Richard Wright fled the South in 1927, two months after his nineteenth birthday. He came directly to Chicago, where by 1932, led by his enthusiastic attachment to a John Reed Club, he had become a Communist. His Communist affiliation brought him eventually into association with a fellow Communist who, like himself, was a Negro born and bred at a considerable distance below the Mason and Dixon Line. Wright speaks of this black fellow-Communist, under the almost certain alias of Ben Ross, in Wright's version of his own experience of communism, which he originally contributed, under the title "I Tried to be a Communist," to the *Atlantic Monthly* in 1944. This so-called Ross, who had a Jewish wife, the mother, by him, of a young son, interested Wright deeply. Wright saw Ross as "a man struggling blindly between two societies," and felt that if he "could get . . . Ross's story, . . . he could make known some of the difficulties in the adjustment of a folk people to an urban environment." Therefore, he persuaded Ross, in effect, to sit for a pen portrait. On occasion he interviewed Ross for hours in Ross's home. Meanwhile, however, the Communist command in Chicago had become cognizant of Wright's interest in Ross and had begun to view his interest with mounting concern. Once aware of the Party's apprehensions, Ross ceased to speak freely to Wright either of his life or of himself. This inhibition of Ross's responsiveness sabotaged Wright's original hopes. Through

81

Ross, moreover, Wright had met some of Ross's friends and, expanding on his original plan, had conceived the notion now of doing, with Ross and Ross's friends all in mind, a series of biographical sketches. Now, however, not only Ross but all of Ross's friends as well had become afraid to talk to Wright as Wright had once had ample reason to suppose they might. Wright consequently altered his intentions. In virtually Wright's own words, after he saw that he could do nothing to counteract the effect of the Party's powerful influence, he merely sat and listened to Ross and his friends tell tales of Southern Negro experience, noting them down in his mind, and no longer daring to ask questions for fear his informants would become alarmed. In spite of his informant's reticence, he became drenched in the details of their lives. He gave up the idea of writing biographical sketches and settled finally upon writing a series of short stories, using the material he had got from Ross and his friends, building upon it and inventing from it. Thus he wove a tale of a group of black boys trespassing upon the property of a white man and the lynching that followed. The story was published eventually under the title of "Big Boy Leaves Home."

Corroboration of Wright's direct testimony in "I Tried to be a Communist," and some further suggestions concerning the genesis of "Big Boy Leaves Home," are supplied in Constance Webb's biography of Wright, which positively identifies Ross as one David Poindexter, a black member of the Communist Party, who had been born in southwest Tennessee in 1903 and had come North when he was seventeen. The family attributed by Miss Webb to Poindexter is the same as that attributed by Wright to Ross. In all the other details which she stipulates, moreover, including Poindexter's status as the original of Big Boy, Miss Webb assimilates Poindexter to the person whom Wright, conceivably in order not to expose a friend and benefactor to possible jeopardy, named as Ross in "I Tried to be a Communist." But when she reports directly on the genesis of "Big Boy Leaves Home," Miss Webb does not parrot what Wright had once said about his determination, if he could, to use Poindexter, or Ross, as an instrument by means of which he could make known some of the difficulties attendant upon the adjustment of a folk people to an urban environment. In this context, as a matter of fact, she makes a statement which would seem to contradict Wright's own about the folk. She says, instead and unequivocally, that in his first series of short stories, *Uncle Tom's Children* (of which "Big Boy Leaves Home" became a part), Wright set himself a conscious problem, the explication of the quality of will the Negro must possess to live and die in a country which denies him his humanity. Furthermore, applying her statement to "Big Boy Leaves Home" specifically, she asserts, within her analysis of that story, that "Big Boy Leaves Home" represents this quality of will as being "only that of the most elemental level—the ability to endure," for, she finally adds, the lesson to be extracted from Big Boy's experience is the dependence of his survival "upon the communal nature of the black community which planned, aided, and organized an escape."

When she says that Wright, in creating "Big Boy Leaves Home" and the other stories in *Uncle Tom's Children*, "set himself a conscious problem," the significant word is *conscious*. In the "Introduction" to her biography, Miss Webb leaves no doubt that the book bears the character of an official life. Wright made of her, she clearly implies, an *alter ego* privy to virtually all of himself that he could communicate to her or anyone. Furthermore, although the word *conscious* does not appear in her declaration that Big Boy's story was planned to demonstrate how his community rallied round him to ensure the preservation of his life, it seems unmistakably clear that here she speaks, too, as a medium who is reporting not only what was in Wright's mind, but also what she would contend he knew was there. She reveals that Wright had chosen a definite thing to do when he wrote "Big Boy Leaves Home," and that he was not confused as to the nature of that thing. Her testimony argues also Wright's own belief that he had substantially achieved his conscious intent.

Writers, however, sometimes belie their own intentions. Sometimes, moreover, what they do actually may well seem better than what they thought they had intended. No one, I think, would argue seriously for a reading of "Big Boy Leaves Home" as an account of an adjustment by an agrarian folk to an urban setting, deeply though Wright once indicated that he was interested in Ross-Poindexter and drenched though he once was in Ross-Poindexter's life and history. If then, however, "Big Boy Leaves Home" is to be read primarily as a parable about the quality of will necessary for the Negro to solve the major problem which he faces in his American environment, and if the message of such a parable centers in an account of the manner in which one Negro community expressed the quality of its will through its capacity to save some of its own, then neither the form nor the content of the parable is aesthetically impressive. "Big Boy Leaves Home" becomes then only an exercise in the depiction of a failure. Its focal point, if not its climax, must then be found in the third episode, for in this episode the representatives of the Negro community do gather, in Big Boy's home. The preacher, Elder Peters, is there, and Brother Jenkins and Brother Sanders, with Big Boy's parents and his sister. They commune with each other. But with what results? Big Boy's father can only berate Big Boy on the folly of his disobedience to his mother's injunction to go to school. The women in the house can only watch the men gathered there in virtually unbroken silence. No one can respond affirmatively to the distressed father's plea for financial aid. The sister has done some service in bringing to the house three outside counsellors. The mother gives Big Boy simple food to take with him when he leaves. Still, it is chance alone and Big Boy's own animal excellences which pave the way for his escape from certain death. No effective aid reaches his friend Bobo. No account is taken of provisions to safeguard Big Boy's family, who, as Big Boy later overhears in his kiln, are burned out of their modest dwelling. The most that can be said when all is done is that Big Boy did elude his would-be slayers and that a fellow Negro, who happened to be going in that direction anyhow, drove him North.

But to read "Big Boy Leaves Home," whatever Wright's original conscious aims, in accord with the form dictated for it by its own development, and to sense its content shaping itself to match that form, and its function emerging as the strong, inevitable concomitant of both, is to witness what well may be one of the three or four finest moments in Negro fiction. Of this inherent form and content it is now high time to speak.

Big Boy's story is shaped into five episodes, conducting a flow of action and related meaning from a point of attack to a conclusion which should round out and justify the whole. This form, at least in its handling here, is flexible as well as fluid. It permits variations of pitch and tone and atmosphere which all contribute to the story's total impact. At the beginning the pitch is moderate. The tone and atmosphere are genial, almost sweet. The function of the content is expository. The identity of the protagonist is established and the condition of all four of the boys involved made known. And beyond all this a theme is adumbrated. For these boys are scholars out of school. They have interrupted their vocation for a holiday of their own making. Still, the fact is clear. They are young, much untaught, and at an impressionable age. To learn, to grow, in other words, in one way or another, is their *métier*. It is hard to see how they should live through any single day without acquiring some new knowledge. In what they are reside the germs of what this tale must be. Then comes the first progression, bringing with itself a proper set of changes. At a swimming hole the white world intrudes. The mood of the first episode is shattered by killings. In a swirl of strident sound and emotions at high pitch and harshly tuned, with corresponding action that is equally cacophonous, a motif of pain and mystery, the ugliness of racistic custom is introduced. Then comes an interlude with a reduction in pitch and a moderation of tone, but without a return to the relative serenity of the introduction, as Big Boy spends a moment with his own kind in his father's house. But this interlude is also prelude, and a fitting one, to the big scene of the story. The big scene, as the logic of the story would demand, is the lynching on the hill, the spectacle of Bobo coated with hot tar and white feathers, burning in the night. This, as we shall see in terms of content, is the moment of truth in the story. It is also the very peak of the wave of form, when pitch and tone and atmosphere all coalesce at their highest points. The story cannot end at such a level of crescendo and fortissimo. It does not; it declines to the low key of its final episode when Big Boy, all passion spent, drifts off to slumber on the bed of the truck that bears him away to the North. But let us return to the lynching on the hill.

I have said that for this story it is the moment of truth. And it is. It is the moment when Wright, whether wittingly or not, gathers up the essence of that which he is struggling to express and stores it all into one symbol and its attendant setting. For the spectacle of Bobo aflame at the stake does constitute a symbol. It is a symbol, moreover, the phallic connotations of which cannot be denied. Indeed, the particularity of its detail—the shape of its mass, its coating of tar, the whitness of the feathers attached to its surface or floating out into the surrounding air—are almost all too grossly and gruesomely verisimilar for genteel contemplation. Whether Wright so intended it or not, the lynching of Bobo is symbolically a rite of castration. It is the ultimate indignity that can be inflicted upon an individual. Such an indignity strips from a man his manhood, removes from him the last vestige of his power and the last resort of his self-respect. In the lynching of Bobo, thus, all lynchings are explained, and all race prejudice. Both are truly in essence acts of castration. It is not for nothing that the grinning darky, hat in hand and bowing low, his backside exposed as if for a kick in the buttocks, seems so much a eunuch. He has accepted in his heart the final abasement, the complete surrender of his will, and so of his citadel of self, to anyone with a white skin. He has capitulated to the most arrogant demand which one human creature can make upon another. This, then, is the true anatomy of racism. It makes no difference where or how it prefers its claims, whether in an apology for its being so adroitly composed as Stark Young's novel *So Red the Rose* or in the blatant conduct of the old-style sheeted Ku Klux Klan. What racism demands is that every white man should be permitted to reserve the right to visit, with impunity, upon any Negro what ever, any outrage of that Negro's personality the white man chooses to impose. This, then, is the symbolism of Bobo's burning body on the hill. But around that symbolism clusters another set of facts put into another pregnant image. For, as Bobo burning illustrates the essence of one indispensable aspect of racism, the mob illustrates another. It is an efficient mob, a homogenous grouping. Yet no one has really organized it. It has no officers and no carefully compiled manual of behavior. Still it operates like a watchmaker universe. Its members know what they are supposed to do, and they do it, as if they were performing the steps of a ritual dance—which of course they are. For that is the real secret of the people gathered around Bobo on his Golgotha. They are responding not only to xenophobia and to an obscene lust for power. They are responding also to an urge equally as neanderthal in its origins. They are acting tribally, even as every lodge brother, black or white or yellow or red, who ever gave a secret handshake and every Babbit who ever applauded a toast-master's feeble attempts at jollity at the luncheon of his service club.

To belong, to conform, and thus to avoid the existentialist nightmare of exercising the prerogative of individual freedom of choice; to be able to contribute all of one's own release of foible and malice to custom that must be followed for the good of the community; to accept the myth that at some time in the misty past a voice, as it were, from some local Sinai spoke to the elders of the tribe and told them how certain things must be done and what prescribed rites must be followed to avert the anger of the gods; thus to be exempted from a sense of guilt at one's own evil; thus to hallow the meanest of the herd instincts; thus to institutionalize mediocrity's hatred of the indomitable spirit and its envy of strength and beauty; this is the pathos, and yet an important part of the explanation, of the capacity to endure of the tribe. This is also as much a part of racism as its lust for power. The castration and the tribalism complement each other. Without either, racism would not be at all exactly what it is. To perceive them, to really take them in, is, as Henry James might say, to see and know what is *there*. And it is part of the excellence of form in this story that Big Boy does see them, that by the story's own handling of its arrangements he is put in such a position that he cannot do otherwise. For, as this story so manages the sense of form which shapes its episodes to place its big scene right, it regulates concurrently another element of form, its control of its own point of view, to the end that at the proper point in the narrative's development the impression it conveys of who is doing the seeing will be as right as the prominence and the substance of what is to be seen.

Thus at the beginning of the story we are aware of, and share, to some extent, in the consciousness of all four boys. But this is Big Boy's story. It is really he whose loss of innocence, as it were, and compulsory education under special circumstances embody all that this story has to say. And so, increasingly, as the story moves from the open country to the lynching on the hill, Big Boy's consciousness becomes the sole point of view. Yet this constriction and this concentration are really the ultimate outgrowth of a rather delicate continuous maneuver of adjustment. Throughout the bulk of his story Wright's handling of his point of view is as dramatic as his separation of his matter into scenes. We watch the characters perform. We hear them talk. From outside their consciousnesses we infer their thoughts and feelings. Yet we identify increasingly with Big Boy, if for no other reason than that we see nothing which he cannot see and hear nothing which he cannot hear. But after Big Boy bids adieu to his parents and their friends and, successfully negotiating his sprint through hostile territory to Bullard's Road, comes to bay at last crouched deep within his kiln, we become more and more intensely one with him. We wonder with him why Bobo has not come, share with him his reverie as he relives the events of his day, mourn with him for the other two friends who have been killed, regret with him that he did not bring with him his father's shotgun, and finally, in fantasy, imagine with him that he is blasting away with that shotgun as he withstands a mob. As white men searching for the Negro "bastards" drift down *his* hill we share, too, his fear, and finally, as the lynch mob gathers, our senses become, like his, preternaturally acute, to watch with him in anguish and extreme distress the torture and destruction of the last of his close boyhood friends. Thus the heightening and the concentration of the point of view join with the elevation of the episode and the power of the symbolism and the imagery to speak in blended voices acting in mighty concert of the inner nature of racism and to trace its roots deep down into the past of human psychology and custom.

It is not a quality of the Negro will which this story explicates, nor is it anything to do with folk adjustment in a city. Far from either. It is, rather, the psychology, and the anthropology, of American racism. It is a lesson given to Big Boy and through him to the world at large. It is a lesson, moreover, which rounds off beautifully both the form and substance of "Big Boy Leaves Home." For the plot of this story represents a progress, not a conflict. Its succession of vignettes combine to form a curious kind of sentimental journey in which Big Boy does leave home; does lose, that is, his relative state of innocence; and does experience an illumination, an exercise in education, that provides him with a terrible, but richly freighted, insight into the adult world.

Reading the Proletarians —
Thirty Years Later

by David G. Pugh

The human memory shows a certain inevitability in selecting what to recall and revive from any previous era. The Gay Nineties: seen in a prism of mauve or yellow, "Buffalo Gals aren't ya comin' out tonight," Little Egypt and San Juan Hill—not the red lanterns and broken necked cranes of the Pullman Strike, the Wobblies, or Coxey's Army on its march to Washington. Pre-World War 1: bathed in the light of Nora Bayes' "Harvest Moon," interurban trolleys on the banks of the Wabash, and Booth Tarkington's Penrod —not the murk of the Jungle west of Halsted Street at the stock-yards, the smells and sounds of the sweatshops and Old Law Tene-ments by the Third Avenue El, or rickety youngsters scrabbling for coal along the mine spurs in Appalachia.

Even the War: it's not accident that Snoopy in the *Peanuts* cartoons dreams of Sopwith Camels, dogfights with Fokkers and the Mademoiselle from Armentieres—not the gassed trenches near Ypres. We have also survived the heightening and shaping of the Jazz Age: speakeasies, John Held, Jr., flappers doing the Charleston or riding in a Stutz Bearcat, and Gatsby watching the blinking green light at East Egg—not the farm mortgage foreclosures, the shriveling of Main Street as cars and concrete made larger areas interde-pendent, or the increasing alienation of individuals from work, neighbors and family.

And now enough people are old enough to recall (but not re-member) the Depression. For some of us it will never quite become a small 'd' depression again. But already we have Batman, paper-back quiz books on trivia, cults of Hemingway and Bogart. True, we are also getting a few collections like Harvey Swados' *The American Writer and the Great Depression* (1966) and a paperbound re-issue of James Agee's and Walker Evans', *Let Us Now Praise Famous Men* (1940), which make concerted efforts to indicate "what it was really like." Daniel Aaron, *Writers on the Left* (1961) attempts to make believable the literary wars of the 1930s; other collections, reprints and memoirs will pour forth to help portray what we have decided to remember of the 30s.

Here rests the nub. If a reader just turned voting age browses through Granville Hicks' collection, *Proletarian Literature in the United States* (1935), he may well find it difficult to maintain that willing suspension of disbelief which constitutes poetic faith. The various publics of the 60s will diverge precisely on this point of believability. This is not a divergence peculiar to the 30s, however; every period evokes (a) nostalgia from those survivors who can suppress the pains and remember the pleasures of an earlier stage in their own personal experiences, (b) antiquarianism patronizingly snuffling and seeking out the quaint and amusing objects (Tiffany lamps, Cigar Store Indians) to flavor a later era as period pieces and to serve as 'conversation openers' or (c) curiosity hungering for material, tradition, and pattern, as part of the usable past for a new generation.

Take a simple little advertisement for a currently fashionable line of young women's dresses. It indicates that, among other attrac-tive qualities, the dress also has "a prim Hoover collar and virtuous long sleeves." The reaction of someone who saw and smelled the patched corrugated-iron, wood and burlap shacks in a local Hoover-ville trash dump may vary a little from those of his daughter's generation. More to the point, as Margaret Mead has pointed out several times, the reactions of the parental generation after World War II to the word, the concept, and the emotional connotations of JOB are quite different from the reactions of a later generation that has grown up in an expanding economy where inflation, consumer credit and insurance practices give a different emphasis to saving and spending. Mortgaging the future, we used to call it, and those of us with such a long memory have also been forced to take an-other look at the relative values of many then vital issues reflected now, thirty years later, in the glare of both Hiroshima and the man in the Moon.

Believability: jobs scarce in any line of work, food destroyed to keep its price up, money scarce, property preserved seemingly at the expense of people—would you believe the possibility of class revolt as Marx and Lenin outlined it? Here part of the hurdle for those accustomed to our current attitudes toward labor unions as social institutions with some tradition themselves (as well as toward the expansion of middle class living style and consumption patterns) can be surmounted by comparing the behavior and commentary coming out of Alabama and Mississippi in the last few years when "outside agitators" march and "stir up our happy local folk"; or the behavior in Watts and elsewhere as looting and destruction attack the property fetishes of the dominant economic class. Another parallel can be drawn from the migrant agricultural workers still struggling thirty years after *The Grapes of Wrath*, even the decade after Ed Murrow's award-winning TV documentary "Harvest of Shame."

The style and form of much proletarian literature adds another dimension to the problem of believability. For one thing, even if a reader under thirty is willing to grant, "OK, that's how life must have been in those days," he may be put off by the flatness of vocabulary and syntax, the obviousness of the style, since many proletarian writers seem to have been devising *agitprop* to be read by the workers. Proletarian poetry, drama and fiction suffer more from this after-effect than some of the reportage or reminiscences, like those of Meridel LeSeuer and Sherwood Anderson. Reportage as a genre has going for it the type of charm and interest old newspapers found lining the bottom of a dresser drawer can have as well as the halo of credibility inherent in journalism or biography—"I was there." Meridel LaSeuer, writing from Minneapolis in 1934 in *I Was Marching* (in Hicks, p. 224) points up the adjustments that a young woman raised with a middle class orientation to individualism and personal privateness found while helping workers during a strike. Her reactions and feelings of belonging and of commitment to action parallel some of the testimony coming out of places like Selma, Alabama.

One common pattern used in proletarian fiction was the building up for group action (often a strike) of sympathetically described workingmen or farmers and their families, disillusioned with the Horatio Alger myth and the ideology of *laissez faire* capitalism.

Strikes are so much more "respectable" now that it is hard to transfer to a newer reader the sense of *risk* and social disapproval, of the possible effects of blacklisting from other employment, that existed then. After all, even public school teachers are striking in some areas today.

The shift in orientation from personal loyalties to collective loyalty involves, first, recognizing differences in the behavior and values of different social classes and, second, delineating them more sharply rather than glossing over or homogenizing them. The frontier, Jeffersonian and Jacksonian political practice, and the unifying experiences of the long public school tradition in transmitting middle class values to all, immigrants to the melting pot, rich and poor alike, support the usual American tendency to consider equality and similarity to be the same thing. To delineate the gulf more sharply, as the proletarians did in order to foster the class struggle, was a reversal. The romantic catalog of working class virtues a reader will frequently encounter seem to many of us a little overdone now, even if we have become used to separate tracks in the public schools, and aware of the circumscribed class structure which makes many suburbs economically and socially sealed off from the full range of American social types. When economic security and trusted social ideals for success failed much of the population after the Crash, the Marxist explanations became attractive to more people, and seemed attainable rather than utopian or merely theoretical.

This genre of strike fiction can be illustrated by the excerpt from the work of William Rollins, Jr., *The Shadow Before* (1934; Hicks, p. 123); the pattern includes an unsympathetic description of management and supervisory personnel, a pointing up of the diverse nationalities among the workers (all cooperating) and the dramatic confrontation and firing of leaders in the union. Not too surprisingly, the passage closes with the singing of the *Internationale* in the factory courtyard. One small turn of style makes Rollins a bit more readable today than some other writers who used the same pattern. The rhythm of the textile machinery in the factory is drawn to give a sense of the tension and pressure building up: "CLAMP THEM ON: SNAP THEM OFF: CLAMP THEM ON: SNAP THEM OFF: . . . UP; down; UP and down." Even such a small stylistic device stands out in surveying some of the fiction written at the time. The more prevalent strategy for the writer was "to give a picture" rendered in some detail, as a verbal description of a photograph or cinematically-based realism shows the setting for the narrative. The kinesthetic selection, the overlay of emotional fatigue is more likely stated instead of being evoked indirectly by the devices of punctuation illustrated above. Consequently, a reader today may find Dos Passos' *USA* with its Newsreels, Camera Eyes and other narrative effects much more evocative to him than the books by more strictly proletarian authors.

Even in a careful craftsman like Steinbeck the dialogue too often seems to be a set of political arguments rather than a real conversation. But, whether in Steinbeck's Salinas valley, Erskine Caldwell's eroded southern hills, or the urban middle class South Side of Farrell's Studs Lonigan, the fiction does give a sense of detail, a sense of place, local color, and sometimes a rendition of local speech patterns or dialect.

Thomas Bell's novel, *All Brides Are Beautiful* (1936), contains many vignettes constructed of the details of city living, desultory conversation waiting at a bus stop in the snow, love's badinage climbing stairs to a second floor apartment, the dialogue of a young married couple (wife working, husband unemployed) setting the alarm clock on a rag rug between the beds to deaden its ticking while getting ready for bed. Their conversation in the pinkish mist from the little lamp on the night table includes his comment to her that women ought to be cold hell against capitalism because (among other things) it tries to make idiots out of them as shown by the kind of slop you find on the woman's page of a tabloid newspaper. Naturally, they should read and support the *Daily Worker*. The strength of Bell's technique is in the apt selection of detail to picture the commonplace actions of urban daily living, and it is not surprising that Hollywood was easily able to turn the plot and some of the photographic details into a three handkerchief movie early in the forties. What was left out, of course, was the special tang of accuracy in expressing a particular political view. Even though he had an ear for the commonplace remark, his urge to fold in the political message flattens the effectiveness for many readers now. His strengths as a genre painter with a built-in tape-recorder for city custom and idiom are still effective, (without the obtrusive politics) in his later novel written during the Popular Front patriotic period, *Till I Come Back to You* (1943) about the family squabbles and the last night together of a draftee and his girl.

The quasi-proletarian writers mentioned previously frequently do a more effective job for the reader today than Bell does because they usually stop short of prescribing a solution for what they describe. When evoking the conditions which cry out for action of some kind, the more rigorously proletarian authors could be quite effective, as in Tom Kromer's outrage in *Waiting for Nothing* (1935; reprinted by Swados, p. 351) at the deputies destroying the food and campfire in a hobo jungle and then cracking the side of the skull of one man while his hungry wife and child look on at the embers and dirt of what had been their uneaten meal. It is when the writers begin to describe idealistically the steps to be taken or the possible Marxist solutions that today's reader really begins to struggle with credibility.

"Reading the Proletarians" — Or is it more accurate to say "Reading about workers who ought to recognize they are proletarians, written by sympathetic artists to be read by unconverted bourgeoisie?" Are these missionary epistles to the non-believer? Or are they *agit-prop* to evoke spirited action by the faithful? Is it written by proletarians (or close observers) to be read by the workers and to sway specific social and economic action? This last tendency had several stylistic effects. Compare for a moment the arguments sometimes heard about children's literature—or literature for children. If this genre is considered primarily as those literary works which children can identify with and possibly enjoy, you have a different rationale for the concept than if it is composed of specially written, vocabulary-graded adaptions of the values in the culture that are considered beneficial for the young. Similarly, material geared for reading by the working class to sway them to action is likely to have been highly specific in place and occasion, plain in vocabulary and in structural techniques, and in some senses curiously moral or puritan in expression when compared to our current fictional output.

Writers who took the short view of their own value when participating in the wars of the left might feel very comfortable (Solidarity Forever) in "reporting" what had happened (or ought to have) so that more workers might imitate it, but, as Daniel Aaron points out and as a look at the writers' congresses of the 30s will show, the Communist party chiefs on the Fourteenth Floor did not always think that writers (unless specifically polemic in journalism or reviews) were very heavy artillery in the class struggle. Many readers capable of nostalgic twinges are likely to object to letting the Communist party in all its twists and turnings completely appropriate the label "proletarian," and also object to labelling the most enduring and effective writers as outside the pale—as quasi-proletarian. Work written for immediate action tends to become dated, however, and the more specifically proletarian a piece is, the more difficulties it has evoking feelings and not just slogans for a reader today.

The feelings evoked and the attitudes described by Albert Maltz in "Man on a Road" (Hicks, p. 116) of a hitchhiker picked up near Gauley Creek, W. Va., who left his family after he found he was fatally ill with silicosis, and was writing a last letter of explanation to his wife, are due partly to the author's restraint and his ability to create a human interchange, not just a Marxist tract. Yes, these things happened; and to discover their impact upon individuals, human beings, in the work of Jack Conroy, Albert Halper or Robert Cantwell and others, as well as the writers mentioned previously, is to acquire some insight into the impulses to react as a group in response to situations. These sometimes almost doctrinaire reactions still affect many of the survivors of the decade in the intensity of their reactions, both pro and con, to such things as the war on poverty, medicare, civil rights and even Viet Nam. Such reading, involving potential incredulity or distaste as it does, can help explain why the scars of the 30s affected some liberals as they did— even if those scars are now pretty well hidden by both affluence and the glaciating impacts of foreign affairs.

Edward Hopper's oil painting, "Summer Evening," shows a young couple standing a little apart from one another under the naked light bulb on the roofed-over open porch of an urban two story wooden frame house, the boy in T-shirt and work pants, the blonde short-haired girl in halter, shorts and tennis shoes. As is usual in Hopper's work, the effect is somber, sad, somewhat lonely. Although the current crop of college students might assume different reasons for the effect (Why aren't they talking in a car, for goodness' sake?), a viewer could, from actual experience (and maybe even from vicarious experience by reading the proletarians), look at it and trigger such questions (not unintended by Hopper) as: "When will there be jobs? Can we risk getting married?" As dear Margaret said, JOB means different things nowadays. So does DRAFT.

The Sweet Savage Prophecies
of Nathanael West

Kingsley Widmer

Nathanael West wrote only four short novels, all published in
the 30s, but those apocalyptic comedies echo far. Precursors of the
despairing laughter now called "black humor" and of several of the
post-30s modes of poetic-naturalism, they also sound out a paradigm
for his decade. Starting with a late dadaistic experiment in the iconoclastic laughter that was an aftermath of World War I, he went on
to raucous political and religious burlesques of the American mythos,
and he ended with a genre study around the dehumanized mob's
hysterical screams shortly before World War II. It is an extreme art,
though now such exacerbated sensibility has become almost normative for sensitive intelligence.

The Great Depression between the Great War and its repeat
performances would seem to demand some such responses as West's,
yet his imaginative grotesqueries are missing in most of his contemporaries, the "social protest" literalists. As so often, the atypical in
its time later provides the better characterization of that time. The
30s in West's work rightly appear as a period of exceptional fraudu-
lence and misery producing bitter disillusionment with traditional
hopes. Especially concerned with the fatuous and machined dreams
counterfeiting that reality, West foresaw the apocalyptic violence of
warped and cheated humanity.

97

A writer's distinctive qualities, of course, should not be reduced to what he neatly echoes for us of his own time and of our placelessness. Appropriate tragicomic response to this joking Jeremiah also requires a sense of unusually artful protest. West's work curiously fuses poetic style and naturalistic subjects, clinical undercutting and prophetic over-reaching, empathetic immediacy and disinterested mockery. No doubt some of this "doubleness" may be related to twists of personality. Though concerned with large moral themes in his work, West—a mother-dominated bachelor until near the end of his life in his late thirties—insists on placing them within a shrewdly Freudian analysis of Oedipal situations. Similarly, his Jewishness contradictorily takes the forms of both anti-Semitic wisecracks and obsessively misplaced Jewish details in each of his books. Reportedly homely and an exaggerated dandy, perhaps such over-conforming encouraged a literary style of ornate parody around meanly representative materials.

Though thoroughly angry in all his work at commercially debased popular culture, he spent years as a dutiful hack in the Hollywood "dream dump." Even the partly leftist political focus of his last two books takes a mocking turn—so antithetical to the prevailing "progressives"—in which he achieves a charity that defies all faith and hope, including the political. West seems to have quietly and bemusedly cultivated violent pessimism. His early death in an automobile accident provides an horrendous personal confirmation of his sense of gratuitous and mechanical human destruction. But perhaps the best images of his contrariety are given by his characters, as when Miss Lonelyhearts reflectively chooses frenzy: "hysteria, a snake whose scales are tiny mirrors in which the dead world takes on a semblance of life. . . . he wondered if hysteria were really too deep a price for bringing it to life."

West's first, and artfully hysterical, novella, *The Dream Life of Balso Snell* (1931), is a verbally polished but wobbly exercise in Dada that satirizes art as a psuedo-sublimation of sex by the incompetent. The iconoclastic theme resolves in a concluding wet dream. Intermittently, the burlesque scenes develop from poet Balso's journey through the Trojan horse of art which he entered by way of the anus. The coy scatological jokes mock the dirty deceptions of the great artistic and rhetorical pretensions: "Art is a sublime excrement."

Most of the *Dream Life*, however, is closet satire. West plays with a parodied life of Christ in terms of a saintly flea, a literary adolescent who fakes a Dostoyevskian criminality in order to seduce his English teacher, the hypothetical suicide of a hunchbacked campfollower of poets, and similar grotesque roles which expose pathetic-fraudulent literary ambitions. This self-mockery of a bookish boy is anti-art, but the basic romantic irony shows too often in the indulgence in traditional grandiloquence, however mocked. To twist one of West's metaphors, the *Dream Life* is an anti-literary protective coloration for a literary animal. The "bad taste" cultivated in such a work provides a despairing humor to color over the "terrible" need for "being more than animals" because we are not adequate animals. Sexual fear is shiftingly disguised as a bitter "laugh at the laugh" of homoerotic and misogynous humor. The demand for vitality, for man brought truly to life, remains an involuted game, as does the cultivated anti-intellectualism of surrealist disjunctions and dadaistic explosions. The *Dream Life* provides an ornately conscious, and somewhat derivative and awkward, assault on what D. H. Lawrence called "the modern disease of self-consciousness."

The Westian way appears set though not perfected in his first work: the artful aggravation of hysteria, the sometimes embarrassed effort to "burlesque the mystery of feeling," the astutely perceived erotic fears and resultant violence, the combined parodying and exalting of suffering, and the harsh undercutting of pretensions to adequate meanings in life. So, too, with the outrageous wit and polish. But exposing the dream life of art remains solipsistic. While a good orgasm might dispel literary fantasies, those of Christian morality, American society and modern counterfeit civilization demand more violent purgations.

Miss Lonelyhearts (1933), West's most polished and profound work, carries the iconoclasm about the dream life into a fuller human anguish. The exploded ideal now goes beyond art to one of the great historic visions—"the Christ dream." With satiric precision, the modern way of the cross is given a debased locale: a neurotic young newspaper reporter, his "advice" column for reader's tribulations which is a "circulation stunt," ordinary human misery re-enforced by the Depression, and the fundamental moral and psychological disorder of our urban civilization. Not only representative incongruities but a corrosive critique of what is now called "mass culture" determines the ambience. "Men have always fought their misery with dreams," but now the dreams "have been made puerile" by falsification and exploitation. "Among many betrayals, this one is the worst." For the corrupted dream finally destroys the whole visionary and passional quality of life.

A cynical-preying editor plays the devil's role, and continues West's mockery of the traditional rhetorics. In several witty sequences, he parodistically poses many of the great Western dream-styles: heroic Renaissance individualism (in a speakeasy full of sodden journalists); the altars of high Art (as a solace to the human needs of poor cripples); "escape to the soil" and the utopia of the "South Seas" (the deceiving cliches of romantic morality); "Hedonism, or take the cash and let the credit go" (the impractical as well as debased traditional fortitudes—including Hemingwayism); and the bathos of culturism, self-destruction and religiosity as answers to human despair. The action confirms and incises the parodies. The young reporter, more deeply involved than he intended in a new awareness of human misery acquired from the letters imploring advice and consolation ("stamped from the dough of suffering with a heart-shaped cookie knife"), bunglingly attempts some of the dream-escapes. The dirty irony is that he does finally succeed in attaining, hysterically, the Christ-dream and the "rock of faith," ending in an all too-human total mess and gratuitous death.

With a fascinated repulsion for the Christianity he sympathetically annihilates, West double-plays the material, shrewdly mixing savage parody with sweet seriousness. The reporter is equally portrayed as a clinical case with a "Christ complex" and as a good man who, by questioning "the values by which he lives," achieves a saintly compassion. With pyrotechnical economy, West develops him as a New England puritan with a history of morbid religious obsession. Miss Lonelyhearts also reveals a painful sexual ambivalence. Women were "not his line," yet he Oedipally makes half-seductions of the sex-teasing wife of the boss he ineffectively hates; and later goes to bed with and ragingly beats the gross wife of a cripple whom he lovingly tries to help. His confused homoeroticism erupts into sadism, into his transcendentalizing passion for "J. C.," and into surreal bits of phallic dreams and visions which turn guiltily violent. Yet Miss Lonelyhearts is also genuinely a "humanity lover," far more victim than perpetrator in his personal messes, and appropriately moved to anger and anguish by the pleas of the suffering and the cruel injustice and disorder of the world. When he struggles to answer "what is the whole stinking business for?" as a cripple puts it, he follows out the Christian self-torturing quest and arrives at Father Zossima's joyous submission to total guilt, going forth "to succor . . . with love" all the cries of human misery and desperation, ending in confused destruction at the hands of the cripple he is going to embrace. West sardonically makes his ordinary-American-Christ equally sick and saintly.

To ignore either the sweet concern or the savage mockery of *Miss Lonelyhearts* falsifies the experience and denies the theme— the defeat in our world of the lonely heart. The archetypal vulgar letters of ordinary people which comprise a significantly large part of the narrative—and neatly counterpoint the surrealism of ordinary reality with the artfully violent tropes of West's description—do not just reveal psychological and socioeconomic problems. The inner and outer Depression but re-enforces unameliorable human misery— cripplings, incurable conditions, unresolvable incompatabilities, total desperations. Suffering is real.

And the available moral visions that claim to confront that reality end by horrendously distorting it. West's insistence on dilemma is pervasive. The heartlorn hero, for example, repeatedly shows a compulsion for order, in the clinical sense—a fixation in which anxiety drives him to trying to "compose" the landscape in rigid rhythmical patterns and hold it that way or to impose geometrical order on the symptomatic confusion of a pawnshop window. But, reflectively, Miss Lonelyhearts also pursues another dimension of rage, man's "tropism for order" which is the demand for coherent human meaning. Here he well perceives that American civilization is producing a counterfeit and destructive order in breaking nature—our civilized "progress"—which in revenge is breaking man. Thus West's clinical dissection of character is *not* reductively used to deny the moral perception of the character. Naturalistic causation and poetic vision truly dwell together. West's pained double awareness belongs with the distinctive achievements of the modern imagination.

Sick confusion fuses with moral engagement. Miss Lonelyheart's fiance, Betty, the sweet and pretty American "girl-in-the-party-dress," whom he both abuses and loves, believes that disorder is sickness and convention is health. She is given her due by West; the pastoral-sexual episode with her is the book's positive scene. But with kind obtuseness she would further answer suffering with maternal chicken soup, his "forgetting" the letters of misery by taking a "nice" job in advertising, and their suburban marriage. "Her sureness," Miss Lonelyhearts comments to himself, "was based on the power to limit experience arbitrarily. . . . his confusion was significant, while her order was not."

Part of Miss Lonelyhearts' agony is the acute perception of the anti-order of our times, the incompatability of his city experiences to any ordering and coherence: "No repeated group of words would fit their rhythm and no scale could give them meaning." And part of his rejection of conventional claims to order comes from a positive vision. Set off by a youthful memory of a child dancing to Mozart, he envisions a whole world of rhythmically moving order—the very antithesis of compulsion—of "every child, everywhere . . . gravely, sweetly dancing."

Miss Lonelyhearts also wants to feel that all would be ordered and whole and simple in the world of suffering if he could "only believe" in Christ and faithfully go forth in total love into the "dream-like violence" of our world. But such faith does not, and cannot, provide a realized and significant order in this society. For West's religious presupposition is, with an edge, the existential one: value is pure subjectivity. Internally, as with Miss Lonelyhearts, this means that authentic religious faith depends on dubious psychic causes; externally, as with the modern American city, this means that the earnest moral gesture devolves into the hysterical destructive joke. While the solacing symbols of the religion of crucified love reveal their causal symptoms in sexual warpings, that heightens rather than denies human needs, within and without. Artistically, the dilemma holds by balancing the playfully artful style with the anguish of hard actuality. For the character, "pity had turned to rage"; for the author, rage had turned to a poetry of compassion, and a self-conscious bitter laughter.

Implicit in *Miss Lonelyhearts,* as the only possible resolution, is a social and cultural apocalypse. Attempts to dramatize this as the violent vengence of the corrupted dreams direct West's remaining works. A *Cool Million* (1934) burlesques one of the exploited dreams, the Horatio Alger pattern, in a rather mechanically deadpan reversal of the stock American success story. In this savage sketch of the rural New England boy who, with sweet stupidity, pursues the sentimental formulas for success (going to the city to make his fortune, practicing honesty as the best policy, etc.) the result is a monochromatic series of jailings, beatings, rapes, frauds, dismemberments and death—all treated farcically. The obsessive piling on of assaults and other inhumanities suggests that the American success myth is so powerful—such an act of faith— that the frustrated heretic-author in the depression is driven to violent blasphemies,

The fundamental corruption he exposes is the "innocent" orthodoxy of our Protestant ethos of work-abstinence-opportunity-righteousness. But West seems to find it difficult to take such Americanism seriously enough to operate the joke machinery, and so he over-does it. Furthermore, he wishes to propound a harsh political future as the final monstrous result of that myth. The destruction of the all-American boy ends in his propagandistic use as a martyr by an Amer-ican fascist movement. This authoritarian manipulation provides the twentieth century reality within the dying myth—a racist, small town oriented, petty-middle-class politics of simple-minded chauvin-ism and resentments—what is now called the "American Right." But West does not give the material its due in human density, does not allow around Protestant-populism's messianic dreams the human need and doubleness he perceived around the "Christ dream" in *Miss Lonelyhearts*. Also, since authoritarianism has never been a unique prerogative of the "right" in "liberal" America, the leftist didacticism —however politically appropriate at times—rather narrows West's prophetic perceptions.

To mock as well as to mouth the Horatio Alger absurdities, and the rightist political deductions from them, does not get at sufficient American reality. A few bravura passages stand free from the con-temptously trite treatment of the trite, such as comic descriptions of regionalist Americana employed in ingenious whore-house decora-tion, some simply accurate images of the machined dime-store taste of the 30s, and a few sardonic gestures from an apocalyptic Indian denouncing our dying civilization. But in this sometimes suggestive book pre-patterned satire (the Alger template) and pat political didacticism (a fascistic take-over) unfortunately dominate. The fine-ly raging and compassionate qualities of West's wit apply only to some bits of the marginal, the bizarre and the pathological imbedded in the ornately ordinary and dead-alive American scene.

The purlieus of Hollywood, therefore, provide apt material for West in his last (and longest) novel, *The Day of the Locust* (1939). Here he develops scenes extensively for the first time—sometimes digressively from his main action, as with a repulsively fascinating "cock fight" and with the bemused portrayal of a vaudevillian who is one of the characteristic Hollywood "masqueraders" (role-players, in current jargon) who no longer knows when he is pretending and when he is living, and dying. The character portrayals go beyond West's usual incisive caricature, though one can't say "in depth" since the melancholy and funny points are the lack of human depth in a society without true communal values.

Thus with Homer, central example of the "lower middle-class" southern California mob of bored and ultimately vengeful parolees from our puritanic heritage. A middle-aged ex-bookkeeper from Iowa and somnambulist product of total sexual repression, entrapped Homer gets effectively foreshortened by West's hyper-visual detailing of elaborate compulsive tics with his hands, pained zombie responses into "uterine flight" and final orgastic release by insane violence. Shambling, anguished, exploited, sweetly confused "automaton," Homer's essential innocence (he goes to bring an aspirin for a woman moaning in orgasm) requires sympathy, even when he deliriously stomps a tormenting child to death in the book's frenzied mob finale. For we see him and, by way of him, the entire mob of the emotionally cheated and resentful as victims of a repressive and fraudulent life-style. The violent dreams of mass-technological culture, represented by the movie premiere which gathers the mob, furnish the ultimate compulsions—and insults.

The mob provides the locusts of West's plague, and the incendiaries of the jeremiadic "The Burning of Los Angeles" which is being painted by the narrator, a perceptive but passive personae of the author. Here, again, we see West's devastating doubleness. The painter-narrator, in spite of his insight and decency, carries the plague; he, too, is one of the sexually defeated, a voyeur of grotesque violence, and a reluctant part of the mob which literally cripples this artist. West's anger is disinterestedly all-inclusive.

The artist-narrator is also hypnotically—and somewhat inexplicably—entrapped by Faye, the childish witch and focus of the unappeasable sexual rage that helps build the violence. Seventeen, puerile, grossly affected—her entire sensibility a serial of "B" movie fantasies and her typical American-pretty-girl narcissism turned grossly exploitative—she, too, is essentially an innocent, a quite depersonalized epitome of a whole culture. "Her beauty was structural . . . not a quality of her mind, or heart"; her sexuality is not an invitation to passion but to fantasy-immolation. Like the fancy whorehouse described in an early scene, she is "a triumph of industrial design" who erotically-destructively appeals to every man in the book. Personification of the technological masturbatory dream, she is intrinsically nothing. And nothing can really happen to this representative pathetic American, neither love nor suffering nor understanding.

The images of Faye suggest a machined doll triggered by mechanical movie fantasies; her vaudevillian father is an "overwound mechanical toy"; Homer is an automated zombie; one of Faye's lovers is described as pure "mechanical drawing"; and so on.

Combined with West's emphasis on speeded-up compulsions, a mostly fabricated (and mis-fabricated) nature, and a society of mechanical responses, this points up his dominant concern with the essence of a mass-technological civilization. The often perceptive recent critics of West (such as Stanley Hyman and Victor Comachero) seem to miss this crucial point, and West's prophetic relevance. The apocalyptic *Day of the Locust* is not just about bizarre Hollywood or idiosyncratic Californiana but, as the narrator suggests, it is about the whole American Age to come.

West's art presents an insatiable human revolt, via sexual violence, against the dehumanizing mechanisms. But as a concerned social moralist in the 30s, he wants to show his crowd as not only victimized by "tedious machines of all sorts" and the counterfeit visions of the dream factories but also of the repressive American past. Perhaps partly because of this, the controlling awareness tends to get off-balanced by digressive materials. Not vaudevillians but, however vividly described, the California cults—a mostly transitory phenomena of the Depression years and not at all confined to California—dissipate prophecy into grotesquery. Similarly, the major shift of point of view from the artist to Homer doesn't just weaken the narrative for technical reasons (as the pedantic critics argue), but confusingly suggests that what is happening is primarily a continuation of the repressive Protestant ethos of Mid-America rather than its machined successor. Even the final mob scene at the movie premiere —one of the most beautifully concrete in literature, strong in literal truth and superior to Zola in its psychology of crowd sexual violence —seems partly intended as the fascist mob of lower-middle-class reaction in the leftist mythology of the 30s.

Day of the Locust, I am arguing, is a brilliant work partly blurred by squaring savage indignation into a too narrow ideological image of the times. Some of the weakening may also come from the author's working within a conventional literary direction—the apparently self-conscious desire to do a "Hollywood novel." As such, of course, *Day of the Locust* belongs with the better images of sadly comic incongruity in that sub-genre (along with Miller, Mailer, Morris, Lurie). Though blurring his prophetic view, West effectively used the Hollywood motifs: the mock-heroic play with contradictory appearance and reality of the studio sets; the brightly satiric yet sympathetic delineations of outrageous Southern California Rococo in architecture, costumes and people; and the charitable awareness of an ornately synthetic and empty life-style. "Few things are sadder than the truly monstrous." West's fine mannerist balance of compassion and contempt is rare.

Day of the Locust describes, with sympathetic mockery, one of the crowds as being in a state of "morbid apathy." Violent hysteria provides the only available simulation of a return to life. Such loss of vitality and selfhood, of the true dreams of passion and heroism, overpowers all. The artist, both within *Day of the Locust* and behind it, can comically throw a few polished stones and mime his angry despair against the mechanical violence of the crowd, but he, too, finds himself absurdly part of the hysteria, screaming with the siren and the mob at the end. That West can treat the apocalypses of the mass-technological civilization and its counterfeited dreams as comedies provides a kind of parody of the ancient metaphysical proof of deity from design: such jokes prove there is a master joker— the sweetly savage nihilist whom we contemplate in his artful mirrors of hysteria. As West's artist notes about a writer, his "involved comic rhetoric" provided a way to balance "moral indignation" and sophisticated acceptance in a lavishly arbitrary and fraudulent society. That was part of what West so well prophesied as intelligent and sensitive response to our world and, I fear, we shall often have to abide by it.

Henry Roth and the
Redemptive Imagination

by William Freedman

Call It Sleep is the kind of book one feels a bit reluctant to write about, at least to "criticize," in the icy sense of that term. To criticize, to analyze, is in a sense to freeze, and Henry Roth's great and only novel becomes too much a part of one's immediate and intimate experience for that. It is, of course, the very personal quality of the book that assured its consignment to obscurity during the golden age of the proletarian novel. Though *Call It Sleep* may be such a work in the sense that it deals with a working-class Jewish immigrant family in Brownsville (and the Lower East Side of New York) shortly after the turn of the century, it is a book about very particular and very painfully real people with very particular and real problems, fears and guilts. No amount of social legislation or reorientation could have significantly allayed the agonizing childhood of young David Schearl, through whose frightened eyes the experience is perceived and through whose tortured imagination it is felt. And no amount of slum-clearance or religious toleration would have quelled the tormented psyche of David's father or made the marriage of the Schearls much more tolerable. The problems are acute, but the obstacles to happiness or even quiescence are personal and psychological, not general and social.

This may mean that the novel offers us no patentable answer to the sufferings of David and his parents, but it does bring us into contact with them as identifiable human beings and establishes an intimacy that I, for one, have too rarely enjoyed in the reading of fiction.

Genya Schearl, David's mother, is a woman of great serenity, nobility, endurance, and love. She is the buffer between David and his violently bitter father and the source of comfort to which he returns, as Huck to the river, but with far greater assurance of an affectionate reception. All the elements of sentimentalism and stereotype are here, and Genya could easily have been turned by Roth into a somewhat younger Jewish version of Ma Joad. She somehow never does, though, and one reason is that she is a flawed human being. She has had a premarital affair—and with a gentile, at that; she reacts with unnecessary hysteria to David's safe return from a brush with tragedy; and she lavishes a debilitating excess of affection, much of it plainly sexual, on her already too fragile child. This combination of major virtues and minor, understandable vices makes Genya Schearl something Ma Joad never quite is—a complex and credible female—and one who had a singular effect on me. Somewhere midway through the book I found myself doing a most peculiar thing. There I was, riffling my eager way through the pages of the Manhattan telephone directory in search of a Genya Roth somewhere on the Lower East Side. (Howard Ribalow's introduction to the Pageant Books edition reports that as of then at least—March 1960—Henry Roth's mother was still living there.) I don't know why I assumed she'd have the same first name, but then there's no accounting for people who look for fictional characters in phone books in the first place, so that's little wonder. It doesn't matter, though, for while I did find a G. Roth in just about the right neighborhood, I never got up the nerve to call or visit her, much as I'd love to and at the time almost had to. Anyway, imagine the look on Gus Roth's face when he answered the door and found me there asking if by some strange chance he was Henry Roth's mother.

Infinitely less endearing but no less persistent in his intrusion into the reader's consciousness is David's father, Albert Schearl. Like his wife, Mr. Schearl is composed of many of the ingredients of stereotype, in this case the villainous father-fiend. Relentlessly domineering, humorless, priggish, bitterly unresigned to what he regards as his deliberate persecution at the hands of shifting symbols of authority and behind them of a malevolent fate, uncontrollably violent, and suspicious of his wife's love and his son's legitimacy, Albert Schearl is his wife's antithesis and, at first, as unsympathetic a figure as one is entitled to meet. As the novel progresses, however, the sources of his volcanic behavior gradually seethe to the surface, and with recognition comes understanding and more than a touch of sympathy. Beneath it all, Albert, the odd man out in a patently oedipal family relationship, suffers from gnawing doubts as to his own masculinity, doubts which he seeks vainly to dispel by repeated acts of aggressiveness and imposition. When Genya, submissive in everything else, threatens to leave him if he persists in mistreating David, he is visibly cowed. His hatred for his son is magnified each time he finds himself thwarted in the alien outer world, each time he loses his job and his masculinity suffers another reversal. His priggish responses to his sister-in-law's vulgar allusions to sex and the female body testify to the same insecurity, as do his perversely fond recollections of the bulls he tended in Austria: bulls "with a shine to [their] flanks and the black fire in [their] eyes." It is only toward the end that we perceive the depths to which his torments penetrate. In the old country, it seems, he had as a boy watched idly as a bull (clearly his own surrogate in another oedipal triangle) gored his father. When, during the final sequence of the novel, he blames Genya's alleged infidelity for the fact that "weeks and weeks go by and I'm no man at all. . . . No man as other men are," we can no longer despise; we can only understand and, to a degree at least, sympathize.

The Schearls, however, for all their humanity, are not after all real people. Autobiographical though the book may be, it is first of all the product of a highly gifted, creative, literary imagination, and the fact that it was the only sustained achievement of what surely must have seemed an inexhaustible literary mind is every reader's loss. Attempting to account for the sudden aridity that overtook him after the completion of *Call It Sleep,* Roth pointed his finger not at the altered and improved social conditions of the proletariat or immigrants and not at the constriction of his personal experience, but, properly, at the failure of his imagination. "I relied almost entirely on the imagination," he wrote to Harold Ribalow, "and when that faded, so did I." Perhaps one of the reasons for its premature exhaustion was its overexertion in this one great work, for in *Call It Sleep* Roth has produced a literary *tour de force.* He has framed with rare success a story of profound social and psychological realism in a mythopoeic outline of symbolic death, redemption and rebirth and rendered both through a subtly complex and symbolic system of light and dark imagery. (Roth wrote to Ribalow, "There is one theme I like above all others, and that is redemption.")

Roth's novel takes us through an agonizing two-year period in the life of young David Schearl—from his sixth to his eighth years—and relives for us the world of his daily experience, a world beset by unsubsiding fears and recurrent attacks of guilt. David has a compelling need to belong, yet he is withdrawn into the frightened confines of his own painfully vivid imagination. He is alienated from his peers; rejected by his father; and petrified by the normal sexual experiences of childhood, his father's seething violence, the prospect of retribution for his guilt (both real and imagined), the largeness and chaos of his physical world, and above all the dark. It is the dark that comes to symbolize all that is ugly and intolerable in David's experience, all that threatens him and from which he seeks to escape. It first and most saliently looms before him in the specter of the cellar (the title of the first section of the novel) at the foot of the stairs of his Brownsville tenement:

> He went out into the hallway. Behind him, like an eyelid shutting, the soft closing of the door winked out the light. He assayed the stairs, lapsing below him into darkness, and grasping one by one each slender upright to the bannister, went down. David never found himself alone on these stairs, but he wished there were no carpet covering them. How could you hear the sound of your own feet in the dark if a carpet muffled every step you took? And if you couldn't hear the sound of your own feet and couldn't see anything either, how could you be sure you were actually there and not dreaming? A few steps from the bottom landing, he paused and stared rigidly at the cellar door. It bulged with darkness. Would it hold?
> . . . It held! He jumped from the last steps and raced through the narrow hallway to the light of the street. Flying through the doorway was like butting a wave. A dazzling breaker of sunlight burst over his head, swamped him in reeling blur of brilliance, and then receded . . . .
> A row of frame houses half in thin shade, a pitted gutter, a yawning ashcan, flotsam on the shore, his street. (Pageant Books, 1960, p. 19.)

The cellar not only crystallizes all his childhood fears in one horrifying symbol: it, or rather a different cellar, is also the scene of his last and greatest guilt. It is the place to which he leads his revered friend and stands sentry while Leo "plays bad" with his cousin.

But darkness is characteristic of more than merely cellars. It is also what David most acutely senses and best remembers about the closet in which he is invited to indulge in lewd sex play by the crippled girl upstairs. And it is also the identifying feature of his despised father, his "dark face," his "black hair," "ink-black hand," "dull black shoe," black milk-wagon horse, and his black whip. Gradually the quality of darkness spreads like an inky stain over David's imagination and comes to stand for everything that threatens him— not only the cellar, the closet, and his father, but Luter, the man who attempts to seduce his mother, sex, sin, guilt, death, and even the devil himself. "Don't step on de black line," David admonishes himself after his terrifying experience in his cousin's cellar. "Touch a crack, touch a cella', touch a cella', touch a devil. He black bugger-unner." Reb Yidel, David's pettily sadistic Hebrew teacher, articulates the deepest fears of his prize pupil when he denounces life as "a blind cast. A blind caper in the dark."

Naturally enough, light is David's salvation, and like its antithesis it is an expanding symbol which characterizes and eventually comes to stand—in the boy's mind and in the reader's—for everything that is redemptive, everything that offers reprieve, however brief, from the torments of darkness. It is the sunlight into which he bursts in his frenzied flights past the cellar door in his Brownsville home and later on from his cousin's cellar on 9th St. It is the sunlight that also lights the roof on which he finds temporary solitude and the "bright yard" that generously separates his stairway from the cellar door in his Lower East Side tenement. It is the candles his mother lights on Friday nights. But most significantly it is the light of God in a variety of transforming manifestations, the source of purification, redemption, and salvation.

Nothing fascinates David like the stories of the light and fire of God, stories to which he is recurrently treated and which he insatiably pursues. He listens enraptured to his mother's story of the Christian peasants who saw a light in an Austrian forest where nothing burned and thought it holy, probably, she explains, because "Moses too saw a tree on fire that didn't burn. And there the ground was also holy." He is even more enthralled by the story he reads in *cheder* of Isaiah and the sin-purifying coal sent from heaven, and he begins to wonder if perhaps he too mightn't be purified by the fire of God. His experiences—more than quasi-mystical—with the dazzling radiance of reflected sunlight on the water (and with the sword he is compelled by taunting gentile boys to drop into the crack of the cable-car power line) convince him that he has indeed seen a coal like Isaiah's:

> Power!
> Like a paw ripping through all the sable fibres of the earth, power, gigantic, fetterless, thudded into day! And light, unleashed, terrific light bellowed out of iron lips. The street quaked and roared, and like a tortured thing, the sheet zinc sword, leapt writhing, fell back, consumed with radiance. Blinded, stunned by the brunt of brilliance, David staggered back. A moment later, he was spurting madly toward Avenue D (p. 340).

"A vision in a crack," the rabbi scoffs; but David knows better.

The book to which *Call It Sleep* is perhaps most frequently compared is Joyce's *Portrait of the Artist,* but the comparison is more apt than is realized by those who make it. For in a very real sense these moments of mystical transformation, of blinding radiance, are moments of imaginative transcendence, experiences through which David momentarily transcends the chaos of his physical universe. Only after such experiences as these is he able to order and deal with his world and accept it for what it otherwise too painfully is. For it is a light he carries with him:

> Look! Is a light! In the corner where baby-carriages—No. Looks like though. On the stairs too. Ain't really there. Inside my head. Better is inside. Can carry it. Funny! Ain't so dark anyway. Ain't even scared . . . . I'm big now. Can go up alone. Can go up slow, slow, slow as I like. Can even stand here and don't even care. Even between the windows, even if nobody's in the toilet, even if nobody's in the whole house. Don't even care. I'm big now, that's why. Wonder if—Yea, all dry now. Can go in now. New underwear she'll give me like the other kids already. For Passover . . .
> —Funny. Still can see it. There. And over there. And over in the corner where it's real dark. It sticks inside all the time, gee, can't never be scared. Never. Never. Never . . .   (p. 351).

These moments of imaginative transcendence are literally David's light in the darkness of his fears, and he understandably comes to view them as the means, if he is to have any, of his ultimate salvation. Seeking them out brings him first to near disaster but ultimately to the redemption he requires.

Only a very substantial bribe could have tempted David to subject himself to the terrors of darkness in his cousin's cellar on his gentile friend's behalf, and Leo's offer is of the only kind that David would yield to. He offers him his rosary, replete with crucifix, an irresistible bribe once Leo has explained that the light surrounding Jesus is Christian light and that Christian light is "way bigger. Bigger den Jew Light," the light of God's coal. But Christ's light proves of little benefit to the Jewish boy, for he is caught in the cellar, an accomplice to Leo's lewd scheme, and his troubles begin to mount climactically. To escape his gnawing guilt he attempts to deny his own identity, to commit symbolic suicide, by informing Reb Yidel that his alleged mother is not his mother at all, merely an aunt, and that he, therefore, is not the person others think him, but "somebody else— *else*—ELSE!" But this of course is merely one more in a continuing series of futile attempts to escape the consequences of existence and action, and it does not work. It only serves to add another to the list of crimes exposed in agonizing succession in a shattering scene in the Schearl kitchen. His fabricated identity, his role in the humiliation of his cousin, and his possession of the execrable rosary are almost simultaneously revealed, and to escape inevitable punishment David flees into the street. He knows his only redemption lies in returning to the scene of his prior revelation and in willingly and defiantly undertaking what he had earlier been compelled to do: to visit the lightless cable-car tracks and create the consuming brilliance once more. This act is more than a quest for temporary release in the dazzling radiance of an electric shock. It is an assertion of his manhood, for it requires him to accept the "double dare" of his gentile taunters, to defy the dark, and to commit a counterfeit sex act which, though of course David does not consciously realize it, will mark at least a partial severence from his damaging oedipal attachment to his mother:

> *. . . he was there, standing between the tracks, straddling the sunken rail. He braced his legs to spring, held his breath. And now the wavering point of the dipper's handle found the long, dark, grinning lips, scraped, and like a sword in a scabbard—* (p. 562)

And the transcendent experience in which he is once again suffused with the incredible power of light and flame produces the desired effect: "Liberty! Revolt! Redeem!" Liberty from the afflictions of consciousness. Revolt against the hostility of his physical environment and his own fears, self-doubts and self-accusations. And Redemption from guilt through the pain of the electric jolt.

By defying the dark and seeking in it the means of release, David comes to grips with something he had glimpsed earlier—that just as coal, God's coal, is found in cellars, so release must be found in the midst of the very stuff from which one would escape. Light must be found in the midst of darkness. The imagination does not literally create, it transforms, and what it transforms are the very materials which Roth has transfigured in *Call It Sleep*—the fears, the anguish, the pain, and the ugliness of life—here a young boy's life on the Lower East Side. The important point, though, is that Roth has transfigured his raw materials without distorting them out of recognizable shape. For the myths of redemption and rebirth are implicit in the story of David Schearl, and both are rendered largely by means of a symbolic image pattern that is part of David's own conscious awareness and that is viewed symbolically by his own fertile imagination as well as by the reader. Such a fusion of myth, symbol, and profound realism does more than raise *Call It Sleep* far beyond the level of most of the proletarian fiction that once obscured it. It makes Roth's novel one of those too rare works of fiction that we can both live and admire, simultaneously.

The Thirties — Poetry

It wasn't a good decade for poetry. It just wasn't. The 30s are skimpily represented in most anthologies, and no one who anthologists seem able to agree must be reckoned a major force in American poetry began to publish in the depth of the' 30s, with the possible exception of Karl Shapiro. Even this exception confirms the melancholy state of affairs, however, for Shapiro's 1935 *Poems* was privately printed, and he did not become well known until *Person, Place and Thing* appeared in 1942. Between Richard Eberhart's first book in 1930 and John Ciardi's in 1940 sprawls a trackless dumping ground of ill-starred ventures into verse.

The Pulitzer Prizes—whatever one may think of them as reflections of excellence—went mostly to the collected poems of men like Robert Frost, who had achieved their reputations earlier. Young poets who were honored, such as George Dillon and Audrey Wurdemann, failed to make a permanent impression.

Several things were responsible for the failure of American poetry to maintain the momentum it had attained in the teens and twenties when the experiments of Eliot, Pound, Jeffers, Cummings, Hart Crane, and Maxwell Bodenheim had attracted attention throughout the world. The depression must bear a large measure of blame. It became more difficult than ever to get such generally unprofitable material as poetry published when even normally remunerative lines of books weren't selling and the most avant garde publishers were joining their counterparts in other wares in bankruptcy. Such a period scarcely evokes a lyric response, either. Poets could not bring themselves to express a confidence they did not feel about the future. "If you could only sing/ That God is love, or perhaps that social/ Justice will soon prevail," Robinson Jeffers chides himself in "Self-Criticism in February" (1937). His darker self replies, "I can tell lies in prose."

The American poetic community had been especially shaken, too, by a catastrophic pattern of its own. Many of those who had burned most brightly in the 20s died by their own hands: Elinor Wylie in 1928, Vachel Lindsay in 1931, Hart Crane in 1932, Sara Teasdale in 1933. All were "poets" in the most glamorously stereotyped concept of the term—vivid individualists of great romantic sensibility, who aspired to create in verse private worlds that would outshine humdrum reality ("The higher vaudeville," Lindsay called it). The suicides—prompted at least in part by the failure of the poets' efforts to realize their aspirations—raised questions in many thoughtful minds about not just the practicality, but even the possibility of poetry's surviving in the waste land.

Ah, "The Waste Land"—that monumental epigraph for an age was another source of difficulty, for Eliot seems to have attracted to his austere banner most of the coolly intellectual, religiously inclined, wryly ironic poets who rejected the world rather than their own dreams and withdrew into the cloister of verse. Few poets have so much inhibited imaginative experimentation in the next generation. Eliot's influence as a critic as well as a poet, furthermore, steered those most interested in the technical problems of poetry away from a concern with the social issues of the time. Those who would once have become Bohemians forsook smock and sandals for Eliot's somberly tailored sackcloth. Not until the fleshly roars of Dylan Thomas were heard from remote Wales was poetry to find again a Romantic voice powerful enough to make itself heard above the incessant hum of the polished prayers of Eliot's ascetic congregation.

Eliot himself enjoyed a very good decade—the one in which he produced the greatest bulk of memorable material. Following the publication of "Ash Wednesday" (1930), the epic of his conversion, Eliot turned to the theatre and gave prospects of new life to the languishing poetic drama in *Murder in the Cathedral* (1935) and *The Family Reunion* (1939). And in the volume of verse collected in the middle of the decade appeared, almost as if an afterthought, "Burnt Norton," which was to become the first of the "Four Quartets" constituting Eliot's last great lyric cycle.

Although these works will probably continue to rank with the greatest produced during the decade, Eliot is not represented in this collection because by the 30s he had become completely disassociated from his native country. A British citizen since 1927, he had begun to write not for his old or new countrymen but for the whole tradition-minded world. He had transcended nationality as his pilgrim in "Ash Wednesday" had the flesh.

Such was distinctly not the case with Ezra Pound, even though he spent the decade largely abroad. His eyes never left his native country from what he deemed exile, and as late as 1939 he made a filibustering tour of the United States during which he tried to badger a number of public figures into reversing the unfortunate course Pound thought this ill-informed land was following under the New Deal. Whatever else the proliferating "Cantos" were, they were surely in the 30s encyclopedic warnings to the United States, comparing our glorious past under John Adams to the ignominious present under F. D. R. In the first of our detailed accounts of American poets at work during the 30s, therefore, Max Halperen appropriately offers us a glimpse of the frenetic activities of poet-turned-propagandist Pound, industriously proving that the louder one shouts the less good he does.

Ez was not, however, the only propagandist active during the decade. The majority of voices were, in fact, raised against the fascism Pound leaned towards as poetry was enlisted in the cause of proletarian revolution. Perhaps the principal trouble with the poetry of the 30s is that propaganda efforts are rarely memorable, and many of the aspiring young versifiers went down with the dogma they embraced. Part of the reason for the thinness of poetry from the 30s in most anthologies is that "proletarian verse" fails to generate excitement today. Yet one could hardly hope to talk sensibly about poetry during the 30s without taking a backward glance at this ill-starred endeavor. In a spirited essay, Sy Kahn, himself an accomplished poet, argues that the work of the best remembered of the enthusiastic radicals, Kenneth Fearing, reveals the essence of the depression years.

A poet who has suffered from his identification with the propagandists—both aesthetic and social—is Archibald MacLeish, who unquestionably served with distinction many causes—poetic and otherwise—during the 30s. Dan Jaffe, another exciting young poet, turns critic to cast a suspicious eye on the usual assumption that

MacLeish changed substantially during the 30s. Jaffe demonstrates a continuity in both the life and work of a man who never gave up the struggle against seemingly hopeless obstacles to make the poet a powerful and respected public figure.

The poet whose work during the 30s perhaps has fared best in later years held himself rigorously aloof from propaganda battle-grounds. I think it is unarguable that no books of American poetry published during the decade have subsequently grown so much in reputation as Wallace Stevens' *Ideas of Order* (1935) and *The Man with the Blue Guitar* (1937). The 30s were clearly not ready for these paradoxical works—austere yet whimsical, coolly ironical yet passionate. People experiencing economic and political chaos wanted certainties, sought panaceas, hoped with Eliot that they might indeed "turn again." Stevens offered only uncertainty and isolation. The world could not bring itself to listen to the poet who as selfish passions made war inevitable could in "The Glass of Water" advise only: "In a village of the indigenes,/ One would still have to discover. Among the dogs and dung,/ One would continue to contend with one's ideas."

To those who hold with this editor that American poetry of the 30s reaches its highest point not in the decade's many timely manifestoes, but in the expression of the timeless concept of reality as incessant individual creation in "The Idea of Order at Key West," Donald Sheehan's lively essay about Stevens' brush with the propagandists will serve to bring into sharpest focus what was ephemeral and what permanent in the art of a turbulent era.

The market for Stevens' poetry remains small, despite much recent critical activity. It probably always will. With an irony to which only a Stevens might do justice, the most marketable product of American poets during the 30s proved not poetry at all, but criticism—of a kind that is still, thirty years later, hailed as "The New Criticism."

This remarkable combination of aesthetic detachment and pedagogical fervor, which—it can be unequivocally stated—has revolutionized the teaching of poetry in American classrooms, was the creation of a group of men, principally John Crowe Ransom, Allen Tate, Cleanth Brooks, and Robert Penn Warren, who had earlier been associated with the "Fugitive" movement, which endeavored to provide the often castigated South with an artistically commendable poetry. The "Fugitives," as they had begun to drift from their base of operations at Vanderbilt University, moved first into politics and economics as enthusiasts for Agrarianism and later—with more authority and success—into the appreciation of literature, because (one is tempted to theorize) they discovered that they could not hope to find an audience for either their poetry or the social theories underlying it until a wide audience was able to read poetry at all.

So extensive and influential were the operations of these crusading Southerners that two essays are needed to examine their labors. To Guy Owen has fallen the less cheerful task of examining the decline of their poetic production during the 30s; to Gene Ruoff, the happier one of summarizing the rise of the New Criticism as poets felt compelled to teach people what poets were doing. Both essayists are Southerners themselves—Owen from tidewater North Carolina, Ruoff from the river port of Paducah, so that both write with a special sensitivity for the aims, aspirations, and disappointments of those who sought to become the artistic leaders in the redemption of a blighted region.

Where are all the others? A great many of the poets who had established themselves earlier continued writing without adding substantially to their reputations or moving in new directions. Edwin Arlington Robinson was still publishing at the time of his death in 1935, but his last narratives are overshadowed by his earlier work. Although Robinson Jeffers produced some of his most haunting short poems, like "Shine, Perishing Republic," during the 30s, he failed to enhance the reputation that he made in the 20s with such long narratives as *Tamar* and *Roan Stallion. Give Your Heart to the Hawks* and *Such Counsels You Gave to Me* seem only further exploitations of the settings, the tone, the rugged forms that he had developed earlier. Marianne Moore and William Carlos Williams were in the curious position of having their most important experiments behind them, their most respected achievements (Miss Moore's "In Distrust of Merits"; Williams' "Paterson") ahead of them. E. E. Cummings continued to turn out the fantastic mixture of typographical eccentricity and sentiment that had made him the undergraduates' favorite, but his poetry of the 30s looks—quite literally—like that of the 20s. Maxwell Bodenheim after 1931 became virtually a parody of his former incandescent self.

How can you omit Hart Crane? admirers cry in anguish. Although *The Bridge* was not published until 1930, the posthumous *Collected Poems* until 1933, they were well known earlier and they seem inextricably a part of the whole desperate gaudy hysteria of the 20s. Read in conjunction with other works published at the same time, they seem already fragments from a world that had exploded.

A much stronger case could be made for the inclusion of an essay on Carl Sandburg's *The People, Yes,* a work expressing a belli-cose optimism in defiance to the defeatism of the times. But this rambling, colloquial chant never commanded the audience that Sand-burg's earlier impressionistic poems had, and we are likely to think of the aging author during the 30s not as poetic spokesman for the inarticulate masses but as Lincoln's biographer.

Robert Frost is an even more difficult problem, for he won two Pulitzer Prizes during the 30s and the book that won the second, *A Further Range* (1936), contains such memorable lyrics as "Two Tramps in Mud-Time," "A Drumlin Woodchuck," "Neither Out Far Nor in Deep." Only in the wryly witty "Departmental," however, does Frost really strike a new note and discover the necessary poetic strategy for dealing with the bureaucracy he despised. Had he been able to develop the vein that he struck in this poem, he might have become in the 30s the rallying point for the forces of the individ-ualist tradition that he later became, but he could rarely maintain his poetical equilibrium when politically exasperated. The 30s were not good years for Frost, as we can see if we read the usually passed over "Build Soil," which he read before both National party conven-tions in 1932, and discover how banally prosy even a great poet can be when he lets polemics overwhelm his art.

Frost, in short, except in a very few poems, failed to develop either his art or his attitudes in the 30s. The best that he wrote during this decade is a continuation of what he had accomplished in the teens and twenties. There seems little reason to examine critically work that fails to do justice to the stature of its writer.

Frost was actually in a kind of eclipse during the 30s. If one said "poet" then, especially to an *au courant* young American, the name that would most likely have flashed into his—or her—mind would have been Edna St. Vincent Millay. "All poets named Edna St. Vincent Millay are major," wrote a *New Yorker* wit. How his waggery puzzles today's undergraduate! No poetic reputation has faded faster or perhaps more unjustly than that of the scintillatingly gallant lady whose candle burned at both ends. Probably the re-action against her has been too intense because so many had to suffer like this editor through endless renditions of "Renascence" and "The Ballad of the Harp-Weaver" at such ill-conceived ventures of the 30s as the "Cultural Olympics" at the University of Pennsylvania.

Yet this book is not the place to redress the balance, for like Frost and Jeffers, Miss Millay failed to move forward in the 30s. The widely read volumes that she published during the decade repeat the patterns and ideas that had been responsible for the meteoric rise of her reputation during the 20s—the era that she epitomized. Even the social consciousness that marks much of her verse during the 30s had been evident—perhaps most effectively expressed—in her writings about the Sacco-Vanzetti trial.

During the 30s, in short, the United States produced a lot of poetry, but not much of it was really fresh and new voices proved unenduring. The times conspired against the lyricist unless like Stevens he chose to sing largely unheard:

> Freshness is more than the east wind blowing round one.
> There is no such thing as innocence in autumn,
> Yet, it may be, innocence is never lost.
> ("Like Decorations in a Nigger Cemetery," xliv)

The 30s were an autumnal decade; the winter of war lay ahead. Innocence was indeed in hibernation; but fresh winds might yet rise from a new direction. Out of a deadly season were to come John Ciardi, Karl Shapiro, Peter Viereck, Randall Jarrell, Winfield Townley Scott, Richard Wilbur.

WARREN FRENCH

Ezra Pound: Poet-Priest, Poet-Propagandist

by Max Halperen

In April, 1939, Ezra Pound came to the United States on a one-man peace mission. "I thought it was monstrous that Italy and the United States should go to war so I came here to stop it," he told a reporter. He buttonholed Senators, Congressmen, anyone who would listen to Ezra Pound as the self-styled voice of reason and civilization. "He's been very mysterious about his comings and goings while in this country," William Carlos Williams wrote, with some fond amusement. But about one matter Williams was not amused: "The man is sunk, in my opinion, unless he can shake the fog of fascism out of his brain during the next few years, which I seriously doubt that he can do. . . . You can't argue away wanton slaughter of innocent women and children by the neoscholasticism of a controlled economy program." Pound did not shake the fog. World War II began in September, 1939, when Hitler marched into Poland (Pound was apparently in the wrong capital if he wanted to prevent the war). Italy entered the war on June 10, 1940; Pound, who had returned to Italy, decided to make another effort to keep the United States out. He broadcast an appeal on the Rome radio. Ironically, the date of the broadcast was December 7, 1941.

Bascially, the broadcast was a diatribe aimed at Great Britain, described as a country not worth saving:

123

> Now, what I had to say about the state of mind in England in 1919, I said in my *Cantos*. . . . I can't say my remarks were heeded. I thought I got 'em simple enough. Words short and simple enough . . . I go on trying to make my meaning clear and then clearer. . . . Things often do look simple to me. . . The pattern often is simple. . . .

Pound does not define the state of mind in the broadcast itself; he apparently expects his listener to look up Cantos XIV and XV. The ground of the argument shifts:

> What I am ready to fight against is having ex-European Jews making another peace worse than Versailles. . . . And in any case, I do not want my compatriots from the ages of 20 to 40 to get slaughtered to keep up the . . . British Jew rackets in Singapore and Shanghai . . . and no number of rabbis and bank clerks in Wall Street and in Washington can do one damn thing for England save to let her alone. . . . Roosevelt is more in the hands of the Jews than Wilson was in 1919. . . .

The news of Pearl Harbor kept Pound off the air for a while, but on January 29, 1942, he returned:

> . . . the United States has been for months . . . illegally at war, through what I considered to be the criminal acts of a President whose mental condition was not, so far as I could see, all that could or should be desired of a man in so responsible a position or office.

The broadcasts continued to July, 1943, the month the Allies invaded Sicily.

Outside of the monitoring stations in England and the United States, few were aware of "Europe Calling. Pound Speaking." The broadcasts became famous only after Pound was returned to the United States late in 1945 to stand trial for treason. In a way, the broadcasts were a grand, or grandiose, gesture. Pound saw himself as the representative of all that was good in Western culture. He had been trying for years to "tell 'em" what was wrong with the West and to point out the road to the good life—a road that was amazingly easy to find. Well, "they" hadn't listened, and now "they" would suffer the consequences. "You are not going to win this war. . . . You have never had a chance in this war." But the responsibility of the intellectual to his society, the responsibility of the clear-eyed one who could pierce the murk of daily chatter and confusion to the realm of truth, did not end because of initial defeat. America had to be told: "For the United States to be making war on Italy and on Europe is just plain damn nonsense. . . ." In the midst of Armaggedon, the voice of sanity could not be stilled: "some things you folks on both sides of the wretched ocean will have to learn, war or no war, sooner or later."

The broadcasts capped almost two decades of furious propaganda for Pound. There was little in them that Pound had not said before—over and over again: The war was a creature of the usurers and profiteers, who now were complacently watching the slaughter while counting their profits and preparing for the next war. It was a war for the gold standard and a "false accountancy system,"a system that kept men from controlling their own financial destinies; money ought to be in the hands of the state, not in the hands of private individuals who profited by lending it out. Only the state could employ money properly—for proper distribution of goods, not for the enrichment of the few. These ideas were as old as civilization. Certain Chinese emperors had been aware of them. The more responsible early American leaders—Jefferson, Adams, Jackson, Van Buren—had, in word and deed, shown their basic awareness. But after the Civil War, bankers and their minions had obscured these truths. American democracy, and American sensibility, had degenerated. Because of the inveterate stupidity and laziness of the American people, the works of the founding fathers were not widely read or reprinted. And surely anyone with any sense could tell that there had been some deliberate suppression. Certain truths were dangerous to the financial overlords of the Western world.

Why had Pound's own tracts, the *ABC of Economics, Jefferson and/or Mussolini, Social Credit, an Impact*—why hadn't they been "used as your text-books?" Why had so many men of wisdom been afraid to speak out or act upon their knowledge? "Ask yourselves." The usurers and profiteers were Jews; their plots had led to the decay of the moral fiber of the United States. A similar process had taken place in England: "you let in the Jew and the Jew rotted your Empire, and you yourselves are doomed by the Jew." Both in England and the United States, the old Anglo-Saxon stock had been ruined by the alien. World War I had been a Jews' war. So was World War II. These truths had been recognized by Hitler and

Mussolini, who were far ahead of the rest of the world in economic reform and had brought their nations to a high level of civilization. Both leaders were humanists. Why were we fighting them?

Such comments are depressingly familiar. They were the commonplaces of the far right before the war, and they have reappeared. But what were they doing in the mouth of Ezra Pound? To the many who felt that Pound was a crackpot, or a charlatan, or a foolish innocent—or all three—the broadcasts simply confirmed, in the most obvious way, what they had always suspected. Pound was forever being tempted by attitudes and positions he had not examined with sufficient care. In the late 20s, Wyndham Lewis found it necessary to dissociate himself from Pound publicly. Pound, he insisted, was a "generous and graceful person"; in fact, "a kinder heart never lurked beneath a portentous exterior than is to be found in Ezra Pound." Moreover, "Pound is not a vulgar humbug even in those purely propagandist activities, where, to my mind, he certainly handles humbug, but quite innocently, I believe." Unfortunately, Pound was too innocent, according to Lewis: "Pound is—that is my belief—a genuine *naif*. He is a sort of revolutionary simpleton!"

Lewis put his finger on one reason why Pound the Fascist, Pound the anti-Semite, Pound the hate-monger, was so difficult to square with Pound in his other guises. For Pound's generosity was legendary. He gave his time, helping Eliot and Joyce get published, acting as a link between European writers and American little magazines, writing letters of advice to any young poets who came his way. He gave his clothes, sending shoes to a puzzled Joyce via a puzzled Eliot. He gave his food, turning all the cats in Rapallo into disciples. Nor was there any way of ignoring the fact that Pound had put his mark on modern poetry, that without him its shape and direction would have been different. In at least one case, Eliot's "The Waste Land," Pound had edited and given final shape to a poem that had in turn shaped almost everything that followed. Pound had also, of course, produced his own body of work, and more than one reputable critic still finds "Hugh Selwyn Mauberley" a better poem than "The Waste Land."

Aside from Pound's generosity, influence, poetry, there was another, more personal, matter to be faced. Pound seemed to be the antithesis of the parochial mind. He would go wherever significance and beauty were to be found—to China and Japan, to Provence and medieval Italy, to the American founding fathers; at the same time, he moved with ease among the moderns. He was scarcely alone in this, of course: Eliot and Joyce carried a considerable freight of knowledge. But unlike Eliot and Joyce, Pound appointed himself schoolmaster to the world. Via letters, translations, criticism, poems, he accumulated educational debts that are still being acknowledged.

Furthermore, Pound did not give way completely to his economic and political obsessions until the end of the 30s, when all Europe wore an air of crisis. The *Cantos* continued to appear, though freighted more and more with Pound's political and economic views: *A Draft of XXX Cantos* in 1930; Eleven New Cantos, XXXI-XLI in 1934; *The Fifth Decad of Cantos* in 1937; *Cantos LII-LXXI* in 1940. The poem was not to be heard from again until *The Pisan Cantos,* 1948, which recounted Pound's experiences in an Army detention camp at Pisa. He saw to the collection of his essays (*Make It New, Polite Essays*). There was more work on the Confucian classics. There were statements of his literary guidelines (*How to Read, ABC of Reading*). There were visiting poets and critics in search of a father. There were concerts to organize, anthologies to edit, Yeats to argue with, cats to feed. He remained, in other words, the multi-faceted man whom one might detest but whom one also might love. Perhaps, then, we ought to rephrase the question suggested above. If Pound was not completely overwhelmed by his obsessions, how did *he* square his propaganda activities with the rest of himself?

Pound, of course, saw no incompatability at all. He boasted, time after time, that he had never changed his general framework of ideas. "One of the pleasures of middle age," he announced in the *ABC of Reading,* "is to *find out* that one WAS right, and that one was much righter than one knew at say seventeen or twenty-three." To Pound, his later political and economic ideas simply helped explain his earlier intuitions. Thus, if the foundations of his taste were basically pre-Raphaelite (Botticelli, not Rembrandt; Gothic, not Baroque), he later insisted that what he found beautiful had been produced in an intellectual climate unfriendly to the usurers and the profiteers. Clearly, Pound felt that his economic and political activities were normal, logical developments of his role as a poet and as an intellectual. And if we want to understand what Pound *thought* he was doing, it is important to understand his view of that role.

He sought, in a very deliberate way, he said, to find what sort of things are transient, what sort of things recur, what sort of things endure. If ideas and forms of enduring value have been lost in time, it is the job of the perceptive artist to revive them, as Pound has revived by translation the Provencal poets and the Confucian classics. It is also the poet's job to pierce the murk of the present to discern what is likely to endure. Journeying through the long past and the short present, Pound in *The Cantos* and elsewhere compares one work with another, one era with another, one man with another, discerning not only differences but similarities in the effort to find what recurs. There are differences of time, place, and temperament, but the perceptive artist is, presumably, capable of piercing these veils to the essential reality behind—the reality of the spirit and the will. Thus, Pound quite consciously and quite ambitiously turns himself into the cultural arbiter of his time.

Now Pound takes a very important step further. He seeks not only enduring literary and artistic forms, but meaningful social and economic patterns. As a sensitive receiver of impressions, as the antenna of his race, the poet is, apparently, peculiarly equipped to discern and define those patterns that make for a decent, orderly society. Thus, *The Cantos* link themselves to certain of man's central aspirations: toward order and the creative life.

Certain temperaments, Pound felt, could be trusted to create lasting art and to guide states toward the good life. The artist and the responsible politician are linked. Such men, Pound asserted, exhibit a reverence for the past, though only for what is useful in it; a sense of responsibility for society and the arts; a clarity of perception that avoids the overly abstract and centers in the concrete; and the will to act upon their perceptions. The will to act is, to Pound, as much a sign of one's genuineness as it is to Sartre. In fact, ideas can scarcely be said to exist until and unless they are seen in action. Ultimately, their life is shown as they work their way into society, becoming part of the unconscious assumptions of the people, seen in its manners and its rituals. "The ideas of genius, or of 'men of intelligence' are organic and germinal, the 'seed' of the scriptures," according to Pound.

There is little in all this to excite comment. In fact, there's a good deal one might agree with: the poet's responsibility for the health of his society, the need for comparison if one is to be certain of his own values, the need to see an idea in action before one judges it. And one can, at least, sympathize with Pound's image of himself as a kind of poet-priest, a carrier of "organic and germinal" seed that must be made to flourish. It makes a nice day-dream.

Paradoxically, much of the trouble lies in the fact that Pound is often right, and carries his sense of certainty into rather dubious areas. In the *ABC of Economics*, we find, in place of "proof," long discourses on the need for responsibility and diatribes on the lack of responsibility among most people; in *Jefferson and/or Mussolini*, a good deal about the ineffectuality and irresponsibility of the Italian intelligentsia.

True, here as elsewhere, Pound is employing his famous ideogrammic method—the juxtaposition, the arrangement and rearrangement, of a small cluster of facts and ideas in the hope that eventually they will break through the layer of dead brain cells that, Pound assumes, surrounds most of our minds, with the further hope that an idea, a seed, may lodge there. Unfortunately, the method is not very convincing. Again and again, where we expect development, explanation, exemplification of the dubious, we get a latticework of Pound's general assumptions, many of which are quite self-evident but few of which prove that Mussolini was a great man or that Pound really knew much about money. One critic felt the "method" was self-indulgent. I wonder whether it might have been self-hypnotic.

Pound's interest in economic and political matters precedes the 30s by a good many years. By the beginning of the 20s he was denouncing usurers, bankers, profiteers, munitions makers. See the early cantos (XII, XIV, XV, XVIII). In Canto XXII, we have a reference to one of Pound's earliest economic mentors, C. H. Douglas, whom he had met in 1918 and whose theories struck Pound with the force of revelation. And what was revealed to the poet-priest had to be preached to the world. Beginning in the 20s, reaching flood-tide in the 30s, the letters poured out of Pound's study. More than one of Pound's literary friends and acquaintances received an abrupt series of questions from Pound: did they know what money was? who made it? who controlled it? Some were impressed. Some were bothered. Some were wryly amused. Henry Miller dedicated to Pound a burlesque pamphlet called *Money and How It Gets That Way*:

> About a year ago, upon reading *Tropic of Cancer*, Ezra
> Pound wrote me a postcard in his usual cabalistic style,
> asking me if I had ever thought about money . . . Since
> then, . . . I have thought about it night and day.

Pound modified his economic theories, and added to them from time to time, but basically they centered on the uses and control of money. In his *ABC of Economics* (1933), Pound asserts that the problem of producing enough goods has been solved. Thus, "probably the only economic problem needing emergency solution in our time is the problem of distribution." Since distribution is effected by money, the problem boils down to that of getting money circulated, which had been C. H. Douglas's assumption. His solution: let the state issue money, in the form of a national dividend, directly to the people. Goods will circulate and poverty will vanish. Pound found an allied theory in the suggestion of Sylvio Gesell: stamp scrip, a form of money that requires the owner to attach, once a month, a government stamp worth up to 1% of the bill's face value; banks, rather than hoard the money, will be in a hurry to rid themselves of it; money will circulate, goods will circulate, and everyone will be happy.

In the *ABC*, Pound felt that perhaps it might be simpler to spread money around by spreading work around—shortening the work day. The state, of course, would see to it that money is carefully adjusted to the work done. And once credit becomes, not the preserve of the bank, but a function of the state—representing the entire people, on whose capacity to produce credit ultimately depends—then taxes cease to be necessary. As the source of money and credit, the state can pay directly—without borrowing—for what it wants done. In fact, this might be another way of assuring that the amount of money in circulation is enough to buy all the goods produced and wanted.

These are simple, clear ideas to Pound. "THE BASES OF ECONOMICS are so simple as to render the subject almost wholly uninteresting." He feels detailed development unnecessary: "The aim of this brochure is to express the fundamentals of economics so simply and clearly that even people of different economic factions will be able to understand each other when they discuss them." Complications arise (A) from the extreme difficulty of foreseeing what will be wanted; (B) from the rascally nature of certain men.

The political implications of his ideas are quite sweeping. Economics is an art, not a science; it requires intelligence, vigilance, honesty. Pound will accept any political system that can put at the top men who are capable of creating the economic environment he describes. With this in mind, we are ready for *Jefferson and/or Mussolini* (1935). Pound came to Italy in 1924. Gradually he grew to like what he saw and to find in Il Duce the economic reformer he sought: "On Oct. 6th of the year current (anno XII) . . . Mussolini . . . told 40 million Italians . . . that the problem of production

was solved, and that they could now turn their minds to distribution."
And that was that. "End of poverty in the Italian peninsula."

The perceptive artist who has looked far into the past and
widely into the present, Pound does not hesitate to insist that "the
fundamental likenesses between" Jefferson and Mussolini "are probably greater than their differences." To Pound, Mussolini was a
man of will, energy, and perception—one of the heroes of *The
Cantos*. And since these heroes are basically artists, Mussolini emerges as one who possesses "the opportunism of the artist, who has a
definite aim, and creates out of the materials present. The greater
the artist the more permanent his creation. And this is a matter of
WILL." Again: "Take him as anything save the artist and you will
get muddled with contradictions." Similar statements might be ap-
plied to Jefferson. Furthermore, Pound feels, the founding fathers
were basically patrician: "Jefferson guided a governing class. A
limited number of the public had the franchise." Both Jefferson and
Adams assumed that the more intelligent members of society would
continue to govern. Since that is no longer the case, and since
Mussolini embodies all the authentic governing virtues, it requires
no great leap to accept Mussolini as the genuine inheritor of the
American revolution. And Italy becomes the only nation in Europe
with the energy to oppose "the infinite evil of the profiteers and the
sellers of men's blood for money." In the second half of the decade,
Germany is added to the list of civilized agents, Pound quoting with
approval both Hitler and Hjalmer Schacht.

While complaining of his difficulty in getting published, Pound
was determined to be heard. In *Poet in Exile*, Noel Stock reports on
the tens of thousands of letters written between 1928 and 1942 to,
among others, Senators, members of the House of Commons, ambas-
sadors, members of Roosevelt's cabinet, even to Mrs. Roosevelt—to
anyone who might help spread the word. At the same time, Pound
edged closer and closer to the intransigent positions that made it less
and less likely that anyone would be listening. He focused more and
more narrowly on the definition of economic terms, on the nature of
money. Since they would not follow him into the Fascist camp, the
followers of Douglas were denounced in an Oswald Mosley weekly
as "Social Credit Asses." The violence of Pound's anti-Semitism
became more pronounced.

At the end of 1941, he addressed himself to the windy Atlantic:
"Europe Calling. Pound Speaking."

Kenneth Fearing and the
Twentieth Century Blues

by Sy Kahn

The poet and novelist Kenneth Fearing died in New York City on June 26, 1961. During his lifetime he published seven books of poetry and seven novels and, quite aside from these works, he also wrote a great deal for the various mass communications media. The poet feared and disdained the power of these media to shape opinion, to obliterate thinking and to emasculate writing; some of his novels and much of his poetry are born of his apprehension and outrage at the spectacle of man's mind manipulated and controlled by the giant voices of mass communication. In poem after poem, shaped by a cool, perfected irony, Fearing gives us a variety of urbane responses to the central terror of man dehumanized. Consequently, it is not difficult to discover that Fearing's books of poetry have a remarkable unity of tone, atmosphere and intention. One may see, as he saw in himself, in the "Forward" to his *New and Selected Poems* (1956), a writer who earned his living by working and writing for newspapers and magazines, radio and television, but who counterbalanced the compromises and simplifications imposed by this work with the authentic observations and feelings of his poetry, written, as he said, "in the margin of whatever light remained."

Although Fearing published his first book of poems, *Angel Arms,* in 1929 and his last in 1956, the major portion of his poetry was

133

either written and published during the 30s or shaped by his impressions of the decade, and no other American poet speaks to us more directly and consistently about the era of the Great Depression. Following *Angel Arms,* he published *Poems* (1935), *Dead Reckoning* (1938), *Collected Poems* (1940), *Afternoon of a Pawnbroker* (1943), and *Stranger at Coney Island* (1948), plus the last collection in 1956, cited above. Except for his first novel *The Hospital* (1929), his novels were published after the decade of the 30s. Consequently, it is Fearing the poet that I wish to discuss, and to indicate how he, as much as any writer and more than most who wrote in and reacted to the 30s, reveals its essence.

Born in 1902 in Oak Park, Illinois, Fearing did not, like many of his contemporaries, follow the expatriate route to Paris. However, following his graduation from the University of Wisconsin in 1924, he went to New York City where he lived and wrote for the rest of his life. His earliest poems were quick to capture the symbols and rhythms of big city life as well as to respond to the fever, desperation and frantic materialism of the 20s, the decade of the cool million. Perhaps F. Scott Fitzgerald's first three novels set the tone and provided the insights into that decade, but true or not, there are striking parallels in the work of both writers. Both sensed the moral decay and human alienation at the center of life as lived by victorious and unshackled Americans during the 20s, and both marked the sinister spectres that haunted busy mankind and that cast dark shadows over the most glittering moment.

The sense of the ominous is a dominant feature in all of Fearing's books of poems, though the face and shape of the threatening spectres shift. In the 20s his men and women are spooked by the fear that the affluence of the decade, the quick fortunes built on inflated stocks, merely gilded a life that had no moral center or stability. When the great bull market died in 1929, and the era of depression began, the characters of Fearing's poems not only still shake from the reverberations of the economic collapse that toppled both fortunes and the dream of eternal security but also they quake because in some subterranean way they sense the shaping of a new disaster, some second coming of a world war. For those who survived the 1929 crash, as well as the decade of the great depression and World War II, there are still new spectres to threaten them. In the poems of the 40s Fearing makes us aware of brutal and coercive forces and devices: the secret police, the informers and intriguers, the listening devices that monitor the individual man and the society with the purpose of rendering each man faceless and efficient. Any eccentricity of the human mind and heart are corrected or erased in order to make the person smoothly fit and remain faithful to a new totalitarian social order; if the customer proves too tough, he can be eliminated altogether. There is little relief for the Fearing man, haunted by the old disasters of the past and threatened by a new conspiracy of ruthless forces dedicated to the principles of subservience and conformity to the will of the state. For the Fearing man, as the books of poetry define his cosmos, every horizon is ominous, and the big clock strikes the hour of doom twenty-four times a day.

In his earliest poems to his last, amid the shifting real and spectral forces, one encounters the terrible image of total human destruction. For example, the early poem "The Drunken Fly" (from *Angel Arms*) concludes:

> Then there is nothing, any more
> But rags and bits of glass in corners,
> And the sound of dust
> Softly raining on an iron door.
> Then there is nothing, and no one,
> The people are gone
> Like an army that has rolled on
> Over deep canyons choked with men.

Almost ten years later, in 1938, at the edge of World War II, the poem "Devil's Dream" (from *Dead Reckoning*) rises at the end to its ironic, apocalyptic statement:

> Because it is not, never could be true
> that the whole wide, bright, green, warm, calm
> world goes
> CRASH.

Later poems handle the basic image somewhat differently. For example, in "Portrait of a Cog" Fearing presents us with one of his numerous business executive types who is vaguely aware that he may be involved in some monstrous conspiracy, "in league with some manic partner whom you have never met," but which shapes a sudden and violent destiny. The man shrugs off his uneasiness, buries it beneath the mounds of business detail. But, writes Fearing,

> When they dig you up, in a thousand years, they will find you in
> just this pose,

One hand upon the buzzer, the other reaching for the phone, eyes
fixed upon the calendar, feet firmly on the office rug.

Then Fearing deepens the irony in the final stanza:

Yes, when they dig you up, like this, a thousand years from now,
they will say: Just as he was in life. A man typical of the times,
engaged in typical affairs.
Notice the features, especially, they will say. How self-assured
they are, and how serene.

Finally, in a poem called "Museum" a group of visitors is addressed
by an anonymous guide who conducts them past a series of tiny scale
models, one one-thousandth size, of typical 20th century business
scenes, "gay, casual" tableaus, that exhibit life previous to later eras
called "the Second Age of Innocence, the Era of the Torrents, the
Third Age of Fire." As the viewers of the future pass on to these
exhibits, the miniature, static models of our age are left behind "in
the darkness." All the types are there: the Executive, Typist, Switch-
board Girl, jovial Attorney, "Each of them comfortable and secure
as in life, each mulling some / personal problem, / Each confidently
waiting for the sun that will surely rise."

Catching casual faces at what seem to be random moments,
Fearing gives us "portraits" of American types at some unspecified
time before some impending but undepicted holocaust. One of
Fearing's favorite ironic devices is to make the subject of his portrait
oblivious to the forces that threaten his precarious existence and the
values and social structure that give him an illusion of safety. Sometimes the character, in a swift and blurred moment of insight, becomes fleetingly aware of some possible disaster which he dismisses.
It is as if a man might suddenly recognize a skipped heart-beat, a
sudden, quick drop in blood pressure, an uneasiness in some vital
function—and then dismiss the symptom because its implication, the
pang of inevitable failure and death, were too unreal, fantastic or
terrible to confront. Anthologizers of American poetry have been
right in frequently including Fearing's poem "Portrait" in their
books. This most famous of Fearing's poems illustrates many features
typical of the poet's work in general, but particularly his gift for
ironic portraiture. However, this typically unnamed type, a sort of
synthetic man constructed out of "R. K. Lambert & Company lenses
framed in gold," "Arndt Brothers necktie and hat," crowned and
bridged teeth, "Mercury shoes, with special arch supports," and who
has a psyche repaired from love's ravages, "it was a textbook case,"

who blithely drives his new car while he is "enclosed in excellent tweed," and who considers, certainly, his soul to be his own, is only one of Fearing's numerous "portraits." There are others of call girls, office girls, charwomen, gangsters, business tycoons, artists, old grads and secret agents. His work provides us with a gallery of portraits, rogues and otherwise, with snapshots, candid and tough, so that we have in all an album of ancestors and relatives of the previous decades, all smiling back at us as if the crash, the depression, the war, as if social and political tyrannies and conspiracies, and death itself could never happen. All the types are kept at an ironic distance; the studies are never intimate, never elaborate. They are images of men and women in motion, caught for an instant, the details and setting arranged with a seeming and deceptive carelessness, but all, in the final analysis, calculated by the poet to deepen the ironic tone and intention of the portrait.

In these poems Fearing is further removed in time than in technique and intention from the work of the earlier American poet, Stephen Crane. Both Crane and Fearing employed free verse, the long, rambling line counterbalanced by the short, thrusting line to render their ironic portraits. The freedom of the line length enables both writers to use the long, discursive line as a method of both disarming and preparing the reader for the short, laconic line, or sometimes series of staccato phrases, which carry ironic power. The technique might be compared to the boxer who uses long and lazy left feints and jabs to set up his opponent for the quick, explosive right cross. Like Crane, Fearing too was a young man come to the same big city, and both may be said to have sought the line and form for their poems that would respond to the pace, tempo and beat of swift and noisy city life. The freedom in form, of course, was first won by Whitman, and in the same city in which Crane and Fearing were to write and publish their work, and in response to city scenes and moods not so essentially different. Whitman, of course, was no ironist, Crane was—but both poets broke ground that Fearing further explored.

Commenting effectively on an era and society through ironic portraiture of general types is also characteristic of the best poems of E. A. Robinson and a few of T. S. Eliot's. Fearing shares with Robinson the technique of using portraiture as a way of rendering a double irony: the poem's and the poet's. Robinson, however, succeeds by giving more intimate details of feature, gesture and dress of his subjects, and in rendering them in more formal and traditional diction, line length, rhyme scheme and structure than Fearing ever attempts. Also, Robinson is far less concerned with the total atmosphere of a time and place than is Fearing. Robinson's characters are at once more particularized and more mythic than Fearing's whose figures are closer to the free and easy line of the impressionistic or surrealistic cartoon.

Between Robinson and Fearing we may draw some revealing contrasts and parallels in their manner of ironic portraiture in poetry, but when it comes to T. S. Eliot, then a real inheritance can be traced. Certainly the images, the free verse, the various dramatic devices of "The Waste Land" helped shape the imagination of a whole generation of poets, and one feels the impact of Eliot's early work in Fearing's poems. There are the same metaphors of dry, empty and forlorn urban life, the same ennui, tensions and apprehensions, and the same indictment of the failure of human values. Hollow men whisper together too in Fearing's poems, but as often as much to undo and betray each other as for mutual support. Like Eliot, Fearing implies the loss of traditional moral and spiritual values. Fearing's poems, however, speak of and to the 20s and 30s with a diction and with a type of free verse, in images and in dramatic situations, that make his poetry much more accessible to ordinary and casual readers than Eliot's richly allusive, subtly accented observations could ever permit. Thus Edward Dahlberg, in his introduction to Fearing's second book of poems, saw the poet as a spokesman for the depressed masses of the 1930s, indicting capitalism and speaking for a Marxist future. For Dahlberg, the poems are "an accusation and a foreshadowing of the doom of the whole capitalistic society," and they "rise and expand into an affirmative Communist statement." Kenneth Fearing, Dahlberg proclaims, is "a poet for workers" who offers "one more piece of documented evidence of the horrible mutilations of human dreams and nobleness under capitalism." Fearing's simplicity and accessibility as a poet makes his work liable to the sort of reading Mr. Dahlberg gives it, but it reveals more about the critic, reading through red-colored glasses, than the work of the poet. Both before and after the highest point of communist enthusiasms in America, Fearing was indicting, it seems to me, not so much an economic system but some basic failures in human imagination and sensitivity, attacking human fear, weakness and cruelty, marking the ironic distances between aspiration and conclusion, hope and despair. "And Steve, the athlete, where is he?" asks Fearing at the beginning of "Class Reunion." Later he provides the answer, "And true that Steve is bald, and broke, and fat?" And so on for all the others in the class reunion who provide a symphony of personal defeats and disasters, not because of the evils of capitalism but rather the inscrutability and malevolence of a fate more Greek than economic:

> White mice, running mazes in behavior tests, have never displayed
>   more cunning than these, who arrived by such devious
> routes at such incredible ends.

Kenneth Fearing wrote poems not manifestos, poems less terse than Crane's, less formal than Robinson's, less literary and complex than Eliot's; he devised a consistent style and attitude uniquely his, and he is a clear and definable voice in the poetry of the 30s and 40s. In broad terms he speaks for an America at the edge of the deep and long abyss of the depression, and during the depression decade; he speaks not only of life in that abyss but also as a Cassandra pointing to the new war whose lights he could see flickering in the distance. In *Dead Reckoning* (1938) Fearing was already reckoning the dead in poem after poem dark with the images of violence and destruction. In that volume, at the end of "Happy New Year," he writes:

> Pour the cocktails
>   it is late, it is cold, it is still, it is dark
>   quickly, for time is swift and it is late, late, later
>   than you think
>   with one more hour to kill, one more night, one more day
>   somehow to be killed.

In Fearing's poems there is much of the sense of waiting: waiting for the next battle, the next war, the next economic or social disaster. The murderer waits to be electrocuted, the girl waits for madness, men wait for death that can never quite be acknowledged as inevitable and real. The moods of waiting and warning alternate and counterpoint, while men look hopelessly into barroom mirrors at 4 a.m., or turn up the juke box, or repeat social rituals that might diminish the spectral warning, evaporate the ghosts under hot lights, bury the future before the future buries them. It was the world of the 30s; Fearing caught the mood and melody and devised the song.

Fearing's poetry is characterized by certain words and images that also contribute to the unity of his work as much as his consistent dark moods and ironic tone and free-verse style. For example, the word "millions" occurs many times, the millions swept by giant forces, manipulated and eventually manacled by the mechanical devices they must serve. Modern industry may force the millions to enslave themselves to the machines they serve, not only for their livelihood but also for what they believe to be their amusement and pleasure: the radio and the gags of comedians evoking instant, mechanical laughter, the thin images of the movie screens, for example, pandering to hopeless, sentimental dreams. (One remembers the lavish musical comedies by which we escaped the oppressive, daily facts of the 30s.) Thus, "fantasy Frank," and "dreamworld Dora," and "hallucination Ned" make brief and false escapes, or, at worst, become automatons blind to terror and deaf to appeal, like robots no longer human or humane. Symbol after symbol of mechanical contrivance standing for the triumph of technology and the death of the spirit appear in Fearing's poems. His imagery is habitually linked to the world of machines and mechanized men, and the metallic and manufactured sounds drown out the human voice. One finds, along with this imagery, a heightened sense of time. Almost every poem employs the diction and imagery of time passing, time waning, time running out. The hands of the clock press constantly on the necks of Fearing's people. They press the poet too, for Fearing always played Cassandra, and time is particularly oppressive to unheeded prophets.

Kenneth Fearing's poems speak for the 30s, for demoralized and threatened men and women, caught between past and impending disasters. A poet of city life, where the tensions of the depression years were felt most keenly, he wrote a tough, simple, hard language and made ironies out of outrage, sarcasm out of despair. Even if the times never suited him, he had talents that suited the times and gave them an effective voice. Regardless of whether Fearing wrote of the 20s, 30s or 40s in his poetry, however, he was always sensitive to deception, whether it was the big lie of mass-think or the lies one tells oneself to avoid some of the unpleasant realities of life in our century. If time, however, undoes every lie and every defense against inevitable catastrophes and personal death, it may also bring change. It is true, writes Fearing in "C Stands For Civilization,"

> You are born but once,
> You have your chance to live but once,
> You go mad and put a bullet through your head but once . . . .

At the same time, in a capitalized refrain in the poem that occurs five times, we may be relieved to hear that not only a decade but also

THE TWENTIETH CENTURY COMES BUT ONCE
ONLY ONCE, AND STAYS FOR BUT ONE HUNDRED YEARS.

Archibald MacLeish:
Mapping the Tradition

by Dan Jaffe

Archibald MacLeish's "Ars Poetica" has probably been more often anthologized than any of his other poems. Almost all anthologies that include MacLeish's work, and that means most anthologies of American poetry published during the last 30-35 years, reprint it. Its lines have been mimicked, parodied, and widely misunderstood. Perhaps no contemporary poem has created such aesthetic rage in some quarters. Few poems have been treated so shabbily, for reasons that have little to do with the poem itself.

Most of the furor caused by the poem concerns MacLeish's final statement, one that has become so familiar that it may soon offend to quote it at all:

> A poem should not mean
> But be.

Those enemies of "modern" poetry who read only enough of it to furnish themselves with ammunition for the onslaught have for years used these lines to prove the effeteness of verse that is not "traditional." One can see them rubbing their fingertips together gleefully as they quote the lines. They remind one of William Buckley appraising a speech of Eleanor Roosevelt. And they were often joined by the Marxian critics who never forgave MacLeish for his refusal to leap to the communist barricades in the 30s.

The standard interpretation runs something like this. In "Ars Poetica" MacLeish advocates a poetry that is self-sufficient, in which texture is more important than idea, a poetry removed from the relevancies of life, a poetry that exists for its own sake and for the sake of an aesthetic elite.

Such an interpretation fails to take into consideration either the context in which the lines appear or the context in which the poem appears, the imposing body of MacLeish's work.

Those who have insisted on the "art for art's sake" interpretation disregard the curious contradiction such an interpretation requires. They maintain that MacLeish is denying the importance of ideas, but at the same time they stress the ideological content of the poem. They maintain that MacLeish denies meaning, but they nevertheless attack his literal meaning. And if one points out this curious paradox they more than likely will reply that it reveals the failure of "modern" poetry to accomplish even the little it tries.

But "Ars Poetica" is a performance of the principle MacLeish states in the final lines. The poem gives the statement what significance it has by dramatizing what MacLeish means by "be"ing. It is essentially a catalogue of images related in tone and linked by declarations. And the declarations serve as a regular reminder that MacLeish is not denying the importance of idea, of theory, of intellectual position. Three times the poem asserts "A poem should be" and goes on to talk imagistically. Then the last stanza opens:

A poem should be equal to:
Not true.

These repetitions make the poem in effect didactic. But is MacLeish insisting on dumping ideas? If so his very didacticism would make that position untenable.

Throughout the poem MacLeish says that poetry should be as real as the images of the world. The images he provides are enormously evocative, full of symbolic potential. They are images chosen not only for their sensory impact but because of the intellectual and mythical ripples they set in motion. "Be"ing then is a larger category than "mean"ing. In the last lines of the poem MacLeish is not shying away from idea, from what is usually meant by "meaning." Instead he indicates that that kind of "meaning" alone is not enough. Message does not make poetry. The poem is first of all an experience; it must have the reality of a happening, not of a statement. But of course, like any occurrence, it may have and probably should have intellectual consequence.

The notion that MacLeish believed poems should have no substantial relevance to intellectual or social written matters seems
ludicrous if one looks at the other poems in *From Streets in the
Moon* (1926), the book in which "Ars Poetica" appeared; for one
soon becomes aware that MacLeish even in his early work revealed
his concern with the outer world, the world of trade and technology.
He was to consider it, to try and capture its meanings. And so in
"Man!" he satirizes the social animal of the twenties:

> LIFE in the vial with Safety Catch,
> LIFE in the Perpendicular Decanter,

In his early books MacLeish experimented with styles, often,
sounded like other poets. But he was more than a literary laundry-
man taking in other writers' washing. We cannot even insist that
all his best early poems were introspective, personal lyrics rather
than social considerations. Some of them certainly were, poems
like "L'an Trentiesme De Mon Eage" and "You, Andrew Marvell."
But others like "The End of the World" are hardly just interior
poems. Very early MacLeish began judging the world about him,
and those judgments make their way into poems written even before
the startling occurrences of the 30s, occurrences that were to make
even the most introspectively inclined aware of the events going on
around them. The first stanza of "The End of the World" makes
MacLeish's view of his society clear:

> Quite unexpectedly as Vasserot
> The armless ambidextrian was lighting
> A match between his great and second toe
> And Ralph the lion was engaged in biting
> The neck of Madame Sossman while the drum
> Pointed, and Teeny was about to cough
> In waltz-time swinging Jocko by the thumb —
> Quite unexpectedly the top blew off:

Although MacLeish develops the circus metaphor without comment,
it is a judgment of the world. And the judgment makes the whole
poem seem strangely prophetic of the way in which the illusions
of the wild 20s shattered on the rocks of depression.

It now seems especially ironic that after the publication of
"Invocation to the Social Muse" in 1932, letters reminded MacLeish
that historically many poets had been men of affairs. The letters
must have been from readers who read the poem's last line, "Is it

just to demand of us also to bear arms?" as the poet's weaseling out of public responsibility. But "Invocation" could only have been written by a man ready to speak publicly. He refers early in the poem to tractors, Marx, and "wars more antiseptic and murderous." He rejects Hoover and "Mister Morgan." In a taunting tone he identifies poets as

> persons of
> Known vocation following troops: they must sleep with
> Stragglers from either prince and of both views.

Whatever his conscious intent at the time, his tone and metaphor suggest disdain for those who take the position he later attacks so furiously in his essay "The Irresponsibles." Further on in "Invocation," MacLeish notes that the poet must speak individually to the individual. He asks rhetorically,

> How to take to one's chamber a million souls?
> How to conceive in the name of a column of marchers?

It seems unlikely that he is recommending a skittish turning away from all causes. Rather he insists on speaking for the single self to the single man, instead of becoming an instrument of the collective. The last line of the poem follows immediately after MacLeish says that the poet is more than a member of a class or a trade. His question about bearing arms is addressed to the Communists. It is a rejection of Marxian doctrine and as such it is the public act of an individual who symbolically bears arms but only as an individual.

In later poems MacLeish pointedly attacked the Morgans, Harrimans, and Vanderbilts. He sounded in Whitmanian fashion the romantic yawp of democracy. He was not standoffish, not the pimple-faced boy at the mixer. He was, in fact, in 1940 to call to task the intellectuals of his time for not speaking out against those who would replace law with force, beauty with cruelty, singleness with numbers. He called those who practice their arts in insulated cells, "The Irresponsibles." Of the men who practiced "academic narcissism," he said, "They emerged free, pure, and single into the antiseptic air of objectivity. And by that sublimation of the mind they prepared the mind's disaster." Nor was such a statement from MacLeish surprising. He had after all during the 30s written a whole series of rather transparent radio plays dealing with the immediate problems of the times. He had gone so far as to write a long poem, *Land of the Free,* which he himself said in a note was

the "opposite of a book of poems illustrated by photographs,"—
"a book of photographs illustrated by a poem." The photographs
were taken for the Resettlement Administration. The poem does
little more than summarize the realizations of a generation that had
seen breadlines form after the stock market crash and the breakdown
of the banking system, who had felt the muscles of industry cramp,
seen top soil wash farms into flood waters and literally millions of
men ride the rails to mealless tomorrows. MacLeish during those
years became the poetic reporter of American deterioration.

MacLeish has never stopped writing those melodic, melancholy
lyrics that first brought him to fame. But as the decades passed he
became more and more the polemicist, more and more interested in
making meaning in the old fashioned sense of that word. All too
often it seemed that he had turned his back on the principle he had
so superbly dramatized in "Ars Poetica."

During the 30s MacLeish set out to do as man and poet what
no other twentieth century American poet has dared. Stirred by
devastating effects of the economic breakdown at home and startled
by the hints of a dangerous anti-humanistic and anti-intellectual
revolution abroad, he set out to make the entire social scene his
domain. He was to try to do Shelley one better, to make the poet
the *acknowledged* legislator of his time.

Even if he had not been a distinguished poet, had not won the
Pulitzer Prize and been elected to the national Institute of Arts and
Letters, his involvement in public life during the 30s and 40s would
have guaranteed him a place in the annals of the time. Beginning
in 1930, he was one of those liberal editors of *Fortune,* a magazine
edited chiefly for the rich, which as Frederick Lewis Allen put it
in *Since Yesterday,* "developed such a brilliant technic of team-
research and team-authorship and trimmed its sails so skillfully to
the winds of conservatism that it not only became a mine of factual
material for future historians but subtly broadened reactionary
minds."

In 1939, despite the objections of the American Library Association and the dismay of the *New York Herald Tribune,* the
Senate approved MacLeish's appointment as Librarian of Congress.
An almost incredible administrator, he reorganized the operation and
direction of the library in his drive to make it "a people's library
of reference." While Librarian he also served as Director of the
Office of Facts and Figures. In 1944 he became Assistant Secretary of State, and in 1945 led the U. S. delegation at the London

Conference that founded UNESCO. This was the same man who had been reminded by irate readers that in the past many poets had involved themselves in public life.

MacLeish did not discard the laurel to put on the Homburg. He was never a literary man graduated into the political spotlight. Nor was he privately a poet and publicly a civil servant. He was both at once. The concerns that he felt as public man revealed themselves in his writing; those that had been revealed in his writing dictated the course of his life.

He returned from Europe in 1929 after five years as an expatriate. *New Found Land* (1930) pointed the direction his work was to take. Like so many novelists and poets he was to seek a definition of America through his work. In "American Letter" he wrote, "It is a strange thing to be an American." He found America strange because of its youth and diversity, because of its challenge and seeming lack of tradition. But in "American Letter" his commitment is clear, "Here we must live or live only as shadows." And yet he feels the old nostalgia for Europe.

It is a nostalgia that will not last. He seeks to replace it by mapping out a tradition. He returns to materials he had almost forgotten were his to work with. It was as if he were returning to old haunts. Five years earlier in "The Farm" he had shown Ephraim Cross driving up the trail from Massachusetts in 1750. Now he was to take to the trail himself, on foot and muleback to follow the route of Cortes from the seacoast to the Valley of Mexico. That trip (1928) and his study of the account of Bernal Diaz del Castillo, *True History of the Conquest of New Spain,* resulted in *Conquistador* (1932) and the Pulitzer Prize.

After exploring at the periphery, he zeroed in. In "Frescoes for Mr. Rockefeller's City" (1933) he pictured America as a fertile nude, "belly . . . flecked with the flickering light of the corn." He contrasted Crazy Horse's love of the land with Mister Morgan's concern with real estate values. He scored the Communists who would replace the experience of the land with the abstractions of Dialectical Materialism.

America's tradition, he came to see, was a tradition of possibility, of promises inherent in the land itself. But, he was to ask himself, have the leaves of that tradition withered? Is the American present a shoot of the original plant? In *Land of the Free* (1938) he notes the disillusionment of the people, their children "canning . . . crawfish in . . . ten cent cans," their voices stilled by company cops, their land blowing out from under their hoes, their independence destroyed by poverty. The poem is an indictment of those who have for their own profit poisoned the tradition. "We wonder whether the great American dream . . . is behind us now." *Land of the Free* ends despairingly; hopes are muted, disappointments emphasized.

In *America Was Promises* (1939) MacLeish assumes a more militant attitude. He also, in a way, reassesses responsibility. He provides not a question but an answer:

> America is promises to
> Take!
> America is promises to
> Us
> To take them
> Brutally
> With love but
> Take them.
> Oh believe this!

MacLeish engaged himself as a public man to fertilize and protect the tradition. As a poet he tried to embody it in his work. Like Robert Frost and William Carlos Williams he sought a technical means of capturing the American voicebox. In the introduction to *Panic* (1935) he discusses the difference between the genius of the American language and that of the English language. He maintains that American is a language of accents, that its rhythms tend to fall rather than rise, are more generally trochaic than iambic. But despite his concern with such problems and despite the fact that he unashamedly introduces idiomatic expressions into his poetry, MacLeish's poems and plays sound more often theatrically American than authentically so. The roll of rhetoric he so often depends on is as far from the voice of the people as the podium is from the street. Let this be read as a general judgment rather than as an absolute one, for there is no doubt that at moments MacLeish accomplishes what he sets out to do. But the task he set for himself was enormous and he succeeds only on occasion in making the kind of poems he called for in "Ars Poetica." As a poet of social consciousness he satirizes more effectively than he dramatizes. And though he seeks to put America into his poems, over and over again the same images appear, the images we find in his early work. Too often he is over-insistent, a shouter and convincer rather than a seducer.

To talk about a writer's failings is not to underestimate his contributions. Archibald MacLeish took the major risk and for that he will be remembered. He is, no doubt, one of the great American lyricists. Even in poems marred by excess he can jolt the reader unexpectedly. In desperate times he sought to revitalize American democracy. What progress we make in part may well be the result of the images he projected.

Wallace Stevens in the 30s: Gaudy Bosh and the Gesture's Whim

by Donald Sheehan

> Shall I grapple with my destroyers
> In the muscular poses of the museums?
> But my destroyers avoid the museums.[1]
> Wallace Stevens, 1935

"The basic shift from an individualist to a corporate society, which is reflected in every present-day activity and in almost every present-day state of mind, has resulted in a fairly complete discrediting of recent literary tradition. . . . There is talk of a new orientation, of 'adjustment,' and so forth. Seminars argue on how to embrace the masses in poetry and on how to accommodate the machine. Poetry circles in writers' congresses discuss the difficulties of embodying social significance in the

---

[1]Wallace Stevens, *The Collected Poems of Wallace Stevens* (New York, 1954), p. 153; the volume hereafter abbreviated as *CP*. Other abbreviations and editions of Stevens' works used here are as follows: *NA, The Necessary Angel* (New York, 1951); *OP, Opus Posthumous* (New York, 1957). Arabic numbers following these abbreviations refer to pages of the volumes on which quoted matter occurs.

personal lyric. Radical changes in society and accepted philosophy urge similar radical changes in literature, so much so that we tend to forget to protect ourselves from assuming that literature begins with us."

So, in 1938, Dorothy Van Ghent bravely attempted to save Wallace Stevens from the condemnations of the decade's ideologies, refashioning Stevens by concluding that he was, as a poet, "interested in observing the material fact, simply because that fact was interesting and beautiful in its own right. This is the human and the naive point of view. It is the point of view of a socialist economy." (New Masses, Jan. 11, 1938) The rhetoric of America's intellectual 30s has long since disappeared: if it survived the shocks of Stalin's first, ghastly purges of Russian artists, the brutal murder of Trotsky, and the Second World War, then the numbing pieties of the Cold War and McCarthyism surely shattered it. Its shrill voice now strikes us as nearly wholly irrelevant to the decade's central concerns; consequently, it is difficult to conceive the real and potent impact this rhetoric had on the artists of the 30s. Only with effort can we see the realities this rhetoric reflected: the vast economic collapse, here and abroad; the protracted violence of the strikes; the widespread, hopeless poverty; the desperate politics of patch-work "new deals"; the long, sickening slide to a cataclysmic war—an age, Wallace Stevens would say in 1948, of vitality "in the sense of being tense, of being instinct with the fatal or with what might be fatal" (NA, 26) On the one hand, with what finally came to be irresponsibility, America's intellectual Left met this fatal age with a passionate commitment to the dream of reconstructing the future through destroying the past. On the other hand, Wallace Stevens—shakily at first, then confidently—met it by affirming his power to create in the very face of wholesale destructions (Marxian and otherwise). In an age that drove its poets to Messianic vocations or Trappist vows, Wallace Stevens almost alone maintained a coherent voice and a significant art.

To be properly understood, however, Stevens' 30s must be seen in the context of his 20s. In 1923, at the age of forty-four, Stevens published his first book of poems: Harmonium. With a few notable exceptions, the book was received with baffled ill-will or with equally baffled praise: both camps agreed that Stevens was an "esthete" and a "dandy" who wrote "pure poetry"—it was simply a question of whether or not you liked your poetry pure. Those few who glimpsed in *Harmonium* the supreme imaginative energy of Stevens' comic diction, bizarre images and odd rhythms, failed to see the real achievement. Instead of a major poetry whose subject was the mind's surprising ways of perceiving (and, thus, of knowing both itself and the world), the 20s saw a slight poetry whose exuberance, gaiety and freedom were simply the newest and most fascinating ornaments of the avant-garde. And this failure, more than anything else, determined Stevens' fate in the 30s. With "defense" taking such forms as Llewelyn Powys' highly mannered gushings—"Listening to his poetry is like listening to the humming cadences of an inspired daddy longlegs akimbo in sunset light against the colored panes of a sanct window above a cathedral altar" *(Dial,* July, 1924) —Stevens was left to the mercies of the century's shifting biases.

When, in 1931, *Harmonium* was re-issued, the revision began. Stevens now became the "decadent," the chronicler of social decay, whose allegiance to "progress" and "social order" was deeply suspect. Then, in 1935, with the publication of *Ideas of Order,* Stevens' second book of poems, the most celebrated encounter of poet and critic occurred. Stanley Burnshaw, reviewing the book in the *New Masses* (Oct. 1, 1935), charged that Stevens' "harmonious cosmos" was "suddenly screeching with confusion," dismissing the book by saying, "It is the kind of verse that people concerned with the murderous world collapse can hardly swallow today except in tiny doses." Burnshaw characterized *Ideas of Order* as "the record of a man who, having lost his footing, now scrambles to stand up and keep his balance" and its poet as one of the "acutely conscious members of a class menaced by clashes between capital and labor" —*i.e.,* the decadent bourgeoise. Now, if we disentangle Burnshaw's literary perceptions from his Marxist rhetoric, we see that *Ideas of Order* does indeed disclose a poet "in the throes of struggle for philosophic adjustment." But the "philosophy" Stevens seeks to adjust in *Ideas of Order* is the poetics of *Harmonium,* and the "struggle" is conducted wholly in the context of his individual search for those poetic forms he cannot, for the moment, find:

> My old boat goes round on a crutch
> And doesn't get under way.
> It's the time of the year
> And the time of the day. (CP, 120)

Ideas of Order is a stark, bitter poetry, filled with a deep loss evident even in the poems' titles: "Farewell to Florida," "Sad Strains of a

Gay Waltz," "Waving Adieu, Adieu, Adieu," "A Fading of the Sun," "Gray Stones and Gray Pigeons," "Winter Bells," and revealed with a profound, literate despair:

> There is order in neither sea nor sun.
> Their shapes have lost their glistening.
> There are these sudden mobs of men,
> These sudden clouds of faces and arms,
> An immense suppression, freed,

These voices crying without knowing for what. . . . (CP, 122) Burnshaw's perception of *Ideas of Order* was fairly accurate; however, his analysis of the cause of its despair, and his Marxist panaceas for it, represent some of the purest distillations of 30s rhetoric. That Stevens was, by 1935, well into a series of extremely subtle shifts in poetic manner was (and is) undeniable; equally, that these shifts in style could in any way be directly linked to the decade's various crack-ups and cures was to simplify to absurdity Stevens' complex poetry. To us, Burnshaw's review represents a criticism falsified by an irrelevant rhetoric of the time; to Stevens, it came to represent the deeper failure of his age: an extreme poverty of the imagination.

Stevens' response to Burnshaw was complicated, extensive and, in the end, a failure. Three months earlier, in July, 1935, Stevens had published in the *Southern Review* a poem that was to form the first part of the longest he would ever write. "The Old Woman and the Statue" (OP, 43) was written, Stevens said, to satisfy his need for "a confronting of the world as it had been imagined in art and as it was then in fact," because "I wanted to apply my own sensibility to something perfectly matter-of-fact." (OP, 219) Now, this need and desire are surely not Marxian-haunted ones; rather, they are any poet's need to disclose himself through the desire to reveal reality. Stevens' 30s, while not unrelated to the decade's crisis rhetoric, were wholly his own years: "If I dropped into a gallery I found I had no interest in what I saw. The air was charged with anxieties and tensions." (OP, 219) Using the old woman to symbolize "those who suffered during the depression," and the statue to symbolize art (OP, 219), Stevens stated his central terms. Just as the imagination's older esthetic forms (a marble equestrian statue in a park) are no longer sufficient to explain reality, so the decade's sufferers—"the bitter mind/ In a flapping cloak"—are unable to shape their reality:

> She was that tortured one,
> So destitute that nothing but herself
> Remained and nothing of herself except
> A fear too naked for her shadow's shape. *(OP, 44)*

On Nov. 2, 1936, there appeared an anthology of contemporary poetry containing Stevens' reply to Stanley Burnshaw: "Mr. Burnshaw and the Statue." Three days later, the poem appeared in book form, now as the second part of the completed long poem, *Owl's Clover*, Stevens' third book. This part of *Owl's Clover* opens with an indictment of Marxism couched in nostalgic, even petulant, rhythms:

> The thing is dead . . . Everything is dead
> Except the future. Always everything
> Is dead except what ought to be.
> All things destroy themselves or are destroyed. *(OP, 46)*

The statue (art) seems "a thing/ Of dank imagination," irrelevant and ugly; but, equally, Burnshaw's politics are unreal in that they deny the "trash can at the end of the world"—*i.e.,* the fact of death. For in death both statue and Marxist politics become

> Parts of an immense detritus of a world
> That is completely waste, that moves from waste
> To waste, out of the hopeless waste of the past
> Into a hopeful waste to come. *(OP, 49)*

The premise of Stevens' 30s wasteland is that those orderings of reality, either political or esthetic, which fail to account for the eternal chaos of change, death and human irrationality are corrupt, unreal and dangerous orderings. (By 1947, Stevens came to identify such imaginative failures as man's essential evil; see "Esthétique du Mal," *CP*, 313). Stevens' way out of the wasteland touches directly one of his constantly reiterated truths: "It is only enough/ To live incessantly in change," for only thus are we faithful to reality.

The third and fourth parts of *Owl's Clover*, "The Greenest Continent" and "A Duck for Dinner" turn on the strangest—and murkiest—set of metaphors Stevens would ever employ. To oppose an ideology of collectivism based on man as a rational being, Stevens posits in part three an ideology based on a collective imagination of irrationality. Symbolically contrasting Africa's rule of blood and irrationality with Europe's sterile and shattered artificiality, Stevens evolves a "sub-man" who lurks beneath the consciousness of us all: "Fatal Ananke is the common god," "Fatal Ananke is the final god":

> He is that obdurate ruler who ordains
> For races, not for men, powerful beyond
> A grace to nature, a changeless element. (OP, 59)

For the only time in his long career, Stevens is here deeply and irrevocably in trouble. "Ananke" is a purely rhetorical assertion and is, thus, as unacceptable as any Marxist assertion. Part four, "A Duck for Dinner," begins by opposing Ananke to ideology through investigating the imaginative roots of the American democratic ideal, and concluding that Marx's "scholar's outline" for the world is "gaudy bosh"—less relevant even than a no longer applicable American past. Stevens' idea of man (Ananke) is the *sub*-historical order of the collective imagination and so precedes any political order; and its esthetics are not that of "the newest Soviet reclame" ("Concerto for Airplane and Pianoforte"), but of the "metropolitan of the mind" of the human race. Yet, Stevens asks,

> In an age of concentric mobs would any sphere
> Escape all deformation, much less this,
> This source and patriarch of other spheres,
> This base of every future . . . ? (OP, 63)

Stevens' ponderous metaphors crack, refusing to mesh within an assertive rhetoric that grows shriller; and Owl's Clover closes with a "Sombre Figuration" (part five) in which Ananke is metamorphosed into a "portent" that finally erupts in the closing lines in a plea for irrationality, a cry for an escape from muddled thought:

> A passion to fling the cloak,
> Adorned for a multitude, in a gesture spent
> In the gesture's whim, a passion merely to be
> For the gaudium of being. . . . (OP, 71)

Owl's Clover failed to fulfill satisfactorily Stevens' stated intent: "to emphasize the opposition between things as they are and things imagined; in short, to isolate poetry"—or fulfilled it too well by attenuating poetry. The oppositions within and isolations of poetry were never happy subjects for Stevens; he continually wrote best of poetry's unities and extensions. In 1936, Stevens published a second version of the poem, cut by nearly two hundred lines; and in 1954, he rejected the poem from Collected Poems on the grounds that it was too rhetorical (see *OP*, xxiii). In attempting to atomize the decade's imaginative failure and to explode its rational rhetoric, Stevens simply invented an irrational rhetoric whose metaphors failed to cohere. Increasingly, Stevens was to find the structure of long poems elusive and difficult; but he was never again to mistake the elaborations of a rhetoric for a metaphoric order. Though *Owl's Clover* is infinitely richer in its details—and so, in the end, infinitely more confused—than my comments indicate, Stevens learned from it lessons of structure and language he was not to forget.

In 1937, Stevens published the poem (in the shorter version) for the third and final time. Now, however, it was subordinated to "The Man with the Blue Guitar," and the book (his fourth) was titled indicatively *The Man with the Blue Guitar and Other Poems.* "Blue Guitar" (*CP*, 165) transforms the "gesture's whim"—irrational, escapist—of *Owl's Clover* into poetic and imaginative energy of major proportions. "Blue Guitar," with its thirty-three short sections of tetrameter lines, represents a clear and complete recovery from the turgid blank verse of *Owl's Clover.* "Blue Guitar" is political in the sense *Owl's Clover* is, in that it concerns itself with the *idea* of man, attempting "to play man number one" upon the imagination's blue guitar: but such playing is only tentative, fully aware of the real power of poetry:

> I sing a hero's head, large eye
> And bearded bronze, but not a man,
>
> Although I patch him as I can
> And reach through him almost to man. (*CP*, 165)

Loosely, almost daringly structured, the poem embraces lyricism and meditation, harsh despair and bright, sure comedy, sometimes atomizing, sometimes fusing its various modes. What holds the variety together is the poem's buoyancy and energy; and from all this poetic force, Stevens says,

> From this I shall evolve a man.
> This is his essence: the old fantoche
>
> Hanging his shawl upon the wind,
> Like something on the stage, puffed out,
>
> His strutting studied through centuries. (*CP*, 181)

Eschewing the nostalgic, rhetorical patois of *Owl's Clover,* "Blue Guitar" creates a language at once its own and its age's, capturing in the image of man as puppet-clown in a dreary world an image both comic and serious. Confronting his decade's most dismal aspects, Stevens evolves a poetry with which to embrace "Oxida," the modern Olympia become a "banal suburb," and so to affirm poetry itself; "It must be this rhapsody or none,/ The rhapsody of things as they are." The poetic imagination returns, cleansed of its rhetoric, to find its proper subject: "Poetry is the subject of the poem,/ From this the poem issues and/ To this returns." And between issue and return, Stevens tentatively suggests, the poem partakes and gives of earth's "True appearances" in "the universal intercourse" of man's mind and the world. Attempting no final integration, "Blue Guitar" fulfills precisely and perfectly Stevens' intent to show "the incessant conjunctions between things as they are and things imagined." The poem's relaxed, almost casual freedom fully affirms the poet's—and imaginative man's—right to exist as he must in a world sick with crises and collapse. By so choosing to be himself, Stevens conquers his destroyers who would engage him in the suicidal logic of their rhetoric. And by creating a poetry beyond the "museums" of his own rhetoric, Stevens discovers himself and makes possible the imagination's survival.

That Stevens survived the 30s is a matter of record—three further volumes of poetry and a collection of essays attest to his continued vitality. That his critics survived nearly as well is not so certain. Stanley Burnshaw attempted in the *Sewanee Review* (Summer, 1961) to explain his earlier position in his midcentury footnotes in article form, recalling the private agonies of doubt that secretly beset the confident Marxist critic of the 30s:

> Not only were the wars within the compound [of the American intellectual Left] frequent and fierce. Even more important: any number of these writers were troubled or torn, each for his private reasons; but the tendency was to keep one's reservations under control, for what mattered was the task at hand—ending the material miseries of the many, extinguishing the dangers of Fascism.

Such footnotes can finally only increase the distance between ourselves and the 30s, and post-mortem explanations by the principals have the curious (if predictable) effect of muddling matters further: "It requires no expertness in Freud to perceive that the present reviewer's concern with Stevens' confusion was at least in part a projection of his own." Confusions tend to be perpetuated, and genuine understanding of Stevens has been slow to take shape—so slow that one assents fully to John Enck's remark in *Wallace Stevens: Images and Judgments* (1964) concerning critics who "make enough mistakes so that Stevens' belief about their getting it straight one day at the Sorbonne sounds like the rankest optimism."

Nevertheless, at the 30s' close, Hi Simons could say in the *Harvard Advocate* that the decade's "destroyers" had in the end helped Stevens' reputation in that his poetry had been treated *seriously* for the first time. The encounter of poet and critic that has come to epitomize Stevens' relationship to the 30s had the net effect of reinforcing the poet's personal reticence at the same time that it deepened his supreme confidence in his art. For Stevens' "destroyers," the Second World War was to be a time of silence, and the postwar an agony of recantation. For Stevens, the war was to dispel the disruptive doubts and obsessive nostalgias of the 30s, and he was to submit its blank violence and the postwar's stunned numbness to a scrutiny savage in its lucidity.

Southern Poetry
During the 30s

by Guy Owen

Let me begin my remarks on Southern Poetry in the 30s by being honest, perhaps ruthless: Southern poetry has never amounted to much. To anyone interested in Southern culture our verse (I speak as a Southerner) offers special problems; perhaps it requires an apology. In the 20s H. L. Mencken labeled us *The Sahara of the Bozart* — but he was a Yankee, and not to be trusted. In 1932, however, one of our own, Allen Tate, wrote as follows: "The historian of Southern poetry must constantly pause to inquire into the causes of our thin and not very comprehensive performance. . . ." Moreover, Donald Davidson commented on the same problem: "The arts of the South in times past took another direction than poetry. They were the eighteenth-century arts of dress, conversation, manners; or, I might add, of handicraft, oratory, the anecdote — all respectable enough and sufficiently recorded to the credit of the South."

The point is that we began late in Dixie, and we tended to lag behind the East and Midwest. The South has never produced a major poet to stand alongside, say Whitman, Frost, or Robinson. (Let me add parenthetically, that in the 1960s we have few poets who can compete with our greatest novelists or short story writers.) Our verse has been, in general, as negligible as Southern music, sculpture, and painting — a fact galling to sectional pride. For this reason, our schoolmarms have tended to over-praise Poe as a poet, as well as such minor talents as Sidney Lanier—contributing to the debasement of our poetic tastes.

It used to be thought that the formation of the South Carolina Poetry Society and the birth of the Charleston Group were the most important events in the history of Southern poetry following World War I. Today, however, we tend to be underwhelmed by the romantic effusions of DuBose Heyward, Cotton Noe and Archibald Rutledge. One has only to read them to see how they led Southern poetry up a blind alley, where the emotions squeezed the intellect out of poetry. (Now, perhaps, the intellect has squeezed the emotions out.)

Anyone who takes the trouble to read Addison Hibbard's *The Lyric South* (1928) is immediately struck by the time lag I have mentioned. Hibbard's Introduction makes no reference to the French Symbolists or the English Aesthetes, nor even the Imagists. With the exception of the Fugitives, Southern poets in the early 20s apparently were unaware of the Chicago Renaissance, to say nothing of those rebellious ladies of the East, Elinor Wylie and Edna St. Vincent Millay, who were burning their candles at both ends. At a time when Cummings, Stevens, Masters, Frost, and Sandburg were charting new roads, Southern versifiers plodded their usual well-worn paths, a generation behind the times. (In another context, Davidson has stated: "The South . . . happily remained some forty or fifty years behind the times.") Free verse was tried here and there by Beatrice Ravenal, Henry Bellamann, and others; but, in general, Dixie poets felt more at ease working with traditional forms and subjects, employing a poetic language that had been effete since Whitman. If they had not read Mallarmé or Baudelaire, it was abundantly clear that they had read the Romantics, especially Keats, Wordsworth, and Tennyson. Others wrote pale imitations of Emily Dickinson and Poe. Sad to say, as late as 1930, Southern poets were still haunted by the ghosts of Timrod and Lanier.

Hindsight always has 20-20 vision. Now we can see clearly that the Nashville Fugitives provided the impetus and the critical background for a genuine Southern Revival. The publication of *The Fugitive* from 1922 to 1925, as well as the Fugitives' anthology (1928), is now seen as an event of major importance. For almost all of our young Southern poets are close kin to the Fugitives: John Crowe Ransom, Allen Tate, Donald Davidson and Robert Penn Warren, to name only the most important. Certainly most of them, in one way or another, have absorbed the critical ideas of Tate, Ransom and Cleanth Brooks. Randall Jarrell, for example, studied under Ransom, and James Dickey under Donald Davidson—and they are our most important post-war poets.

The Fugitives deliberately set up a "counter-current" to the Charleston Group and "the high-caste Brahmins of the Old South." They deliberately turned away from local color and old legends, odes to Robert E. Lee and pretty pictures of nature, as well as vague worn-out poetic diction and soporific rhythms. In fact, they were belligerent when Harriet Monroe, the editor of *Poetry,* suggested that they mine the Southern region and produce what they felt would be a provincial art. As Davidson wrote, "The picturesque charm of the Carolina Low Country was one thing, but the pugnaciousness of the western South, still 'half-horse, half alligator' and ready to fight all comers, was another thing."

What did the Fugitives strive for in their poetry then? They taught us how to combine the old and the new, using old forms and rhythms with fresh, more realistic subjects, adding a richly textured language and irony. They were bitter enemies of romantic clap-trap, sentimentality, vagueness, abstraction. As Louis Untermeyer has written, "An outstanding excellence of the Nashville Group was its free use of discord — juxtaposing the traditionally-poetic and the common colloquialism, and the establishment of a sharp-edged diction. In thought as well as technique, it emphasized intelligence; it insisted on adult poetry as against the plethora of petty, thoughtless, and immature verse written by adults." With the Fugitives, Southern poetry came of age.

In his special Southern issue of *Poetry* (May 1932), Allen Tate served notice on the effete and romantic verse collected in Hibbard's *The Lyric South.* For although he included a typical pastoral poem by Lizette Woodworth Reese and an inevitable anti-scientific sonnet by William Alexander Percy, he featured poets not recognized by Hibbard: John Peale Bishop, Saville Clark and John Gould Fletcher. More striking were the three "fractured" sonnets of Merrill Moore, a satiric blank verse poem by Donald Davidson, and two strong selections from Warren's brilliant Kentucky mountain series, as well as Tate's own "The Anabasis," in his erudite latinate style. It was not a distinguished issue, yet the thrust in the direction of a more modern approach to poetry is evident.

Furthermore, the point is driven home by the three brief essays by Tate, Warren and Davidson. Warren lets it be known that he will have nothing to do with DuBose Heyward or Hervey Allen, who "have used local color and legends of the South, but their concern seems primarily to be with the romantic possibilities as such." Davidson is more truculent; glancing at *The Lyric South*, he notes, "It almost amounts to this: that a poet cannot be Southern without behaving like a fool; and if he tries not to be a fool, he will not be recognizably Southern."

In the 30s Southern poetry matured, though the decade began with two notable setbacks. Ransom, the most talented of the poets, quit writing verse. In addition, too much of the energies of the Nashville poets was diverted into writing about and campaigning for the agrarian movement, which was led by Ransom and Davidson.

This commitment to rescuing Southern society and stemming the tides of Northern industrialism represents a dramatic change in the Nashville poets. In their Fugitive days (over by 1925 when they stopped publishing *The Fugitive*), they had taken little interest in the society around them. As the name they took for themselves implies, they sought to escape into the world of the aesthete. As *The Fugitive's Reunion* (1959) indicates, their meetings at Nashville were given over to matters of poetic technique, to reading and criticizing their poems and selecting the work for the next issue of their little magazine—not to economics, politics or theology. If anything, they tended to disassociate themselves from the South and its art as much as possible.

However, even before the publication of their Fugitive anthology, a number of the Nashville poets were growing concerned about the loss of ante-bellum values. They were galvanized into action in response to Northern attacks on the South during the notorious Scopes trial. Davidson, for example, was outraged when he discovered that Yankee journalists could be hostile towards Tennessee's tall men, excoriating their fundamentalism. To answer the charges against the South's provincialism and backwardness, he proposed the symposium which resulted in *I'll Take My Stand* (1930).

At this point it seems pertinent to note that not all the Fugitives joined in defense of subsistence farming as the way to achieve the good life. Only four men belonged to both the Fugitive and Agrarian movements: Ransom, Davidson, Tate and Warren, although they were the most important and wielded a good deal of influence.

To *I'll Take My Stand* Ransom contributed "Reconstructed But Unregenerate," an essay in which he defends Southern conservatism as being founded on "European principles" and attacks — among other things — the idea of progress, science and technology, a dehumanizing industrial society, and a liberal humanitarianism. From England Robert Penn Warren sent a paper on the Negro problem which stated a conservative position he has since reversed. In Davidson's truculent "Mirror for Artists," he viewed with alarm industrialism's threat to the artist, contending that only a stable, religious and agrarian culture can produce an art worthy of the name. Finally, Allen Tate in "Remarks on the Southern Religion" undertook to re-state a number of propositions from Ransom's *God Without Thunder,* more particularly man's need for myth and dogma. Tate argued that the Southerner must use politics "to re-establish a private, self-contained, and essentially spiritual life." (See John L. Stewart's *The Burden of Time* for a discussion of the fallacies of these four essays.)

Horace Gregory in *A History of American Poetry 1900-1940* called the Southerners' agrarianism and other group activities an example of "conspicuous waste." This is hardly fair, for if the Agrarians failed to stem the tide of technology and industrialism—and atheism—in the New South, the myths which they created of the Old South nourished much of their best poetry; and, one might add, *I'll Take My Stand* is more widely discussed today than ever before.

But to turn away from agrarianism, what, more specifically, was happening to Southern poetry in the 30s? One need comment, I think, only on six poets.

First, John Crowe Ransom, the able leader of the Nashville group, stopped writing poetry. Today it is easy to see a falling off in his third collection, *Two Gentlemen in Bonds* (1927), a dryness and chilling intellectuality—especially in the title poem, a rather dull sonnet sequence. Perhaps Ransom came to realize the repetitiousness of his carefully wrought ironic little dramas, feeling that he had done what he could in that particular mode. In any case, by the end of the 20s he was deeply involved in agrarianism, theology, and the aesthetics of New Criticism. More and more of his time was given to writing brilliant critical essays, and after he moved to Kenyon College in 1937, to editing the influential *Kenyon Review.* There was little time for poetry; still, Ransom, always seeking a classical perfection in his verse, continued to revise the poems he had written in the Fugitive years. *Selected Poems,* published in 1936, contains no new work, but it is the greatest single volume by a Southern poet during this decade. (In the 60s Ransom continued revising poems that had already become classics, almost always improving them—though often at the cost of sacrificing their Ransomic flavor.)

Of all the Fugitives, Donald Davidson had the most inflexible, stubbornly conservative mind. During the 30s much of his energy was turned away from poetry to writing belligerent essays defending the agrarian South, misguided onslaughts against Northern industrialism, Southern liberals, progressive education, etc., later published in *The Attack on Leviathan* (1938). Long after Ransom had abandoned agrarianism for the hopeless cause that it was, Davidson stuck by his guns. Indeed, he has allowed himself to write in defense of segregation in the South, a fact that has brought charges of fascism against him and militated against his best poems finding an audience today. For example, the modern reader is put off by such lines as the following from *The Tall Men* (1927):

> Black man, when you and I were young together,
> We knew each other's hearts. Though I am no longer
> A child, and you perhaps unfortunately
> Are no longer a child, we still understand
> Better than others. There is a wall
> Between us, anciently erected. Once
> It might have been crossed, men say. But now I cannot
> Forget that I was master, and you can hardly
> Forget that you were slave. . . .
> Let us not bruise our foreheads on the wall.

Davidson is clearly the most "South-conscious" of Southern poets. His poetry stems from a strong nostalgia for the past, the days of his Tennessee pioneer ancestors and the heroic figures of the Civil War. Unquestionably he has a genuine feeling for his "tall men" and the wilderness, and in such poems as "Fire on Belmont Street" his fury against the evils of the modern city lends dramatic power to his blank verse lines. One who takes the trouble to read *Lee in the Mountains and Other Poems* (1938), Davidson's most memorable book before *Poems* (1966), will discover how far the poet has come from the derivative and romantic verse of *The Outland Piper*. It is unfortunate that Davidson's reactionary views are alienating his audience in the 60s, for his sinewy blank verse narratives are among the best written in our time, and such poems as the meditative "Lee in the Mountains" and "Hermitage" are notable achievements.

Allen Tate was the most productive of the Fugitive-Agrarians during the decade, no doubt, too, publishing the most significant new poetry. His *Selected Poems* (1937) contained the best work from *Mr. Pope and Other Poems* (1928), *Poems: 1928-1931* (1932) and *The Mediterranean and Other Poems* (1936). Tate, like Ransom, has always taken pains to revise his early verse, and his later collections show the care he took to perfect his work, revealing a kind of disciplined violence. It is not difficult to see the signs of growth in his poetry—in spite of the energy that went into his novel *The Fathers* (1938) and *Reactionary Essays on Poetry and Ideas* (1936).

Tate from the early Fugitive days was the most experimental of the group, precipitating, at times, sharp disagreements among his fellow poets. In fact, he seemed to enjoy playing the role of *enfant terrible*, shocking his elders with his rather decadent early poems—as well as his violently yoked images, arcane allusions, his latinate style and general obscurity. It was Tate who introduced T. S. Eliot to the Fugitives, later quarreling with Ransom publicly because he attacked *The Waste Land* in a review. Tate had been led to Baudelaire through the writings of Ezra Pound, and if the French Symbolists had a perceptible impact on the striking imagery of the Fugitives, this foreign influence came through him.

In the 30s it became clear that Tate was to be the most cosmopolitan of the group, the least southern. For a while he lived in New York and was a close friend of Hart Crane. As his poetry matured, he became less obscure and more controlled—though he is still the most difficult of the group. Turning away from his first poetic wild oats, he became obsessed with the problem of belief, of faith in a modern world dominated by science and technology. His search led him finally to Catholicism; along the way he wrote some of the finest poems on religious mysticism of the time, for example "The Seasons of the Soul," which has been compared to Eliot's *Ash Wednesday* and *Four Quartets.*

Tate completed the most important poem to come out of the South during the decade in 1936, a work which owes a good deal to Eliot. This is his famous "Ode to the Confederate Dead," published in an earlier version in 1928. Set in a confederate cemetery, its theme is solipsism, the locked-in self-love that paralyzes modern man in an unheroic age of unbelief.

As John L. Stewart has noted in *The Burden of Time: the Fugitives and Agrarians,* Robert Penn Warren served a long apprenticeship as a poet. The 30s were not his most fruitful period, but at least when the decade was over, he had found a style that was neither Ransom's nor Tate's. During the period Warren produced little poetry because he turned to writing fiction and edited the texts that put New Criticism in American classrooms: *An Approach to Litera-*

ture (1936) and *Understanding Poetry* (1938). In the 20s Warren had begun writing verse in the "grand and romantic" vein, apeing, like so many young Southerners, Swinburne and the English Decadents, no doubt tainted by Cabell's eroticism. He also went in for a heavy diet of Pound and Eliot—here Tate was his guide. During his stay in California, however, Warren began to appreciate his native Kentucky as fit material for poetry; he also became steeped in Shakespeare and Dante, according to him the two major influences on his verse. In the early 30s he was writing imitations of Marvell, employing metaphysical modes in such poems as "Bearded Oaks" and "Love's Parables." In 1935 Warren's first collection of poems was published in an edition limited to 165 copies. *Thirty-six Poems* is an undistinguished volume in which the poet tries the voice of numerous masters, yet it includes a few poems in which Warren is his own man: for example, the Kentucky Mountain Farm series. In the 40s his lines would become more open, and he would make greater use of native materials.

John Gould Fletcher was not included in *The Lyric South* because he had spent so much time in England, where he was an important contributor to the Imagist movement. However, he did contribute to *The Fugitives,* as well as *I'll Take My Stand,* on occasions attended their meetings and was championed by the Nashville poets. In 1933 he returned to America, his famous "colored" symphonies behind him. Settled in his family home in Little Rock, Arkansas, he began making greater use of a Southern background in his verse, especially in such poems as "Down the Mississippi" and "The Old South." Although *XXIV Elegies* was published in 1935, he had spent twenty years writing the book, one poem for each hour of the day— some of them inevitably tedious enough. The poetry which he was writing in the 30s employs the "grand manner," but the rhetoric is more subdued than in his *Irradiations.* Fletcher won the Pulitzer Prize for his *Selected Poems* in 1939.

Finally, John Peale Bishop continued his desperate search for his own voice, finding it in only a handful of poems. As Robert W. Stallman wrote, "Bishop's poetry is the collective catch-all of the chief fashions which his age made current. His derivations and echoes . . . constitute a catalogue of contemporary poets: Pound, Eliot, Yeats, Tate, MacLeish, Cummings, W. C. Williams, Wallace Stevens, Paul Valery; even perhaps Edith Sitwell and Hart Crane." Pound and Eliot were the main influences in *Now With His Love* (1933), Yeats and Tate predominate in *Minute Particulars* (1935), Yeats becoming the major influence. Of course, Bishop freely admitted his imitation of other poets, and no doubt it is easy to dismiss much of his work as mere skillfully-turned echoes. Yet a dozen or so of his poems are still very much alive, a number of his best from the 30s: "Speaking of Poetry," "Young Men Dead" and "Colloquy With a King-Crab."

Briefly, how did Southern poetry differ from that of the rest of the country? For one thing, we did not produce a Lola Ridge or Kenneth Fearing or much of anything that would fit into the proletarian anthology *We Gather Strength* (1933). Freud had little impact; the Orient none. At a time when Muriel Rukeyser was writing the work collected in *Theory of Flight* (1935), poems that according to Stephen Benet had "fed on the quick jerk of the news-reel . . . the take-off of the plane from the ground," Davidson was fleeing the smoke and traffic of the urban world into the past of his Tennessee hunters, and Andrew Lytle in *I'll Take My Stand* was suggesting that the Southern yeoman "throw out the radio and take down the fiddle from the wall." One has only to juxtapose Sandburg's *The People, Yes* to the work of Tate or Ransom to see how dramatically Southern poetry differed from that of the East or Midwest. For although the Fugitives were damned as "modernists," it is now easy to see how conservative they generally were in their approach to poetic forms and diction.

To conclude, Southern poetry during the "political decade" repeated the national pattern. The 30s were not as interesting or fruitful as the 20s. New talents were not being discovered; Randall Jarrell was the only poet to begin to publish significant work. During the decade some of our best poets—notably Warren, Davidson, and Tate—matured, but the ferment of the old Fugitive days and the heady excitement of the Agrarian controversy were missing. Still by 1940 Southern poetry was firmly in the mainstream—which it decidedly was not in 1920. And in spite of Davidson's fears, it had joined the mainstream of American poetry without totally losing its identity.

The New Criticism: One Child of the 30s That Grew up

by Gene W. Ruoff

The New Criticism would seem to have been a part of the literary and academic scene long enough—thirty years by most accounts, even more by others—to have reached a comfortable, secure maturity. It has remained, however, a surprisingly controversial approach to the study of literature. The New Critic appeared at the time of his greatest notoriety, the late 40s and early 50s, to be almost a product of the quaint mythology of that period—Captain America to his followers, the omnipresent Subversive Pinko to his foes. This phenomenon is particularly strange because college literature departments are not, typically, centers of seething factionalism; British and American literature specialists, medievalists and modernists, even bibliographers and poets, manage to coexist in urbane tranquility. To be sure, the new critical controversy has by this time abated considerably: a new essay by Cleanth Brooks, the *bête-noire* of early opponents of the movement, no longer calls forth automatically the wrath of Douglas Bush, the dean and guardian of traditional literary scholarship. The peace, though, is deceptive. It is based more on mutual tolerance than mutual understanding.

To the student who has remained relatively ignorant of the dialectics of critical quarrels, and this blessedly includes most students, the entire subject of the new criticism must seem a tangle. Even the

169

simplest treatments of the movement are littered with names— T. S. Eliot, R. P. Blackmur, Yvor Winters, I. A. Richards, Kenneth Burke, John Crowe Ransom, Allen Tate, W. K. Wimsatt, Cleanth Brooks, William Empson, and Robert Penn Warren at the very least. Ransom, who named the school in *The New Criticism* (Norfolk, Conn., 1941), centered his discussion on Richards, Eliot, and Winters, all of whom figure only tangentially in contemporary discussion of the field. In one influential and generally helpful guide, *A Glossary of the New Criticism* (Chicago, 1948), William Elton states that "strictly speaking, there was no 'New Criticism,' as its enemies supposed, but several new criticisms mingled with several old ones." This is a just, balanced observation, but it is hardly likely to reduce confusion.

Elton does, however, use a phrase that provides an admirable entry into the subject: "The Revolution of the Text." At the center of the New Criticism is the belief that the proper task of the critic is to study the text, the piece of literature itself. As a consequence of this belief, the New Criticism rejects the study of literature in terms of something else: the life or psychology of the author, the spirit and beliefs of the age or nation in which he lived, or the artists, contemporaries or forerunners, who presumably influenced his work. New Criticism lumps together those who study literature in any or all of these ways as historical critics. New Criticism embodies the principles stated above almost as a platonic ideal, and it seems to me most appropriate to call a particular commentator a New Critic to the extent that his work demonstrates his allegiance to this ideal. Several attempts have been made to approach the problem from the other direction, to study the alleged New Critics empirically to determine their shared aesthetic principles. Most notable of these studies are *The New Apologists for Poetry* (1956) by Murray Krieger and *The New Romantics* (1962) by Richard Foster. The failure of such analysis, perhaps, lies in its assumption that New Criticism was a movement in aesthetics, an attempt to derive an organic theory of poetry. It was, and is, at its most influential, nothing of the kind. George Watson, in his brilliant little book, *The Literary Critics* (1962), stresses the non-theoretical aspect of the movement: "The real merits of the school are not to be studied in its attempts to theorize. It is rootedly pragmatic and particular, a way of teaching rather than a formal doctrine, and based upon an urgent impatience with academicism rather than upon any coherent principle."

Such "urgent impatience" may seem strange today, for books of incisive criticism are being written which use firm historical groundwork. One must look more closely at historical criticism as it existed in the 1930s to see the New Critic's reason for rejecting so strongly the accepted methods of literary inquiry. Consider, for instance, a typical article from the prestigeous *PMLA* (December, 1936), "The Symbolism of the Wind and the Leaves in Shelley's 'Ode to the West Wind' " by I. J. Kapstein. It is not a well known essay, but as an example it proves instructive. The closing paragraph summarizes the study, and I quote it in full:

> There were at least five distinctive elements, then, in the composition of the "Ode to the West Wind": (1) the stimulus of the natural objects, the Wind and the Leaves, as he [Shelley] observed them earlier in his life and more immediately in the Cascine Wood; (2) the philosophic-literary association of the Wind and the Leaves as he encountered them in Homer, "Ecclesiastes," Spenser, Dante, Lucretius, and Holbach; (3) "Prometheus Unbound," which expressed his extensive conscious beliefs of what the Wind and the Leaves already signified for him in the depths of his unconscious mind; (4) the death and rebirth of his ideas as exemplified by the "Revolt of Islam" and "Prometheus Unbound" respectively; and (5) the birth of his son, a living symbol of his own regeneration, and so associated with the ideas of rebirth and regeneration symbolized by the Wind and the Leaves in "Ode to the West Wind."

Kapstein discusses the symbols in terms of the poet's present life, past experiences, conscious mind, unconscious mind, reading in past literature, and use of them in other works. The essential critical act, the New Critic might say, would be analysis of the two images as they assume symbolic value and operate in the context of the poem. Kapstein nods slightly in this direction early in the essay, when he gives a one-paragraph paraphrase of the poem, in which he sets forth the accepted standard interpretation. The New Critic would ask several questions about the method of his study: Is this mass of information necessary to an understanding of Shelley's poem? Does it set straight any complications in it? Does not, in fact, the scholarly paraphernalia the writer is employing stand directly in the path of approach to the poem as a work of art, keeping him from considering it as such?

The almost religious fervency with which New Criticism announced its beliefs is best understood as a reaction against the shallow pedantry it found in studies like Kapstein's. New Critical terms often have an inquisitorial ring: they condemn the heresy of historical relativism (the belief that aesthetic values change according to time and place), the didactic heresy (the belief that poetry provides "lessons" for the reader), the intentional fallacy (the study of a work in terms of its author's presumed or even explicitly stated intention). The rhetoric of New Criticism was not balanced or polite; it was a rhetoric of militant rebellion against a complacent, firmly entrenched academic establishment.

The student may find it difficult to understand why such a movement in criticism should have begun in the 30s, a time, we are given to understand, of unparalleled artistic and intellectual involvement in the politics of social change. A purely aesthetic critical school deriving from this period must seem an anomaly. But "history," one might recall, was not only the domain of the scholar; it was the rallying cry of Marxism and, for that matter, all political thought left of center. Brooks and Warren, the New Critics who have proved most influential, were considerably right of center in their political beliefs. They had earlier been leaders, along with Tate and Ransom, of the Southern Agrarian movement (for a lucid account of the fortunes of this group as "Fugitive" poets, conservative agrarian reformists, and New Critics, see Alexander Karanikas, *Tillers of a Myth*). The New Critics' rejection of historical relativism in academic scholarship is equally, if not explicitly, a rejection of Marxist criticism, which judges past and current literature according to its awareness of and involvement in the class struggle. Pure aestheticism itself could, in the 30s, be a political act: a refusal to surrender literature to extra-literary, sociological evaluation.

Despite their anti-historicism, the New Critics suffered little abuse at the hands of the left. Perhaps the critics of the *New Masses* had written them off during their agrarian days as incorrigibly decadent conservatives. It is more likely, though, that the new criticism escaped such scrutiny through a quirk of timing. New Criticism's first journal, the *Southern Review*, made its appearance in mid-1935. Within a year leftist attention was focusing on the civil war in Spain and the internecine struggle of the Moscow treason trials. By the time Ransom founded the *Kenyon Review* in 1939, the second of

New Criticism's major voices, the entire left was being splintered by the shock of the denunciation of Leon Trotsky, the intellectual giant among the architects of the Russian Revolution, and the non-agression pact between Stalin and Hitler, the former arch-enemy of the united left. It is little wonder, then, that New Criticism encountered little socialist opposition. If it was noticed at all, it must have seemed a small thing indeed.

And it would still be, in terms of its impact, a small thing if it had remained simply another critical movement. It expanded its arena, however, to include the classroom as well as the critical quarterly. An educational bias was apparent even in the forerunners of the new critics. Ransom has said that the movement "very nearly began" with I. A. Richards, the British critic and linguistic psychologist. Richards' most important work, *Practical Criticism* (1929), grew from a classroom experiment, in which he studied the ability of a group of Cambridge University students to read poetry. He found that they consistently misunderstood lines, let their personal beliefs interfere with their appreciation, and considered simple, overtly sentimental and didactic works superior to the poems of Shakespeare and Donne. For all their "superior" educational background, they had never learned to read a poem. The cry for critical training in literature was taken up in the United States by R. S. Crane, who published in the *English Journal* (October, 1935), his essay "History vs. Criticism," questioning the assumption, "cherished by many professors of literature, that most if not all of their researches in literary history can be defended, not as history merely, but also as a 'fundamental prerequisite' of criticism." If we want criticism, he goes on to say, "we must have principles, we must have sensibility, we must have such learning as is indispensable to the proper reading and interpretation of texts, but that is all: of literary history as such, in its distinctively genetic and narrative aspects, there is seldom need to take account."

The followers of Crane, the neo-Aristotelians of the University of Chicago, were hampered in their influence by the appearances of their criticism being limited, almost solely, to *Modern Philology,* a thoroughly academic journal. The criticism of the southerners, on the other hand, appeared principally in the *Southern Review* and *Kenyon Review,* both broadly literary and cultural. The fiction of Warren, Katherine Anne Porter, Mary McCarthy, Eudora Welty, and Caroline Gordon, coupled with the poetry of Tate, Ransom, and such outsiders as Wallace Stevens, certainly enhanced the reputation of the criticism in the journals. Such a frame could have "made" a far less appealing picture. More important, though, these two journals were reaching the undergraduates, graduate students, and young instructors who were receptive to new techniques for studying and teaching literature, and from whose lists the apostles came.

Probably the most crucial force behind the power of New Criticism, as it was advanced by Brooks and Warren, was the publication in 1938 of their textbook, *Understanding Poetry*. Karanikas suggests that this was "the first time in literary history that a textbook has also been a potent force in criticism." The authors preface their anthology with the frank statement that "This book has been conceived on the assumption that if poetry is worth teaching at all it is worth teaching as poetry." They enforce their approach by doing away with the normal chronological subdivisions, using instead purely generic categories that place side by side verse ranging from folk ballads to contemporary works. They follow many of the individual works with extensive analyses that show graphically the way a critical approach to poetry works, and set a standard by which the teacher's effectiveness could be judged, both by his students and by himself. More than any other work of New Criticism, this book served to shift radically the concentration of teaching from the artist and his age to the text. Few books, and few critical movements, can claim equal results.

The Thirties — Drama

"The Fabulous Invalid" they called it, but the American theatre rarely had it so good. We face when we turn to the drama an embarrassment of riches. This section of this survey of the achievements of the 30s might be greatly expanded: Robert Sherwood demands attention along with Maxwell Anderson, Lillian Hellman rates consideration as well as Clifford Odets, the experiments of Thornton Wilder and John Steinbeck possibly attracted even more attention than William Saroyan's. More difficult lines had to be drawn here than in dealing with fiction or poetry. In the long run, as always when merits yield to no objective determination, the tastes and interests of the contributors determined what would be included. All would only agree that these essays on the American drama of the 30s are but a partial introduction to a rich and rewarding subject.

Apparently few critics of the decade realized how much was being achieved, for many looked back longingly on the glorious 20s. Actually little has survived from the 20s. We have now enough perspective to see the significant difference between the decades. The American theatre was dominated during the 20s by its first—still unchallenged—genius, Eugene O'Neill. None of the playwrights who were active principally during the 30s can stand beside him; yet never in this country's history have so many of a slightly lesser mag-

175

nitude been active at the same time. The critics of the 30s spent too much of their time in a vain search for another O'Neill to appreciate the rich and varied fare that was being offered them.

Two of O'Neill's most memorable achievements, of course, belong to the 30s: *Mourning Becomes Electra* (1931), the awesome triology that reshapes Greek myth against a somber New England background and is perhaps the apex of O'Neill's achievement as a tragedian; *Ah, Wilderness* (1933), the mellow autumnal drama that is perhaps his supreme comic achievement. Both of these works, however, are culminations of the playwright's great productive period during the 20s. Even before he won the richly deserved Nobel Prize in 1936, O'Neill, wracked by illness and personal tragedy, had lapsed into a long silence. His contributions to the 30s have little direct relevance to the troubled times, dealing rather with periods already vanished when they were produced—the "Great Barbecue" of the post-Civil War years, the era of Edwardian complacency early in the twentieth century.

The "Best Plays" collections scrupulously edited by Burns Mantle greatly ease the critic's task by spreading before him a year-by-year account of the travails and triumphs of the American theatre. While the rigid format of the volumes by demanding ten "best" plays every year obliged Mantle to celebrate much that was transient and trivial, it can be said that—as far as this editor can determine—Mantle never overlooked or even seriously underrated a play that has any enduring claim to attention.

As Mantle's selections indicate, the shining light of the American theatre during the 30s was not the fading star of O'Neill but the ascending one of Maxwell Anderson. Eight of Anderson's plays appear in the "Best Plays" volumes of the decade—often leading the selections: *Elizabeth the Great, Both Your Houses, Mary of Scotland, Valley Forge, Winterset, The Star Wagon, High Tor, Key Largo*. It is remarkable that one writer—laboring besides to introduce an alien poetic idiom to the American stage—could produce all these works and four more besides; yet no single one seems as impressive today as it did when it was premiered. Fittingly, therefore, Jordan Miller opens this section on drama with a consideration of the reasons why the reputation of this playwright who promised to supplant Eugene O'Neill during the 30s has since diminished.

Robert E. Sherwood's star shone almost as brightly during the 30s as Anderson's. Five of his plays are included in the Mantle volumes: *Reunion in Vienna, The Petrified Forest, Idiot's Delight,*

Abe Lincoln in Illinois, There Shall Be No Night. Through these five one might trace the whole aesthetic and political history of the slowly dying hopes of the 30s. In the long run, however, Sherwood's reputation has proved a little more fleeting than Anderson's, his concerns a little more timely than timeless. The plays that were once such delights are unmistakably period pieces today. Since Sherwood —who turned after the 30s to political writing—has also recently received part of his due in the first volume of John Mason Brown's biography and Baird Shuman's critical study, his demands for attention seem less urgent than the unduly neglected Anderson's.

Both playwrights were members of the group of five that in the fall of 1938 launched the Playwright's Producing Company, which for a time displaced the Theatre Guild as the leading play producing unit in this country. This co-operative endeavor of successful dramatists (Elmer Rice, Sidney Howard, S. N. Behrman were the others) to stage their own works is but one of several important evidences that the 30s were the decade of corporate action in the theatre. An earlier venture was the Group Theatre, a rebellious offshoot of the Theatre Guild, which from 1931 to 1941 attempted to bring to the United States, a theatre that, as Gerald Rabkin explains in *Drama as Commitment,* was viewed by its founders as "a necessarily collective art," in which "esthetic questions of style and production could not be separated from the problems of a *group*."

Ultimately, as Rabkin explains, the Group Theatre failed because "its ideals were inimical to the hard facts of commerce" and it "could not survive the demands of impending global conflict." This country was not yet ready to support a commercial theatre of such single-minded intensity, although the spirit that motivated the Group was to blossom into many of the Off-Broadway theatres of the 50s. The Group Theatre did, however, produce during its short life a major playwright, Clifford Odets; and it is for works like his *Waiting for Lefty, Awake and Sing,* and *Golden Boy* that the Group is still remembered. Odets was not a great playwright, but he was unquestionably the most skillful theatrical propagandist of an age of propagandists. Robert Griffin, with three decades' perspective, looks back on these perhaps most representative works of the Thirties' Theatre of Outrage to take the measure of the man and the times that produced them.

Perhaps Lillian Hellman will outlast Odets; *The Children's Hour* and *The Little Foxes* produce more impact today than any of his works. They will never become period pieces as long as malice and greed make the world wobble round. Yet their very enduring qualities makes the need to re-examine Odets most urgent. One feels that Miss Hellman's best work can look out for itself and justifies also overlooking her less successful efforts.

By far the most interesting of the theatrical organizations to flourish briefly during the 30s was the Federal Theatre Project, an offshoot of the much criticized Works Progress Administration. This ill-starred venture was the federal government's first timorous and tentative effort as a patron of the theater. Although other ventures of the 30s clamor for attention—the resolutely doctrinaire Theatre Union, Orson Welles' much-publicized Mercury Theatre, the International Ladies' Garment Workers Union's flirtation with theatre that produced the delightful *Pins and Needles*—none of their stories seems as permanently significant as that of the first government effort to subsidize American theatre, motivated regrettably more by a need to create jobs than an aspiration to create art; and no one is better qualified to tell this story than Gerald Rabkin.

Not all playwrights of the period were associated with groups; individual experimentation also flourished. The season of 1937-38 brought, in fact, two of the most important and enduring American dramatic experiments: John Steinbeck's dramatization of a novel that he had written to be performed as a play, *Of Mice and Men,* and Thornton Wilder's bare-stage evocation of America's small town heritage, *Our Town.* Either play deserves attention as a remarkable tribute to the creative vitality of the legitimate theatre during the 30s, but James Justus chooses to examine rather the work of another celebrated and even less categorizable writer who threatened (that seems the only appropriate verb) even more than Steinbeck or Wilder to remodel the theatre of the late 30s in the image of his own fancies—William Saroyan. Saroyan, you say? Oh, yes, whatever became of Saroyan? The answer seems to be that he simply dribbled away his talents in too many experiments that showed no development in his vision. In his day, however, to borrow a famous phrase from Edna St. Vincent Millay, he gave "a lovely light." While most of his plays seem consigned to the obscurity his detractors predicted, *The Time of Your Life* still flourishes as perhaps the supreme theatrical example of the rowdy, irresponsible optimism that is a persisting American characteristic despite the warnings of the worrybirds.

Others plead, too, for attention. After a fallow period, Philip Barry, one of the most successful playwrights of the 20s, blossomed again late in the 30s with *The Philadelphia Story* and *Here Come the Clowns*. Sidney Kingsley moved to the forefront of the American drama with *Men in White* (1933) and *Dead End* (1935), but failed to retain his place. S. N. Behrman—one of the Playwrights' Company—was the darling of sophisticated theatre-goers. His *Biography, End of Summer*, and *No Time for Comedy* remind us that Americans were able to keep laughing through the depths of the depression, as do also James Thurber and Elliot Nugent's *The Male Animal*, Clifford Goldsmith's *What a Life!*, and Claire Boothe's masterfully catty *The Women* and *Kiss the Boys Goodbye*.

But Americans laughed longest, loudest, and hardest at the collaborative products of the remarkable team of George S. Kaufman and Moss Hart, beginning with *Once in a Lifetime* (1930) and ending just a decade later with *George Washington Slept Here* (1940). It is ironic that the least successful production of this unique team was *The Fabulous Invalid* (1938), in which they wept nostalgically over the very institution that they played the largest role in saving from invalidism.

Both men were successful separately. Kaufman was already a famous theatrical figure in the 20s, and even during the 30s he produced hits in collaboration with Morris Ryskind (*Of Thee I Sing*), Edna Ferber (*Stage Door*) and Katharine Dayton (*First Lady*). Hart, it is true, got his big break when Kaufman agreed to help revise a spoof on Hollywood, *Once in a Lifetime;* but the junior partner also wrote librettos for musicals like *As Thousands Cheer* and (later) *Lady in the Dark*. Together, however, they reached the pinnacles of their careers. Although *Merrily We Roll Along* (1934), a satire of successful sell-outs in which the action none too merrily rolls backwards, was only tepidly received during the depths of the depression, the delightful burlesque of the New Deal, *I'd Rather Be Right* (1937), with George M. Cohan as a dancing image of F. D. R., the stunning patriotic spectacle of *The American Way* (1939), and the caustically riotous farce about the authors' own thinly disguised celebrity friends, *The Man Who Came to Dinner* (also 1939), were both at the time and in retrospect the highlights of the American comic theatre during an unfunny era.

But the greatest work of the team and—I am more and more inclined to suspect as the years pass— the most revealing literary clue to the dominant American temper of its era was *You Can't Take It With You* (1936). Nothing makes more incredible reading today than the contemporary reviews that dismissed the play as "deliberately banal," "all absurdity," "a parlor game," "not a good play but the best entertainment in town." One critic actually had the lack of perspicacity to link the play with another called *Brother Rat* and to observe that "perhaps neither will be remembered twenty years" after their premieres. (The notices of a Broadway revival in 1965 were more glowing than the original ones.)

Perhaps because, as Brooks Atkinson put it in the *Times,* "the sheer irresponsibility" of Grandpa Vanderhof's attitude "irritated theatergoers with responsible minds," none of those who attended the first performance seemed to realize that this work provided the best answer to the questions that have most puzzled later students of the 30s, "Why didn't this country succumb to the fanatical rightist or leftist political movements of the 30s? How did Americans keep their equanimity?" This answer is that Grandpa Vanderhof and his fantastic brood of candy, fireworks, and trouble-makers not only entertained but embodied that segment of the American public that actually guided our perplexing course through the 30s. Delightful as it is, *You Can't Take It With You* is a play with a moral—the same moral as Voltaire's *Candide*—"Cultivate your garden . . . Work without theorizing." Americans still wanted to cheer the tax-dodger who could afford to loaf, to believe in the triumph of fun over the Puritan ethos, of the dedicated craftsman over the manipulator of intangibles like stocks and bonds, of individuality over the system. *You Can't Take It With You* embodied these beliefs in the kind of hilarious, breathless, apparently aimless romp that Americans loved to see upon the stage.

Americans also especially loved musical comedies with scores by Irving Berlin, George Gershwin, Jerome Kern, Cole Porter. The musical theatre of the 30s has, of course, been overshadowed by the much more spectacular one that Richard Rodgers and Oscar Hammerstein II launched in the 40s with *Oklahoma!* Little from the 30s lingers in the repertoire of our summer musical theatres. *Of Thee I Sing*—a product of the formidable talents of George Kaufman, Morris Ryskind, and the Gershwin brothers—blazed a trail by becoming the first musical to win a Pulitzer Prize, but its timely political satire has not as much amused later generations as it did the original patrons.

The only musical work of the 30s that has not just retained but bolstered its position in recent years is that climactic work which Richard Rodgers and his earlier collaborator, Lorenz Hart, devised from John O'Hara's cynical tales of the comeuppance of a heel—*Pal Joey.* Theatre-goers of the 30s preferred the pleasant escapism of *Anything Goes* and *I Married an Angel;* but disillusioned post-war audiences have found the uncharacteristic toughness of *Pal Joey's* "black comedy" characters and lyrics more to their taste.

Not all the drama of the 30s unfolded on the traditional stage. Other media began to bid for the limelight. Originally it had been hoped to include in this collection an essay on the development of American films during the 30s, but it soon became apparent that the achievements of the first decade of the talkies would require a comparable book of their own to do them justice. We close our survey of the literature of the 30s, therefore, with an appreciation of a genre that was distinctly a product of the decade—radio drama.

When the 30s began, radio was still generally regarded as a toy; by the end of the decade, it had established itself as the most influential mode of communication and had even—through Orson Welles' notorious "Invasion from Mars" broadcast of H. G. Wells' *War of the Worlds*—frightened the country nearly to death. Patrick Hazard, one of the most enthusiastic historians and critics of "newer media," takes us on a nostalgic whirlwind tour of an art that was just beginning to realize its potential when it was destroyed by the advent of television. His essay reminds us that even in the bleak 30s one artistic form flourished as at no other time; certainly in two decades television has not created anything like the effective drama that radio did during the single decade of its dominance.

Those 30s—they were theatrical years! Melodrama ending in catastrophe.

WARREN FRENCH

Maxwell Anderson: Gifted Technician

by Jordan Y. Miller

When Joseph Wood Krutch was offering his Columbia University lectures in modern drama in the late 40s, Eugene O'Neill and Maxwell Anderson were both living contributors to the New York stage. At a time when newcomers Williams and Miller were just beginning to enliven the postwar theatre, the names of Anderson and O'Neill were still the big ones, survivors of the between-wars decades that had seen American drama rise to world prominence. In a statement which may or may not have been original with him, Prof. Krutch drew a sharp and still pertinent distinction between these men when he said, "The difference between O'Neill and Anderson is that O'Neill is a genius while Anderson is merely ingenious."

In any evaluation of Maxwell Anderson in the 30s it is difficult to avoid comparison with Eugene O'Neill for the obvious reason that no other writers of American drama remotely approached their levels of productivity and skill. Yet, in almost every way, they were as dissimilar in what they accomplished as they were in temperament and personality. In the brooding, introverted, socially isolated mystic of O'Neill lay a kind of giant dramatic force, somber, overwhelming, preoccupied with the tragic nature of the universe, and expressed in a ponderous but wholly compelling style. In Anderson, on the other hand, active, outspoken, willing to argue publicly the merits of his work with any dissenting critic, resided a facile theatrical skill, directly concerned with contemporary social forces and the appealing melodramatics of history, and set down in poetry, prose, or even song, in a style effectively attuned to the popular eye and ear. In one, the single mindedness of a dramatic artist driven almost in obsession to ponder the ways of God to men—the drive of genius, if you will. In the other, the unrestricted variety in theme and form of an accomplished theatrical technician displaying the immediate attractions of polished ingenuity.

Now that it is becoming academically respectable to include American drama in the study of western literature, it is a significant fact that while O'Neill has become acceptable as a subject for advanced scholarly study, Maxwell Anderson remains in the background, of secondary importance, concern with his work lagging behind the rapidly developing critical interest in Williams, Miller, or even Edward Albee. Standard anthologies do, of course, include representative pieces such as *Winterset* or *Elizabeth the Queen,* but Anderson's reputation has fostered no posthumous revival of interest in his work such as centered around O'Neill more than a decade after his death.

This situation is, one might venture, somewhat strange, considering the generally high quality of the works of Maxwell Anderson and the impact which many of them made during his lifetime. Anderson, like O'Neill, was a man of unquestioned artistic integrity. He was devoted to his profession with much the same energy which prompted O'Neill to affirm early in his own career that he wanted to be "an artist or nothing." Anderson, too, knew what he wanted to do, and the goals he wished to achieve. When he left his journalistic trade to become a serious theatre professional, he became, long before his participation in the Playwright's Company, a conscientious dramatic artist as well. He could write fine melodrama, strongly effective social protest, or even delightful and imaginative nonsense, in addition to being able to devise a viable form of historic pageantry. Tragedy was not beyond him, and he was able to turn out comedy or slapstick farce with equanimity. He was far more unbound than the mystic O'Neill, and more varied, say, than Williams, lost in the midst of a decadent female South.

And yet, where are the *Strange Interludes* or *Electras,* the *Glass Menageries* or the *Streetcars,* the *Salesmen* or the *Crucibles,* or even the *Virginia Woolfs* from the list of over thirty plays by Maxwell Anderson? Something there is that lacks. Anderson, as Krutch im-

plies, was a maker of distinctively stageworthy dramas of great originality, sacrificing the permanence of art to the timely, and temporary,
facility of ingeniousness.

The only possible place to begin a discussion of Maxwell Anderson is the rousing, cursing display of the hard drinking, fornicating
American fighting man of World War I that was exploded in 1924
before a shocked public in *What Price Glory?* Anderson's hand was
not, to be sure, the only one, for his fellow journalist and war veteran
Laurence Stallings helped to create this memorable piece. But it is
the play which first brought the name of Maxwell Anderson to the
popular mind while launching him permanently on his play-making
career.

What Price Glory?, we hardly need emphasize, broke the long
established romantic stage traditions of war and the soldier who fights
it that had dominated the American stage since 1798, when William
Dunlap created his impossible artificial portraits of Washington,
Bland, and the title figure in *André.* Here, instead, for all to witness,
were the filth, grime, blood, fear, hate, suffering and pain of combat,
but further, and more important, were also revealed the wild abandoned pursuits of sensual pleasures practiced by the man in the
front line who must kill or be killed, and who celebrates with a
primitively wild joy the fact that he has thus far remained alive. The
earthiness of the language and the basic human, if animalistic, drives
of the men involved catch the essence of the abominable work of war.
There is no doubt that the primitive feuding and blasphemous roars
of Capt. Flagg and Sgt. Quirt mirror reality, or that the preference of
the men under them for the body of the strumpet in the nearest
bistro to any idealized concept of defense of flag and country is
authentic.

The trouble with *What Price Glory?* is that, for all its destruction
of the traditional stage image of the soldier, it ultimately remains as
romantic as anything out of the past that it meant to avoid. These
men ride greasy motorcycles instead of white chargers, and they fight
a stalemated war in foul trenches instead of galloping forward in spine
tingling bugled charges, but they are men who, in the last analysis,
will always come through and who will, for all the coarseness of their
exterior, reveal the genuine heart of gold. As long as we have the
Capt. Flaggs to fight our wars and the Sgt. Quirts to limp after them
shouting "Wait for baby!", all will be right with our world. The play
in its time was "new," and it was unquestionably "different." In structure it is demonstrably well done. Still, the gaps are evident. Char-

acters, although memorable, lack the emotional depth so badly needed to display the havoc that warfare creates within a man's soul as he must order men to die or to perform as beasts day after day in a life monstrously insulting to their intelligence. Theatrical incident, while grimly lifelike, only succeeds in revealing the impossibility of literal interpretation of battle upon the stage. *What Price Glory?* remains significant as a stage milestone, but the more closely one scrutinizes, the more one discerns too much alarum and excursion, too much noisy romanticizing of men and deeds—that is, too much effect for its own sake. To say the play is "dated" is not quite right, for its subject remains as important as ever. It is certainly not naive, for the men who wrote it knew intimately of the life they described. The term? One might say it is simply too pat, perhaps somewhat shallow, no longer able to move emotionally. Remaining a good play, a significant and impressive play, it demonstrates too much of the playmaker and not enough of the dramatist, missing by a narrow but clear line the mark of greatness.

Although Anderson was seldom absent from the New York stage during the remainder of the 1920s, none of his next seven plays had any of the impact or permanence of *What Price Glory?* Except, perhaps for *Saturday's Children,* a not particularly effective piece of social protest, or *Gods of the Lightning,* an over-contrived melodrama based on the Sacco-Vanzetti case, nothing of that five-year span can be given serious critical consideration today. The picture changes abruptly, however, with the new decade. Anderson's next thirteen appearances, including a highly successful musical comedy, brought his greatest critical success and established him as a dramatist of considerable artistry. Although he never achieved the international reputation accorded O'Neill during the same period, he was, within his own country and to no little degree elsewhere, one of the very large literary figures of the 30s.

History provided Anderson with the greater part of his strength during this most productive period. The first two of his three "Stuart" plays, *Elizabeth the Queen* and *Mary of Scotland,* are the best known, but the intrigues of the Hapsburg court in *The Masque of Kings* and widely separated incidents in American history found in *Night Over Taos* and *Valley Forge* are in many ways no less significant. All of them, in addition to their recognition of the potent dramatic values to be found in the imaginative portrayal of how it all might have been, are singularly important because they represent a good portion of Anderson's ventures into verse, for which, in the long run, he may be most remembered.

There is, however, a paradox herein. Although there must be praise to Anderson for the dignity and the sense of decorum which he brought to the contemporary American theatre in his verse plays, there is also in each of these romances the continual awareness of the lack of artistic depth. Throughout one recognizes the validity of the fairly lofty themes, and approves the choice of action to accompany them. The subject matter befits the poetic line, for each story is laid in a locale of some distance in time, providing the appropriate aura for the "unrealistic" diction of poetry, and each is inhabited by characters of considerably high personal bearing. But difficulties remain. Elevated themes and stately language cannot completely hide the evidence of theatrical skill and facility, of adroitness and, ultimately, of ingenuity. The end result is that all of these plays are basically great theatre. None of them is great drama.

In the Stuart plays particularly there is a considerable feeling that something is not quite ringing true. The character development and the intense dramatic conflicts of the confrontation of the principals are many levels above any Anderson play from the 20s. There is a sure hand present in the evolution of the melodramatic situations, none of which ever get out of hand nor remove the audience from its strong empathetic relationship with human beings caught in impossible, often fatal, circumstances through no fault of their own save the level of their birth. History is treated with respect; the might-have-beens themselves are wholly plausible. The problem, then, becomes one of a kind of pretension. To read the dialogue as it stands gives one the feeling that too often Anderson is consciously creating "poetic tragedy" out of whole cloth through the simple expedient of placing excellent and rhythmic prose in a broken verse-like line, then asking that we follow a series of pseudo-Shakespearean romantic intrigues to match. It seems clear that the plays aspire to tragedy, and there can be no doubt but that the destructive inevitabilities are intrinsically tragic. They emerge, however, as romances; the protagonists, poetic diction and elevated stature notwithstanding, do not mount the required heights. The power is lacking, though the effort to place them there is strong and laudatory.

Night Over Taos benefits most from Anderson's poetic approach, but it shares with *Valley Forge* a kind of strained heightening, a reaching for effect that becomes more of an end in itself than a dramatically strengthening factor. The exotic setting of the revolt of the Spaniards in New Mexico and the tragically catastrophic end of a noble family combine to create an atmosphere eminently compatible with poetic speech. Further, the period of the republic's greatest hour of trial, dominated by the giant father figure of George Washington, is an equally fit subject for the dramatic poet. But the promises never materialize in either play. Characters become wooden; they seem, especially in *Taos,* to be too consciously aware of the language they are asked to speak. Given the atmosphere of Elizabethan England in the Tudor plays, and an assumption, inaccurate or naive that it may be, that people somehow "talked that way," the language does not intrude in the same jarring fashion. If Anderson in *Taos* is attempting to catch the rhythms of Spanish conversation through the artificialities of English verse, he fails. If he is merely creating the sense of aristocratic high estate, he becomes much too contrived. Fortunately, he turns to verse more sparingly in *Valley Forge,* relating his tale of scavenging rebels and their high principled leader in mainly conventional prose style. When the poetic line does arrive, however, it disturbs, rather than soothes, and must share with *Night Over Taos* the lack of success in reaching a satisfactory plateau above normal dramatic routines. The quality of verse in these plays seems far more artificial than in the Stuart plays; at times, which cannot be said for the others, it even strikes one as wholly inappropriate. The term is unpleasant, but what comes forward seems better termed a bastard art lacking in unified artistic direction, the product of ingenuousness rather than dramatic genius.

Anderson's strong attraction to the romance of history did enable him to create a pair of dramatically strong characters in his version of the dynastic problems of Franz Joseph and Prince Rudolph in *The Masque of Kings.* The mystery of what happened at Mayerling has wide popular appeal in its sentimentality, and sinister courtly intrigue provides as much a chance of dramatic success as the romances of Elizabeth, Essex, or Mary Stuart. Although there is the constant threat that it will fly off into the rarefied atmosphere of a Viennese operetta, *The Masque of Kings* remains firmly on the ground, mainly through the sympathetic central figures of emperor and prince. The poetic dialogue becomes more natural, too, than in *Valley Forge* or *Taos,* and with far less of the weakening pretensions that mar the Tudor plays.

It was in mid-decade, however, that Anderson wrote what is beyond question his masterpiece. The play most often associated with Anderson's name is *Winterset* (1935), one of the finest American plays of any decade. A fortunate combination of Jo Mielziner's superb setting, Burgess Meredith's greatest acting role, and Anderson's successful amalgam of his most effective poetic diction and best articulated tragic theme effected one of the decade's outstanding stage productions. The polish of facile ingenuity may still be evident, but *Winterset* is Anderson at his dramatic and theatrical best.

The story of the Sacco-Vanzetti case, so arbitrarily and hysterically handled in *Gods of the Lightning,* has become only a framework here. Into the basic plot structure are introduced characters of considerable depth, tense and well-managed melodramatics, and a highly effective statement of the theme of humanity's tragic nature. Man, be he young as Mio, must combat or be subdued by the forces of unfathomable evil; or, be he old as Esdras, must suffer and ceaselessly endure the same, unable to rationalize or explain it all away. Moreover, by a touch undeveloped in other plays, Anderson writes into *Winterset* a poetry of noble dignity, carrying a conviction almost totally lacking elsewhere. We are not even asked to assume that we are in a "poetic" world of Tudor England, revolutionary America, or nineteenth century Austria. Instead, *Winterset* places us in the hazy nightmare world of twentieth century gangsters and crumbling tenements, of monstrous impersonal bridges and monstrous personal deeds, where instant love may develop between two youngsters who hardly know its meaning, but who perfectly comprehend its death-bringing force. We are placed in a modern world, but a modern world of wild improbabilities, where murder victims seem resurrected and conscience-stricken mad judges hold court. Everything is arbitrary, everything is unreal, and for this reason, everything so easily fits into the style; the verse, however and whenever spoken, fits equally comfortably, without intrusion. We are in a real-unreal world of injustice, violence, and pointless death. We know this world, but shudder to recognize it. It is a world of the most completely unpoetic sort, yet what it does to men in its grips can inspire poetry. *Winterset* adds up to a thoroughly acceptable stage piece, movingly tragic, touchingly romantic, unquestionably poetic.

In *Winterset* Maxwell Anderson's sense of ingenious theatricality has become his most positive asset. It makes no pretense of aspiring to the awesome Greek-ness that O'Neill's *Electra* or *Desire Under the Elms* displayed. It avoids the mystic, bypasses elemental passions and reaches instead for touching sentiment. In the portrayal of the doomed lovers and in the design of the background against which they act, Anderson displays his best abilities. When he does attempt to draw modern parallels of classic themes, as in the play of the following year, *The Wingless Victory,* the flaws once again become apparent.

In this latter-day Medea, Anderson has created a formidable heroine in Oparre, but the rest of the play fails to rise beyond the level of an interesting parallel to a great classic tragedy. The comparisons with O'Neill's success in *Mourning Becomes Electra* are distinctly unfavorable, for O'Neill was able to transcend the artificialities of his close Aeschylean imitation to create a viable dramatic tragedy. Anderson does not rise to the occasion he has chosen, in spite of a memorable female protagonist of near tragic stature. She has been placed in the midst of a hopeless situation in which the petty stupidities and prejudices of narrow-minded provincialism viciously destroy with none of the awesomeness of gods amid the rumblings of Olympian storms. The cold, unyielding family and community, and the husband who ultimately joins them, Jason-fashion, do not carry the impact and tragic conviction of *Winterset's* marvelously grand little people. Nobody is "noble" in *Winterset,* yet the central figures rise to a nobility beyond their inferior status. *The Wingless Victory* ends with ingenious melodramatic effect, but nowhere is there adequate flesh to cover and give body to the mythical skeletal framework.

Of the remaining two important plays of the decade, *High Tor* and *Key Largo, High Tor* must be grouped with *Elizabeth, Mary,* and *Winterset* as Anderson's best remembered and critically most important plays. Among all thirteen, good, bad and indifferent, eliminating the special case of the musical adventures of Peter Stuyvestant in *Knickerbocker Holiday, High Tor* contains almost every one of Anderson's most skilled theatrical devices. The end result is a unique combination of whimsy, fantasy, slapstick, romantic comedy and melodrama that provides a little bit of everything for everybody, while very nearly getting tied into knots of disturbing confusion through the writer's delight in expressing his own cleverness. On the whole, however, one must judge *High Tor* an acceptable *tour de force,* because in the end it delights more than it disturbs, and its message of dismal human shortsightedness, corruption and brutality is plain enough. This is a simultaneous dream and nightmare world, where the gangsters of *Winterset* are bumbling fools, and the lovers fight between themselves over principles of natural beauty and ordinary decencies. Even though the audience must occasionally back and fill to close the gaps between dying philosopher Indians, highway patrolmen, bank robbers, and funny Dutchmen from a ghost ship three hundred years old, Anderson's imaginative inventiveness, combined with more of his familiar and once more appropriate verse style, has created a piece of almost pure theatre.

At the close of the 30s the dress rehearsal in Spain of the ultimate disaster that engulfed Europe brought Anderson once more into direct involvement with men at war. In one respect *Key Largo* becomes superior to *What Price Glory?* because it investigates certain of the causes and effects attendant upon the act of warfare and the responsibilities of men to themselves and to each other in considerably more depth and with fewer pyrotechnics. Yet even then it is another distinguished failure. Its heavy reliance on the blacks and whites of the struggle taking place between the conscience-driven King and the conscienceless gambling punk prevents a truly satisfactory development of character or exploration of dramatic situation. The facedown is too patently theatrical, and the final catastrophe far too plainly telegraphed. There is an acceptable point of morality in *Key Largo,* true; after all, honor does mean something, and a man must sometime come to grips with himself, even in the face of death, forced into determining what he is and what he is capable of, in spite of his shame.

It is unjust to end consideration of the plays of Maxwell Anderson just as the new decade of world war and international ideological combat provided him with material for some of his greatest popular successes. *The Eve of St. Mark* in 1942, mostly inundated in maudlin sentiment, contains Anderson's best character creation in the compassionate, brilliantly comic figure of Francis Marion. *Joan of Lorraine* (1946), followed by the third of the Tudor plays, *Anne of the Thousand Days* (1948), and the highly sensitive musical adaptation with Kurt Weill of Alan Paton's *Cry, the Beloved Country* in *Lost in the Stars* (1949), enhanced Anderson's reputation as a conscientious theatre artist. Even into the 50s, when *Barefoot in Athens* (1951) and *Bad Seed* (1954) brought critical acclaim on the one hand and box-office popularity on the other, the name of Maxwell Anderson retained its importance. But the final estimation of his position in American drama must still rest with the larger proportion of his work appearing in the 30s.

In the cold figures of Broadway commercialism, Anderson was only moderately successful, a lesser light in terms of cash receipts. Eliminating the more than 400 performances of *What Price Glory?*, no play by Maxwell Anderson before 1940 could muster over 200 performances except *Mary of Scotland* and the comedy-fantasy, *The*

Star Wagon. Others struggled to reach even a basic success level of 100 nights; many faded away with less than 50. The majority of the most serious plays—*Night Over Taos, Winterset, The Masque of Kings, High Tor, Key Largo*—must all be considered commercial failures.

In spite of all that has been said here, however, it is impossible to judge Anderson as a critical and artistic failure. Virtually every aspect with which we may find fault in any given play deserves strong praise for the attempt it makes to bring artistic integrity to the growing body of American dramatic literature. The collected works of Maxwell Anderson have a striking effect in their variety, and they impress one as the product of a sincere artist. They are not, however, the product of a gifted thinker, but of a gifted technician. The genius that could have turned subject, theme, or form into a drama of permanent, universally appealing literature is not there. The plays remain instead the end product of studied ingenuity.

On the Love Songs of
Clifford Odets

by Robert J. Griffin

I once thought the best way to approach Odets's significance as a spokesman for a decade would be to compare his most famous work, *Waiting for Lefty,* with a more recent landmark in stage history, *Waiting for Godot.* Both are fairly short but "big" plays, diverging conspicuously from the norms of theatrical traditions; both represent an unfulfilled waiting for a somebody, perhaps of no extensive importance in his own right, whose failure to appear is centrally important; both treat suffering, or at least serious frustration, and a kind of universal befuddlement. Of course it is their differences that furnish some justification for discussing each as a sign of its times. *Waiting for Lefty* erases the line separating actors and audience, while *Waiting for Godot* presents a cast of characters and a series of activities so singular or out of the ordinary—very well, so absurd— as to increase the usual sense of theatrical distance (though heaven knows this doesn't allow us to jubilate, "Very puzzling, but clearly of no particular pertinence to the world *we* live in"). If the one seduces its audiences' emotions, the other wittily assaults their intellects. Perhaps each play in its distinctive way is meant to arouse sympathy, perhaps ultimately self-sympathy, but in Odets's the one awaited is simply a man, "one of us," and we know at the last what has happened to him, while in Beckett's, who or what is Godot,

193

where is he? Probably the most essential difference is that at the end of *Lefty* there is no more waiting. Further similarities and differences—for instance, the differing concepts of the downtrodden, the exploited—might be worth exploring, if our primary interest is the temper of the times that these two plays represent. But for several reasons I am now persuaded that a detailed comparison cannot adequately serve the purpose of the present essay. For one, the plays may be too thoroughly dissimilar to permit point-by-point juxtaposing that is really meaningful in the way of critical analysis; the resemblance of the titles is thin stuff to build on. For another, we may be too close to *Godot* and its decade to judge its representativeness—and I freely confess that I am not yet able to figure out exactly what kind of forest Beckett's trees add up to. Above all, it seems to me that concentrating on *Lefty* alone is bound to give a distorted image of Odets's career in the 30s.

Still, *Lefty* has to be taken into consideration. It was the first play of his publicly produced (on January 5, 1935, at the Civic Repertory Theatre), and though only a one-act play originally slated for a one-time performance—it was subsequently given in a series of benefits at the Civic Repertory, became the talk of the town as part of a regular production on Broadway, and soon thereafter a must for every social-minded theatrical or reading group in America, not to mention some abroad—it signalled loudly and clearly the emergence of an important new playwright. It therefore has quite rightly the place of honor in the collection I take as my text: Odets's *Six Plays,* published late in 1939 and containing not only his major productions of the decade but also the best work he ever did. *Waiting for Lefty,* though formally more unconventional than any of the others, was in its youthful mixture of values a pretty accurate forecast of the longer plays to follow.

The basic format of *Lefty* is a union meeting. On the bare stage are a committee of workers and the head of the union of taxi-cab drivers, off to the side is a gunman in the pay of this confident, porcine bully of a leader (named Fatt!), and actors or "voices" representing members of the union are planted in the audience. Within this framework of a meeting Odets has sketched several pre-meeting flashbacks, views of the various backgrounds of this moment of decision: a hack, one of the committee members, and his wife arguing furiously over what to do about the snivelling poverty they have been reduced to; a "lab assistant episode" showing how another committee member was once a promising technician, forced from his good job by his conscientious objections to grossly unscrupulous practices; a young hack and his girl at the point of break-up because of her family's objections to a suitor who "ain't got nothing" to support a wife on; an "interne episode" showing another come-lately driver forced from his profession by the political skulduggery and anti-semitism of a hospital board. Finally, when the tide is already beginning to turn against the racketeering leader and his henchmen, word arrives that the absent Lefty has been found "behind the car barns with a bullet in his head." That does it. And if the play is produced with as much as half-hearted enthusiasm, even a presentday audience will find itself joining in the final cry of STRIKE that brings the play not so much to a close as to an explosion of aroused sentiment.

Lefty is a period piece, but it is not "dated" beyond capacity to affect. Though its overt, practical issues are (hacks, forgive me) no longer of desperate importance, and its globs of sentimentality are now much easier to perceive and disparage, it is still a stirring piece of theater. It was never really as revolutionary a piece as its anti-Left critics said. The actual strike it was based on had, after all, taken place the preceding year. The "Communism" of its social principles was no more specifically Marxist than, say, the mocking of middle-class hypocrisy in *Main Street* and the plea for humanity and the uniting of the oppressed in *The Grapes of Wrath*. The play was an incitement, but not to the violent overthrow of the government (the man in the White House seemed to be headed pretty much in the right direction). Nor was it very revolutionary in form. Episodic structure is as old as drama; bare stages and audience involvement were more or less commonplaces of the agit-prop theater of the early 30s. If there was anything "new" about *Lefty* as a work of agitational propaganda, it was the successful incorporation of realized human emotions in some of its close-ups. This was the different kind of involvement that Alfred Kazin has testified to in *Starting Out in the Thirties* (1965):

> Nothing could have been less like the declamatory heroics
> of German Communist sailors portrayed at the Theater
> Union, or the gloomy editorials in the "living newspapers"
> of the Federal Theater Project, where you had only to look
> at the social dummies parading the stage . . . to know that
> the choreographers of the Social Theater were putting
> their usual ciphers through their paces again. . . . (pp. 81-82)

Another eminent American critic, Van Wyck Brooks, has noted the perpetual need of youth—both young people and young nations —for "romance," a gallant cause or distinctive mode of life that demands more than mere lip-service to an easy allegiance. America began with the romance of national revolution, later came the romance of abolition, then the romance of gigantic money-making; when, after the romance of saving the world for democracy was suffocated in cynicism, the attempts to resurrect the money-making dream aborted, the depressed 30s very naturally, inevitably took up the romance of a search for social justice. Communism was its extreme ideological form and the new Russia its exotic objective correlative. Lest we forgot, the hellzapoppin freak shows of the McCarthy days reminded us that this romantic complex engaged the sympathies of many of our best artists and intellectuals. This does not mean that Odets and his fellows sold their souls for a mess of Marxist party-lining. The Group Theater company of which Odets was a part — partly a product — offered plays by a diverse lot of authors, Maxwell Anderson, Paul Green, Sidney Kingsley, J. H. Lawson, and Dawn Powell, as well as all of Odets's plays written during the decade. Odets himself was only fitfully, youthfully and romantically, very imperfectly Communistic with a capital C. He knew approximately as much about dialectical materialism as he knew about corporate finance. But labels are handy. If a man thinks that a strike may be warranted when sweet reason fails, if he likes the idealistic, brotherly ring of a word like "comrade," the easiest thing to do is file him under C; and the Waspish critics had no qualms about filing *Till the Day I Die,* the fervent anti-Nazi play that Odets wrote to fill out the bill of an evening of serious entertainment with *Waiting for Lefty:* "If you want to register an emotional protest against Nazi polity, Mr. Odets requires that you join the Communist brethren." Balderdash—unless we assume that the *New York Times* reviewer meant the emphasis to fall on *brethren;* for the play is primarily a *cri de coeur* against Hitlerian oppression in Germany, and secondarily a plea, not for Marxism per se, but for a united front to oppose the impending enslavement of all Europeans, tomorrow the world. The far-left press, at any rate, knew better; even *Lefty* was received with serious reservations, and *Awake and Sing,* Odets's first full-length play, was considered a "come-down," an "unimportant play," certainly nothing like good propaganda or Socialist Realism.

Actually the form of *Waiting for Lefty* is, as Odets himself noted in an interview recently published in *Harper's Magazine* (September

1966), "very rooted in American life": "what I had semi-consciously in mind was the form of a minstrel show . . . [with] an interlocutor, end men, people doing their specialties, everyone sitting on the stage, and some of the actors sitting in the audience." His strike play was revolutionary, then, chiefly in the sense that he had taken an old form, an indigenous convention, and put it to the service of class-conscious humanitarianism. *Awake and Sing* was likewise revolutionary not by virtue of some vaguely apprehended political theory occasionally shadowed forth in a topical slogan, but in the new life that it brought to the stage. What was very un-vaguely apprehended was a vital milieu, the pulse and guts of the lower-middle-class life that Odets knew, regretted, and loved. Again, Alfred Kazin is my witness to the effect of the play on the romantic youth of the thirties:

> In Odets's play there was a lyric uplifting of blunt Jewish speech, boiling over and explosive, that did more to arouse the audience than the political catchwords that brought the curtain down. Everybody on that stage was furious, kicking, alive—the words, always real but never flat, brilliantly authentic like no other theater speech on Broadway, aroused the audience to such delight that one could feel it bounding back and uniting itself with the mind of the writer. . . . Odets pulled us out of self-pity. Everything so long choked up in twenty thousand damp hallways and on all those rumpled summer sheets, everything still smelling of the cold shattered sand littered with banana peels under the boardwalk at Coney Island, everything that went back to the graveled roofs over the tenements, the fire escapes in the torrid nights, the food, the pickle stands in the shadow of the subway and the screams of protest—"I never in my life even had a birthday party. Every time I went and cried in the toilet when my birthday came"—was now out in the open, at last, and we laughed. . . .
> Sitting at the Belasco, watching my mother and father and uncles and aunts occupying the stage in *Awake and Sing* by as much right as if they were Hamlet and Lear, I understood at last. It was all one, as I had always known. Art and truth and hope could yet come together—if a real writer was their meeting place. . . . (*Starting Out in the Thirties*, pp. 80-82)

For some reason, no longer very clear, Chekhov's name began to crop up in discussions of Odets. Harold Clurman has pointed out in his Introduction to *Awake and Sing* (reprinted with two other introductions in the back of *Six Plays*) that the work of Sean O'Casey provides better analogies. Odets's work shares with O'Casey's a kind of improvisational quality, the sense of realistic spontaneity in the impulsive talk and action, "tenement tenderness," and the playwright's deliberate inclusion of the inconsequential because it may be this accident, that diversion or avoidance of issues which really counts in the lives portrayed. "Poverty, or at least life-long economic pressure among city persons who still manage to get along 'respectably,' " says Clurman, "produces a certain lack of order, a confusion of physical details with spiritual crisis which to the outside observer must appear just as laughable as it is saddening" (p. 422). This natural comedy present in *Awake and Sing* and Odets's three other full-length plays of the 30s saves them from that morass of sentimental melodrama which the two shorter plays do not always avoid. When Odets set himself the task of staging the realities of middle-class life in an American city, he managed to show selected segments of that life with a wise wholeness of vision. I mean, though he may have a humane social gospel to announce, his "message" does not mislead him into oversimplifying the experience he is dealing with: the issues he may treat simplistically, but not the facts. Bessie Berger, the mother of *Awake and Sing*, is on the one hand a frightful materialistic tyrant, and on the other an admirably gutsy, far from unfeeling pragmatist—not one or the other, but both; her daughter Hennie is at once a self-sufficient bitch and a sufferer who has earned the right to run off with a man she can really love; the play ends on a note of hope, but it is a hope hard won, hope that must be taken in the context of all the muddle and turmoil that precede it. And it results not from specific political doctrine but from love of life; which is to say, a sense of human potentiality to prevail whatever the obstacles, and a love for all people who are capable of loving.

Paradise Lost (first presented by the Group Theater at the Longacre, December 9, 1935—what a year!) deals with problems at a higher level of middle-class frustration. It is even more "poetic" than its predecessors because its characters are more clearly epitomes or symbols as well as interesting individuals. It attempts, as Clurman puts it, "to be true in the naturalist's sense, and visionary in the artistic sense" (*Six Plays*, p. 427). Once more, at the last, in the midst of chaos, comes affirmation; the end of the play is really a better beginning. *Golden Boy* (1937) is yet further along the road of visionary naturalism, very nearly downright allegory. In treating a career in the "fight game" of professional boxing, it seeks to symbolize a universal struggle for a secure place in the world. Joe Bonaparte's necessary suppression of his finer instincts or natural self, his reduction to the condition of a commodity, his futile effort to find solace in romantic love—all these elements and many more signify in a microsomic way. The note of hope? Joe's labor-organizer brother Frank fights not as a loner, a blood-letting entertainer, but as part of a forward-looking consolidation of fellow men; by joining in a group identity, refusing to accommodate to the demeaning exigencies of the status quo, he has become a free man. Odets's last play of the decade, *Rocket to the Moon* (1938), is not so easily deciphered. Here is no political pointing whatsoever and scarcely any hint of social conscience. But then this strain of thought and hope in the 30s had more or less run its course. *Rocket to the Moon* at least retains the vitality of characterization and that core of humanitarianism which gave life to Odets's more propagandistic plays—the love of man as a seriously flawed but corrigible being, able to snatch hope from the jaws of despair and to prevail by recognizing the possibility of positive action and the urgency for sharing.

It is possible—I believe it is quite certain—that Odets became an imaginative spokesman, a "poet," of the romance of the 30s because his personal sentiments and aspirations mirrored the decade's captivating ideals. His deep sense of frustration and the need to belong, to be a member of a Group, for instance, was a natural match for the problematical dreams of social justice achieved through united action. Thus his major plays of the period provide symbolic action in two distinct but complementary ways: they dramatize a social "protest that is also prophecy," and they enact, imitate the structure of, some crucial event or circumstance in the playwright's own life. *Waiting for Lefty* celebrated a public cause, and also (I'm quoting again from the posthumous article in *Harper's*) "matched my conversion from a fellow who stood on the side and watched and then finally, with a rush, agreed . . . that the only way out seemed to be a kind of socialism. . . ." He rewrote the third act of *Awake and Sing* to give Ralph Berger a more "affirmative voice in the end"; the affirmation reflected a growth in the hopes of social-idealists, and "the change had occurred in me, too—a growing sense of power and direction." *Golden Boy* represents, in addition to the universal struggle I have (borrowing from Clurman) tried to sketch, the author's personal struggle with the material temptations of Hollywood, temptations he could not single-handedly overcome. In 1961, two years before his death, Odets lamented that the post-30s years failed to provide him with "positive, ascending values to which a play can attach itself." His own proper decade was a different matter. The salient problems and dreams of that era awakened responsive chords in the personality of Clifford Odets, awakened a singer. The voice sometimes quivers mawkishly or strains for a high note of enthusiasm, but it is a living voice that we can still afford to listen to.

The Federal Theatre Project

by Gerald Rabkin

The history of American theatre from the Provincetown Players to the present has been simultaneously the history of Broadway and of alternatives to Broadway. At the moment, the fabulous invalid seems to be sinking even faster than usual, and Broadway seasons pass without one financially or esthetically successful "legitimate" play (fine word, legitimate!). Community and academic theatres from Washington and New Haven to Dallas and San Francisco consequently have accelerated their efforts to break Broadway's theatrical monopoly, with varying, if encouraging, degrees of success, attempting to provide alternatives not only to Broadway but to New York City as well, to create a viable, professional, decentralized American theatre, to destroy the image of the regional community theatre as an amateurish diversion or a minor league stepping-stone to the majors in New York. After all, the proponents of the new theatres argue, unlike England and France—which have always looked to London and Paris for cultural leadership—we are an enormous nation steeped in regional pride, jealous of our local prerogatives. Why, then, can we not have, like Germany or Italy or Yugoslavia, noncommercial subsidized theatre which arises out of the needs, aspirations, and talents born of regional diversity?

The answer is that for a brief four years we had such theatre. The Federal Theatre Project, which was founded in 1935 and which was killed by Act of Congress in 1939, was conceived and operated on a scale which in retrospect seems almost incredible—that is, when its accomplishments are recalled at all. By an act of collective amnesia we have almost expunged the memory of the project from our theatrical consciousness, perhaps because it invokes dread memories of depression: breadlines, bank failures, farmer's revolts, and hordes of unemployed. How many articulate contemporary theatregoers have any idea of the enormous scope of the project, surely one of the largest co-ordinated theatrical experiments in the history of the world? In New York City alone, for example, the Federal Theatre operated five major units—the Living Newspaper, the Popular Price Theatre, the Experimental Theatre, the Negro Theatre, and the Try-Out Theatre—as well as a host of smaller, subsidiary units—a one-act play unit, a German unit, an Anglo-Jewish theatre, a Classical Repertory unit, a Poetic Drama unit, a vaudeville unit, a children's theatre, a puppet theatre, a Continental Repertory unit.

But the accomplishments of the Federal Theatre were by no means limited to New York City, although the activities of the New York Regional Theatre naturally bulked largest. Across the entire United States, in theatres, stadiums, arenas, improvised tents, in thirty-five individual states, living theatre was brought back to the people; all in all, during the four seasons of its existence, the Federal Theatre produced over 1,200 individual productions in every section of the country, employing, at its peak, over 13,000 theatre personnel. The list of its productions covers no less than fifty pages in Hallie Flanagan's history of the project, *Arena*.

Nor were the Federal Theatre's activities exclusively productional. Among other services which the project offered were (1) the encouragement of local community drama and dramatic training; (2) the establishment of the National Service Bureau, which, among its many activities, read, wrote, and translated plays, sent synopses, scripts, and bibliographies to the field, and conducted theatre research; (3) the publishing of its own periodical, the *Federal Theatre Magazine;* (4) the creation of a Federal Theatre of the Air, which presented approximately two thousand programs a year, all released through regular commercial stations and networks; (5) the development of psycho-drama experimentation in various municipal hospitals; (6) the establishment of playwriting contests in CCC camps and in colleges. Conceived and operated in this way, the Federal

Theatre was much more than a play-producing organization; it had to meet, on all levels, the needs of the communities which it served and to which it offered a myriad of services.

How did such an ambitious enterprise arise? And why has its example been so disregarded? For the answers to these questions we must look to the unique social influences of the Depression. The Federal Theatre did not arise out of the government's sudden dedication to the vital social importance of theatre and drama. The pragmatic American character has been eternally distrustful of the non-utilitarian. To this day our law-makers are largely guided by the conviction that art must pay its way. No, the Federal Theatre arose from economic necessity, not esthetic or social theory. The noble experiment was based upon the fact of unemployment. In the spring of 1933, the most urgent problem that President Roosevelt had to face, once the banking crisis had eased, was the stark problem of relief. There were upwards of fifteen million unemployed and nearly six million persons on state and municipal charity rolls. The problem of unemployment was particularly difficult for the artist, for art—within the context of breadlines and soup kitchens—must have seemed the most dispensable of commodities. It is estimated that 40,000 show folk were destitute during the Depression, and their situation was made even more desperate by the fact that they could not turn to part-time employment in anticipation of the next theatrical job— "temporary" jobs just did not exist. Thus the theatre person, already the victim of technological unemployment created by the rise of the motion picture, not only found job opportunities increasingly scarce (in the summer of 1933 New York sustained only five productions), but was denied the traditional economic alternatives.

To meet the relief needs of the unemployed, Congress passed the first Relief Act on March 31, 1933, which, in addition to providing relief for unemployed adults, set up the Civilian Conservation Corps with the object of finding jobs for unemployed youth. Six weeks later Congress established the FERA (Federal Emergency Relief Administration) for the purpose of granting federal funds to states to assist in caring for the unemployed. On November 9, 1933, Congress established the CWA (Civil Works Administration) for the purpose of creating four million jobs for men and women desperately in need. In all of these agencies, the emphasis was upon immediate need, and theatre people were among the recipients of this emergency aid. The inadequacy of the initial, hasty, relief projects was soon recognized, however, and on April 8, 1935, Congress passed a bill authorizing a new approach—based upon the experiences of FERA and CWA—to the problem of unemployment. The WPA (Works Progress Administration) rejected the concept of the dole; it attempted to remove the stigma of relief by the implementation of three departures from earlier methods: (1) only employables were to be taken from the relief rolls of the states; (2) to these employables, work was to be offered *within their own skills and trades;* unemployables were to be returned to the care of the states. Thus the preservation of both the skill and the self-respect of the worker was viewed as the corollary of the alleviation of economic want. It was deemed important not merely that the worker received financial assistance, but that he work in the field for which he was trained. Since it had been learned upon investigation that thousands of unemployed artists were engaged in various relief activities for which they were basically unfit, it was decided to establish projects in order to provide proper work for the artists in their respective fields. Thus were created the major Federal Arts projects—in Art, Music, Writing, and Theatre.

But while the project had its origin in economic necessity, it was soon apparent that its director, Hallie Flanagan, and her subordinates (chosen, it may be noted, largely from the ranks of the noncommercial theatre) conceived of their task as more than the administration of relief. "The arts projects were being set up to deal with physical hunger," wrote Mrs. Flanagan, "but was there not another form of hunger with which we could rightly be concerned, the hunger of millions of Americans for music, plays, pictures and books? Were not these aspects of hunger a part of the same equation which it was our job to solve?" Thus, the directors of the Federal Theatre Project accepted the essential functional premise of the theatre's creation, but they were not satisfied with this premise. They wanted to create out of the fact of unemployment a theatre which would not only serve the entire nation in many ways, but which would be expressive of the attitudes and needs of the age. At the heart of the Federal Theatre lay an idea which co-ordinated its multifarious aspects, and which made it deserving of the title of a "Theatre": that art is an integral and necessary part of the social community. In a very real sense, then, the Federal Theatre reflected the social ferment which gave birth to the left-wing Theatre Union and molded the development of the Group Theatre and other socially committed theatre groups of the 30s. The essential requisite of art was conceived as the fulfillment of the social need which had brought it forth. Hallie Flanagan maintained that if the theatre were to be a vital social force, it could not afford to ignore the implications of social change. The theatre, in her view, had to grow up.

The dual aims of the Federal Theatre—the satisfaction of immediate economic need and the creation of a vital contemporary theatre—were to some extent contradictory. For one set of aims—relief, popular appeal, commercial revival—was necessarily impermanent, while the other set—the training of actors, the improvement of public taste, the stimulation of the writing of meaningful contemporary plays—was permanent. If the conflict between providing relief and producing vital drama was manifest at the beginning and throughout the experimental stages, that conflict intensified when wholesale dismissal for economy forced a decision between relief cases and continuation of work by those best qualified to perform it. If the purpose of the project were solely relief, it would be logical for the competent to be discharged first, since they were most likely to find work elsewhere. But what theatre could survive on the basis of the dismissal of its most talented performers? The amazing fact is that the Federal Theatre was able to maintain the acting level of its productions despite these very basic difficulties.

The dilemma was reflected administratively; while Mrs. Flanagan and her assistants were striving to concentrate upon the permanent aspects of the theatre they were attempting to create, it was impossible wholly to extricate the Federal Theatre from the nationwide WPA network. The WPA officials—usually businessmen pressed into civic duty—knew little of the exigencies of the theatrical profession and could not understand why the handling of the arts projects should differ in any particular from the handling of any other WPA project. Moreover, in the later stages of the project distrust of the Federal Theatre arose within the ranks of the WPA itself, a distrust which occasionally manifested itself in overt or covert censorship, and in the discontinuing of the *Federal Theatre Magazine,* which expressed the point of view of people on the project. With Harry Hopkins no longer in charge, the Federal Theatre found itself talking to increasingly unsympathetic ears. Thus the association of the Theatre Project with the WPA presented another series of obstacles to surmount. It is a tribute to the energy and indefatigability of Mrs. Flanagan and her co-workers that despite these difficulties the project was able to record a substantial achievement.

The Federal Theatre faced one other great liability: it was forbidden by law to advertise, and thus was denied the opportunity of both informing the public of its theatrical wares and of answering the attacks of its opponents. These attacks took two basic forms. On one hand, the Theatre—and the entire WPA project—was accused of "boondoggling" and shovel-leaning, of wasting the taxpayers' money. On the other—and this charge was ultimately instrumental in the denial of funds to the Federal Theatre—the Theatre Project was held to be a hotbed of radical activity, the plays it presented were described as "communist inspired." Significantly, few of the more virulent attacks upon the Federal Theatre came from the theatrical profession itself (except for a few old-guard producers like Brock Pemberton). Most came from the intransigent right, such as the Hearst press, which termed the project "an adjunct to the New York Leftist literary junta." The fact is that because of its governmental support the Federal Theatre was particularly vulnerable to political attack. Moreover, by virtue of the WPA directive forbidding any coherent public relations policy, the project was unable to respond publicly to its critics, with the familiar result that denials never caught up with the accusations.

As for the charge that the leadership of the project was communist dominated, it was recognized by all responsible critics that the accusation was manifestly absurd. No more substantial charge was ever leveled at Hallie Flanagan than the fact of her "subversive" penchant for theatrical experimentation. In fact, she repeatedly pointed out to her subordinates on the project that she would not tolerate the use of the Federal Theatre for the promulgation of any specific political platform. She objected to—but characteristically made no attempt to censor—certain of the political implications of the Living Newspaper's production of *Injunction Granted*. When separate productions of Sinclair Lewis' *It Can't Happen Here* were in rehearsal in twenty-five different cities, the following memorandum went out to all projects throughout the country:

> . . . avoid all controversial issues—political angles of any degree—special appeals—racial or group appeals—or interferences in any of these directions since Federal Theatre is interested only in presenting good theatre, neither adopting nor assuming any viewpoint beyond presenting a new and vital drama of our times, emerging from the social and economic forces of the day.

Of course, it was to some extent naive to assume that such a vital, contemporary drama as that desired by the directors of the project could totally avoid assuming *any* political viewpoint, and the Federal Theatre plays inevitably reveal various social concerns and solutions. But the tenor of its directive is clear: the directors of the Federal Theatre aspired to a nonsectarian social drama, a drama which affirmed the necessity of facing social issues, but which avoided a dogmatically consistent political position upon these issues. In the case of a government-supported theatre such a position was obviously a necessity. But the problem was further complicated by the scope of the Federal Theatre and its avowed principle of non-censorship (if the principle was not always scrupulously followed it was more the fault of nontheatrical WPA or governmental action than of censorship by the project directors themselves). Plays were chosen by the individual regions involved, subject to approval, rarely denied, by the Theatre's central directorate. Thus, unlike the Group Theatre, the Federal Theatre's plays were not chosen by its directors; although the National Service Bureau—the Theatre's official play-reading unit—recommended plays to the various localities, the choice was generally left to the regional directors. Despite the fear that subsidized theatre might result in direct political control, the facts reveal otherwise. *Fortune* magazine spoke for many observers of the project when it noted: "The Arts Projects have been given a freedom no one would have thought possible in a government-run undertaking. And by and large that freedom has not been abused." (The two major exceptions: the banning of the Living Newspaper's first production, *Ethiopia,* because Mussolini was represented as a character; and the ban on Welles' and Houseman's production of Blitzstein's *The Cradle Will Rock,* which served as the catalyst for the formation of the Mercury Theatre.)

The quantitative accomplishment of the project thus speaks for itself. What, however, of the quality of Federal Theatre productions? Francis Fergusson speaks for many who attended the project's performances: "Many of its productions showed all too clearly the signs of the chaos in which they had been put together. But the best of them had a style which triumphantly accepted the precarious situation, an immediate and headlong vitality which I will never forget." This style was clearly discernible in Orson Welles' two famous productions of *Doctor Faustus* and the Negro *Macbeth.* T. S. Eliot's *Murder in the Cathedral,* receiving its first American production, was another of the project's major successes. But a perusal of the list of Federal Theatre productions reveals a basic deficiency: the conspicious absence of significant original plays by contemporary American dramatists. This inability to persuade established playwrights to write for the project combined with the lack of success in developing any striking young playwrights of its own represents the Federal Theatre's greatest failure. Unlike the Group Theatre, the project produced no Odets or Saroyan. Of the many original plays it performed none has remained dramatically viable; *Altars of Steel, The Sun and I, Chalk Dust, Class of '29, Prologue to Glory, Battle Hymn*—obscure footnotes to American dramatic history. The reasons are several. By the time of the formation of the Federal Theatre many theatre groups already existed to absorb established playwriting talent, most significantly the Group Theatre. The older successful playwrights, Maxwell Anderson, Robert Sherwood, Elmer Rice, S. N. Behrman, and Sidney Howard, had formed their own production unit, The Playwrights' Company, and continued to work within the confines of Broadway. As for new talent, perhaps four years is just not enough time; it took the Group five years to produce Odets.

Paradoxically, the Federal Theatre's most significant dramatic accomplishment was represented by a genre which was necessarily ephemeral: the Living Newspaper, like the entire project, was the product of economic necessity and social purpose. The immediate cause for the adoption of the form was the necessity of dealing with a problem peculiar to the project, a surplus of manpower. Unlike almost every other theatrical group the Federal Theatre had the problem of using the thousands of actors and technicians on the relief rolls. At the very moment that the directors of the project were pondering this dilemma, the Newspaper Guild of New York City was looking for a way to absorb some of its own unemployed in the Federal Theatre. Out of this dual necessity arose the decision to produce dramatizations of the news with living actors, light, music, and movement. Such a form was ideally suited to the needs of this project: first, it solved the problem of the use of personnel; second, its emphasis on production allowed the directors to minimize the deficiencies of some of the acting talent available; third, it appealed to the project's spirit of dramatic experimentation by creating a unique theatrical form; and, fourth, it served the project's social ideal of speaking articulately upon contemporary social problems.

In such works as *Triple-A Ploughed Under, Power, One-Third of a Nation,* and *Injunction Granted,* the Living Newspaper attempt to create the theatrical equivalent of the film documentary, another characteristic genre of the period; in the former case, however, the material of art was not the juxtaposed celluloid images of reality, but rather the formal verbal recreation of this reality through fact and comment theatrically expressed. Light, music, staging—these were the formal media through which the Living Newspaper worked. The durability of the form from an esthetic point of view rests not in the various plays which were presented, for these, being living *newspapers,* were intended to serve only an immediate function; the form's durability rests in its theatrical principle, in the *conception* of news theatrically expressed. The validity of the form remains, as such contemporary theatre documentaries as *The Oppenheimer Dossier* and Peter Weiss' *The Investigation* indicate.

Although the themes of the Living Newspapers were more reformist than radical, there can be no doubt that they created powerful enemies instrumental in the final closing of the project. Such opponents as Representative Martin Dies, who was shocked by the "vulgarity and profanity" of several project productions, and Representative Everett Dirksen, who called the work of the Federal Theatre "salacious tripe," waited for the propitious moment, and when it came, acted. The Federal Theatre did not die a natural death; it was killed by Act of Congress on June 30, 1939. The ostensible reason for the denial of funds to the Arts project was economy, but this reason is belied by several facts: all the Arts projects used less than three-fourths of one per cent of the total WPA appropriation, and the appropriation *was not cut one cent* by the termination of the Federal Theatre; the money was simply distributed among other WPA projects. Furthermore, there was no opposition from the theatrical profession itself. Letters and telegrams poured into Washington from the greatest names in the American theatre, as well as from the major theatrical unions, urging the continuation of the project, and New York's drama critics sent a joint letter to Congress maintaining that "the theatre project in New York . . . has been on the whole an institution of great value to the life of the community." The project was ended primarily for political reasons, because enemies of the administration saw in the issue of communism within the project a means of embarrassing the New Deal. And the administration itself, fighting hard for its social program, could not risk the sacrifice of much of this program by demanding the continuation of the Arts projects. That the accusations against the project were largely unfounded was not important to its critics; they were not concerned with the record, and, in fact, resolutely refused to accept the theatre's invitation to attend performances of its plays. The following exchange between Representative Starnes of the Dies Committee and Hallie Flanagan, who had petitioned repeatedly to be allowed to answer the charges brought against the project, clearly reveals the caliber of the attack:

> Congressman Starnes: (quoting from Hallie Flanagan's book, *A Theatre is Born*) 'the workers' theatres . . . intend to remake a social structure without the help of money and this ambition alone invests their undertaking with a certain Marlowesque madness.'
> You are quoting from this Marlowe. Is he a Communist?
> Hallie Flanagan: I am very sorry. I was quoting from Christopher Marlowe.
> Starnes: Tell us who Marlowe is, so we can get the proper reference, because that is all we want to do.
> H. F.: Put in the record that he was the greatest dramatist in the period of Shakespeare, immediately preceding Shakespeare.
> Starnes: Put that in the record, because the charge has been made that this article of yours is entirely Communistic, and we want to help you. Of course we had what some people call Communists back in the days of the Greek theatre. I believe Mr. Euripides was guilty of teaching class-consciousness also, wasn't he?
> H. F.: I believe that was alleged against all of the Greek dramatists.

We are closer to home now; normalcy was returning. As the decade came to its close, as the economy improved, the social forces which converged to create the Federal Theatre were dissipated. As the relief aspect of the project diminished there were those who proposed its continuity on a permanent basis. A Federal Arts Bill was introduced for the creation of a Department of Science, Art, and Literature. But the ideal was short-lived; the belief that the government had a responsibility towards the arts was, with the Federal Theatre itself, plowed under.

William Saroyan and the Theatre of Transformation

By James H. Justus

Zip! Walter Lippman wasn't brilliant today;
Zip! Will Saroyan ever write a great play?
—*Pal Joey*

Lorenz Hart's question in 1940 contained its own implied answer: *no*. In the 60s, though the answer may still be the same, the Saroyanesque play as a unique amalgam of sentiment and fantasy deserves the attention of a new generation of readers. From the beginning, critics praised Saroyan for his freshness, irreverence, and promise, and from almost the same time condemned him for vagueness, egoism, and lack of discipline. In the 30s alone, both praise and condemnation could be sufficiently and indiscriminately confirmed by a long list of short fiction—seven major volumes—and two produced plays in 1939, *My Heart's in the Highlands* and *The Time of Your Life*. Before the decade was over, despite the favorable reception of the two plays and the wider popular success of the stories, perhaps only Saroyan himself maintained a consistently favorable opinion of his contributions to American literature.

Like Steinbeck, Caldwell, Farrell, and the dramatists of social protest, Saroyan had a distinctive voice which spoke of and for the 30s. But where others were unremitting in their castigation of specific evils of American capitalism, Saroyan was merely occasional in his accusations. However deeply he felt about fascism and the abuses of political power, the literary treatment was usually generalized and moral. Placed against the programmatic social protest of Maxwell Anderson's *Winterset* (the moneyed classes pervert justice) and *High Tor* (the business world is ruthless in the name of economic progress), Paul Green's *Johnny Johnson* (the military and its mad supporters crush men of good will), John Howard Lawson's *Success Story* and Clifford Odets' *Golden Boy* (capitalism corrupts individual integrity), a play like *The Time of Your Life* seems mild indeed. Saroyan suggests, hints at, alludes to specific social wrongs, and then nearly always in comprehensive moral contexts (such as the deadening effects of materialism) which tend to dilute the anger with nostalgia and irony. A characteristic speech is the closing line of *My Heart's in the Highlands;* after their eviction, when Johnny and his penniless father take to the road, Johnny says: "I'm not mentioning any names, Pa, but something's wrong somewhere."

It was clear to The Committed that Saroyan was not effectively angry—he could not write *The Grapes of Wrath,* for instance. Neither was he interested in exploring the potential revolutionary spirit of the rural or urban dispossessed in the manner of *Studs Lonigan* or "Kneel to the Rising Sun." Most clearly, he was not interested in ideology — the determining motive behind *Awake and Sing!* or *One Third of a Nation.* Moreover, Saroyan was too bumptiously independent, he was too addicted to the vitality, rather than the privations, of children and immigrants, and he indulged himself too freely in a rhetoric that could only inspire fantasy and dreams. The Saroyan method, made clearer in the 1940s and after, is finally not frontal, but oblique; and the major mood it establishes is not anger, but poignancy.

Lack of money—and therefore food and shelter—is more the occasion for sorrow at The Way Things Are and indefinable longing than it is for a plea to correct those things. In *Love's Old Sweet Song* (1940) even the pathos of the uprooted is changed into vaudeville as Cabot Yearling, fresh from Oklahoma with a pregnant wife and fourteen children, claims squatter's rights to an already occupied house. If Saroyan is remembering the plight of the Joads here, he gives Steinbeck little comfort for his role as their chronicler. Accompanying these Dust Bowl paisanos are a *Life* photographer and a newsman who keeps saying things like "The pitiable plight of these unfortunate people is not the concern of one man alone, but of the whole nation." Furthermore, the view is conservative when it is not merely comic; Cabot denies that he is unfortunate, proclaims his proud integrity, and boasts of being able to "shift for ourselves, the same as ever." Only in his best play, *The Time of Your Life*, does Saroyan resemble those dramatists who were choosing viably realistic situations which invited larger, symbolic readings. For all their differences, Harry Van of Robert Sherwood's *Idiot's Delight* and Gimpty of Sidney Kingsley's *Dead End* both anticipate Joe of *The Time of Your Life*: the little man of essential decency who understands the human predicament and who despite that gloomy knowledge idealistically clings to the hope of man's improvement. Entrapment, the common informing metaphor in the lives of those people herded together in a remote Italian lodge and the tenements along the East River in New York, fails to be the dominant metaphor for the habitués of Nick's San Francisco saloon simply because the hopes for escaping the trap are more stubbornly voiced.

Since the early 40s the familiar Saroyan stories have continued to flow, a few novels have appeared and been variously received; and plays both produced and unproduced, with seemingly tireless admonitory prefaces, have been published—all reminders that Saroyan is not only still around but that he is still the same old Saroyan. And, except for the tone of his non-dramatic work, which has grown increasingly solemn and self-conscious, and a few stories written in bile, Saroyan's is indeed the same voice heard in the 30s: there is grief aplenty, but man is a miracle, and merely living confirms life's miraculousness. That which seemed so distinctive to the spirit of the 30s no longer strikes us with the same relevant hopefulness, although such an observation may say more about our times than it does about Saroyan's themes, which were and still are largely prescriptions for ills which the author sees as endemic to no particular time.

* * *

In both his narratives and his dramas, Saroyan's sphere of significant action is a theatre of transformation in which he presents a celebratory enactment of man's affective victory over the timid conventionalities, compromises, and evasions of his life. He sings of man's release into a new vision of the "miracle" of the rebirth: "Let him walk and talk and think and sleep and dream and awaken and walk again and talk again and move and be alive." His vision ("the glorious truth of mere being") is never passive; it activates other men into new areas of awareness. Saroyan's vision receives full—if rambling—definition in the hortatory confessions of the memoirs, *The Bicycle Rider in Beverly Hills, Here Comes/ There Goes/ You Know Who,* and *Not Dying:*

Life may or may not be a tragic thing—the question is "still open." Man is captured only once, at birth, "only that capture is also a setting free." Merely living, "an enormity not to be slighted," involves wholeness—good vision, good hearing, swiftness of mind and spirit, laughter, "the fact of *being.*" Although man is an "accident" on the earth, an element of the "deliberate" is sufficient to compel him to correct the "wrongs of the accidental" in him and to "cherish, accept, recognize, employ, extend, enlarge, improve, and thrive upon the accidental *rights* which were also born into him, the principal one of which is to continue. . . . " Because the "each" of anything is unique, man must honor other men, whatever possibility may be discovered in the "less great, the non-great, the antigreat, the anonymous, the unimportant, the insignificant, the useless, the unfortunate, the ill, the mad, or the wicked." His duty is to live fully, forever pushing aside irrelevant boundaries and dedicated to finding himself, others, the world, time, and space as a "dramatic, satisfying, and good" experience.

This vision of man—a premise in *The Time of Your Life* but a force which competes riotously, luxuriantly, with the action itself in most of the other plays—is conventional enough, though its sources are perhaps more complex than in most writers who share it with Saroyan. Behind this vision are the stoicism of an enduring minority in a new land, the Biblical sense of humility and joy in contemplating God's creation, the sincere arrogance of the special man who has been mystically touched by grace, the received literary-philosophical conventions of nineteenth-century Romanticism.

Out of these varied backgrounds—and from Saroyan's own experience—comes the persistent and often sentimental reverence for the innocent, the helpless, the down-and-out. In summoning up his wild array of con men, unknown artists, exuberant youths, impractical Greeks and Mexicans, sad Jews, dreaming streetwalkers, unemployed actors, and indigent drunks, Saroyan has always celebrated a single type of which these are representative: the beautiful people. Silent or incorrigibly loquacious, they are those who understand the mystery of being, treasuring the rare moments of illumination. And they are not *merely* representative, for while Saroyan is insistent on the miracle of life itself and its essential wholeness, the intensity of his scorn is in proportion to the world's demonstrated indifference to individuals. His people tend to be extravagant, eccentric, improbable—even those little people of decency and honesty whose simple minds and kindly hearts should make great claims on the world's attention.

If Saroyan's concept of the beautiful people tends toward the simplistic and the sentimental, his picture of the world they must live in is complex, involving the forces which at once assault them maliciously and test them providentially. If they survive the sheer facts of incompleteness, disease, violence, indifference, and the pervasive fear of death, their beauty is earned and is thus worth Saroyan's effort to celebrate it. In *My Heart's in the Highlands* the reminders of human misery—the gnawing need for cheese, bread, fruit—impinge upon and constantly threaten the superior claims of art—the medium for transforming loneliness into community. In *The Time of Your Life,* the transients attempt to impose the order of charity in the artificial world of Nick's saloon, but constantly intruding is the disordered chaos of the great world where there is, in the Arab's reiterated observation, "No foundation. All the way down the line." The disinterested generosity of Joe extends to all those bruised by the world, but the hurt is more persistent than the healing. There is a touch of the futile and the desperate in the facile way Blick is dispatched; the bullying forces of evil, made more horrible by public sanction, are even here, in Saroyan's most realistic play, routed by concerted wish-fulfillment. Barnaby Gaul of *Love's Old Sweet Song* reminds Ann of the "great troubles" of man—panics, famines, floods, hurricanes, and "fury and stupor in the heart." He reminds the *Time* salesman that he brings "news of world-wide madness and horror to the living every Friday," but the only antidote Gaul can offer is the con man's nostrums—bottled hope that will somehow cure disgrace, disease, and wretchedness.

Saroyan's examples of forces and alliances which threaten man are less often social than moral—not banks and loan companies, but "wretchedness," not Hitler, but "the madness of war," not Wall Street, but "despair in the heart." When the mice in *The Beautiful People* (1941) cry for a lost brother, Owen, a writer of one-word novels, advises his sister Agnes not to interfere: "Things end. They change. They spoil. They're hurt. Or destroyed. Accidents happen . . . Sooner or later everybody's got to know that death is with us from the first breath we take." But despite this mature realization, Owen is an artist of affirmation who reaches the peak of his awareness when he can write a *two*-word novel, *My Brother*. Jonah the father proclaims: "We are alive with all things alive, from the mite to the whale." The transforming power of love extends to the inarticulate boy with whom Agnes falls in love. When she complains to her father, "He's bewildered and shy and full of terrible sorrow, and his shoes don't fit," Jonah replies: "But his feet within them do." Misery and joy are in delicate balance always, but Saroyan insists upon the poet's right to change whatever in the world is changeable, to preside over man's potential rebirth. *The Beautiful People* is the most obvious of Saroyan's parables of man's necessity for love, the transforming agent; the victory of its action is worthy of awe: "Aye," says an old drunk, "the wonder and the beauty of it."

In this theatre of transformation, Saroyan's most familiar technique is that of first juxtaposing, then merging, two orders of reality: the eccentric, the unusual, the singular, and the familiar, the usual, the commonplace. In the astonished mingling of the two orders comes the blurring of distinctions, and mankind stands revealed in unity as the eccentric grows familiar and the familiar becomes an object of awe. It is not only a twentieth-century version of what the poets of *Lyrical Ballads* were striving for; it is also the triumph of a faith in both unity and variety—the residual tradition of Emerson and Whitman. A waterfront saloon may be the natural arena for the banal—prostitutes, longshoremen, and ordinary but persistent young men who risk their nickels in telephones and pinball machines —but it is also the stage of opportunities, not only for the swaggering Kit Carson with his endless flow of tall tales, but also for Joe himself, who believes the stories and whose commitment is to the daily "rehearsal" necessary for "man to get to be himself."

Saroyan's theatre of transformation is any place where the world's misfits and outcasts gather together in huddled need and where, often, the world's proud spiritual cripples—bankers, vice-presidents, voice teachers, construction workers—also wander in to reveal their even greater need for rebirth. It may be an ordinary house in Bakersfield or Fresno, a bar or an apartment in San Francisco, a New York restaurant, or a vacant theatre itself. And presiding over the ceremony of rebirth is Saroyan's priest, touched by madness or grace, God's own elect who points the true way. He is Jasper MacGregor (*My Heart's in the Highlands*), Joe (*The Time of Your Life*), Barnaby Gaul (*Love's Old Sweet Song*), Jonah Webster (*The Beautiful People*), Michael Sweeney (*Sweeney in the Trees*),

Jim Dandy (*Jim Dandy: Fat Man in a Famine*), the King (*The Cave Dwellers*). In Saroyan's dramatic enactments of these romantic premises, it is perhaps inevitable that the results are so often maudlin. The Good Heart has ever been a difficult notion to make interesting, and Standing in Awe of Life is easier to affirm than it is to render.

Saroyan has always been fond of saying—and the early critics were eager to agree—that his work is of its time and place, its particular moment of reality. That his work should reflect the desperate days of physical and spiritual unease is only natural. There is disillusion and there are suggestions throughout his work of the 30s of the larger world outside the California setting: the threats of dictatorship, oppression, and hatred organized for war. In its aggressive optimism and its very popularity, *The Time of Your Life* arrests the mood of America in crisis, particularizing genetic evils and celebrating the momentary but fragile victory of charity and good will.

But unlike Dos Passos, Farrell, and most of those writers who lost moorings, found new ones, and lost even those in the 30s, Saroyan was relatively untouched by social disorder and political disenchantment. Moorings he had and kept. His disillusion, hurt, and fear were not the exceptionally personal ordeals of most of his fellow writers. The difficulty of earning one's precarious way and making orderly lives in the midst of dominant American social and political patterns were for Saroyan givens of life. The Armenian community, in conjunction with other minority groups, made itself felt in the whole processes of Saroyan's attitudes toward life and, so naturally with Saroyan, his attitudes toward art. Endurance, no mean virtue, became a matter to be understood; withstanding the cruelty of the world became a matter for ingenuity and laughter. The claims of "the others" always impinge on those of "the beautiful people," and the confrontation is often tender and sentimental but sometimes corrosive and brutal. If laughter is the characteristic response to such situations, it is often laughter that verges on crying.

The close identification with his origins which has constantly shaped Saroyan's vision of man—endurance in the face of the great trial of living and the "miracle" of simply being part of humankind—has also shaped the form of his work. What man is and does is reflected in everything of Saroyan's: the short fiction, the novels, the plays, the memoirs, the songs. More often than not, the organization is not related to cumulative development of character and plot but the smaller units of form: the set piece of rhetoric or incantation, tableaux vivants enlivened by music, the tall tale, the fable, the anecdote, the interlude, the vaudeville "set." It should not be surprising for those now accustomed to the plays of Genet and Ionesco that Saroyan characteristically uses the play as a kind of repository in which all these formal units meet, mingle, and compete. But for an occasional grim exception—such as his first dramatic attempt in 1935, *Subway Circus,* and the brutally pessimistic *Hello Out There* of 1942—Saroyan's plays are spectacles: the grand assembly, the concatenation of voices and types, the particulars, eroded and made featureless, reduced to their generalities. Man in his clumsy and wobbly experience on earth is made to order in a handful of types. There is a profusion of faces and masks, shifting identities, caricatures, stereotypes: all representative of Essential Man. The fleshing out is done according to the patterns of myth and dream, not those of realistic character portrayal, a strategy which permits extreme individuality to function as emphasis for the common strain beneath it. The shifting, jostling juxtaposition of the real and the unreal not only justifies Saroyan's cheerful borrowings from the theatrical traditions of expressionism and surrealism, but also points up the technique, if not the substance, of what has turned out to be the dominant theatrical mode since World War II—the theatre of the absurd. Saroyan's plays—the sunny absurd—are dedicated to the underlying principle that though man's living may be tragic, his dying certainly is not. Saroyan investigates how many may best live, and the formula in *Jim Dandy* is characteristic—plunging beyond the mere acceptance of man's lot *(be-beget-begone)* is the resolution that comes of enlightened rebirth: "I will confound time and change with love and patience."

*   *   *

Saroyan may never write "a great play." His scorn of the commercial theatre and his indifference to the formal conventions of the genre render his exercises in the drama interesting, stimulating, provocative—and also platitudinous, unintegrated, impressionistic. But they are of a piece; they celebrate repeatedly the miracle of what one character in *Jim Dandy* describes as "that perfect defective thing whose breed is man." Saroyan's strengths are also his weaknesses—whimsy, spontaneity and improvisation, the exploitation of all the tag-ends and scraps of man's vitality as a human and social animal. They belong to a tradition of highly structured formlessness that recurs now and again and finds common cause in such diverse phenomena as the *commedia dell' arte* and the plays of Ionesco and Beckett.

Purists who suffer through a Saroyan play may find comfort in Gide, persuaded as he was—at least in 1920—of the impossibility of making a theatre piece into a work of art; but if the play can be thought of as a vehicle of man's celebration of himself, Saroyan must be suffered. In Saroyan's incantatory world, what is hurt and imperfect in man is transformed by love into a celebratory ritual which defines his potentialities for a "good" survival. Everyman's rebirth, like Fishkin's in *Jim Dandy,* proceeds from the lament over the cosmic trick of having to inhabit "this Fishkin flesh" to the song of transformation: "This world's home and we are lucky tenants of the house." The sentiments are stubbornly cheerful as prescriptions for survival in a mad world. They reflected the needs of the 30s, but Saroyan persisted in his belief that those needs were more general than specific and did not somehow disappear at the end of that decade. Out of the vagaries of whimsy and moralism, Saroyan has always demonstrated an agile sense of experimentation in structure and form in his art, but he has never seen fit to alter his theme: "To have been born is surely our end. To die is beside the point. And to live is our pleasure and law."

The Undiscovered Art:
Drama on and off
American Radio in the 30s

by Patrick D. Hazard

"Radio had its faults but at least it never led the American people around by their eyeballs. It let them see for themselves." Archibald MacLeish, *The American Story.*

A. William Bluem coined an apt phrase, "the forgotten art," for radio documentary's sad post-TV eclipse—in America alone, we sadly remind ourselves. As one compares the relative development of radio drama as a unique literary genre in America and Britain, a better epithet for that neglected phase of the sound medium might be "the undiscovered art." Defenders of American radio argue that the soap opera was a dramatic form "ideally" suited to the low intensity, episodic attention of the female listener-as-washer-and-ironer. And serial comedy in the hands of a low-keyed wit like Goodman Ace left us spoonerised scripts from the "Easy Aces" series which still amuse me. And if you want to define drama loosely enough, Mae West's "come up and saw me sometime" skit with Charlie McCarthy which earned NBC an FCC slap on the wrist is a play of a vestigial kind. But of drama worthy of that proud name, *i.e.,* demanding a minimum kind of seriously sustained attention, of the level BBC policymakers rightfully preened themselves about, the American listener had precious little choice: a plethora of Hollywood dominated translations, noble but abortive experiments like

221

The CBS Radio Workshop, and *causes celebres* like Orson Welles' very free variation on H. G. Wells' *War of the Worlds.*

Radio drama as a unique challenge to the creative sensibility as experienced by the young Tyrone Guthrie seems never to have arisen in America until almost a decade and half after the medium went national through networks. True, Deems Taylor and Edna St. Vincent Millay inaugurated the new CBS radio network in 1927 with a radio version of the new opera, *The King's Henchman,* but that was Cultural Ribbon-cutting, an esthetic rabbit's foot for hoping the Muses wouldn't get in the way of the money karts coming down Madison Avenue, a kind of exercise in exorcism. For radio was first, last and always an extension of the domestic appliance industry. Which is not necessarily to knock it utterly; the masses cannot become cultivated autonomous patrons until they are beyond the margin of bare economic survival. Mass production is as essential a part of the infrastructure of abundance as mass education.

The portable or midget set turned radio from a luxury in the free-spending 20s to a domestic necessity in the cash-poor depression —no piddling accomplishment. Radio's 9,000,000 homes before the Crash in 1929 had swelled to 29,200,000 in 1940. The total number of sets in use quintupled from 10,500,000 in 1930 to 54,-000,000 in 1940. Car radios, selfcontained aerials, and push button tuning were developed to keep up demand in a saturated market.

Between 1920 and 1925 "radio" drama consisted mostly of amateurs presenting short vignettes from a studio or plays broadcast direct from a legitimate theatre. In the latter, announcers tried from the wings to make up for the maddening aural lulls of pantomime with whispered explanations of what was going on on stage. Radio was still a long way from drama.

In the spring of 1925, however, a man and wife vaudeville team playing the Chicago vicinity were talked into creating some skits for a WENR program known as "The Smith Family." They were not very well received, but they started something—the serial story, a continuous narrative presented in daily episodes—that would become a basic staple of radio programming. That unsuccessful couple, Marian and Jim Jordan, later achieved fame and fortune as Fibber McGee and Molly. Their future competitors Sam 'n' Henry did use the new format successfully that same year over WGN and then went to the opposition NBC station WMAQ as Amos 'n' Andy in March 1928.

The writers of "True Story Hour" (1928) were among the first to recognize—through their pioneering use of the first-person narrator—that radio had to devise techniques of its own. Kay Van Riper's "English Coronets" from KFWB (Hollywood) also broke fresh ground. Rudy Vallee's "Fleischman Hour" (October, 1929) was the first to bring established actors and actresses of the caliber of Helen Hayes and Walter Huston to radio in original sketches that paid well and gave many new writers a toehold in the new craft.

The history of America radio drama is largely the history of experimentation in the use of sound. The ingenuity of the radio sound effects man is still impressive to recall. When WGN put on "The Pied Piper of Hamlin," it simulated the squeaking of thousands of rats by twisting resined corks on glass and the scratchiness of their feet by passing short ends of insulated wire over a marble surface, the rubber doing for the tiny pads of rodent feet, the wire making like eentsy toenails. Sand falling on lettuce equalled rain, crinkling cellophane was fire, blocks of wood could do for marching feet, the frequent sound of a human head being clunked was enacted by thumping a melon.

Not all such innovations were equally successful. For example, a Chicago producer ran into trouble one night with fancy lights intended to wow the audience. The new WGN studio built next to the Tribune Tower in 1935 had a theatre in which splendid stage lighting effects could be changed from the control room to divert the studio audience. One day an agency man had the bright idea of typing the more dramatic parts of the script on red paper ("to spur the actors to new heights"). As Blair Walliser's radio play reached its climax, the border lighting cues happened to call for red. As the color deepened into scarlet, the lines typed on red paper disappeared into the night!

Davidson Taylor believes it significant that the first successful play for radio was one that Rupert Hughes wrote for BBC in which the action took place entirely in the total dark of a mine disaster. "But poets in America," Taylor continues,

> have, on the whole, been very remiss in failing to realize that radio re-establishes with the public the contact which made the troubadours and their humbler colleagues socially significant. The wide social function of poetry could be restored through radio, if poets would only prepare themselves to use it.

Equally little attention was given the preparation of early sound effects. Anybody who was around created them until late in the 20s. The rise of radio drama, however, made a sophisticated approach to "ear scenery" imperative. By the end of 1949, the ten key network stations in four program originating cities (New York, Chicago, San Francisco, Hollywood) employed an all-time high of 121 full-time sound specialists.

Robert B. Turnbull, author of *Sound Effects* (1951), believes that Arch Oboler was one of the few radio writers who really understood the aesthetic potential of sound in the new medium. After Oboler's first radio play, "Futuristics," was aired in November, 1933, he took over the Wyllis Cooper series "Lights Out." After his first script, "Burial Service," sent transcontinental chills up and down the nation's spineless addicts to mystery, he was given *carte blanche* to pursue fantasy, stream of consciousness, and other devices. One of his experimental plays for NBC, an adaptation of Dalton Trumbo's sensational novel *Johnny Got His Gun,* Turnbull calls "a milestone in the imaginative use of the radio medium."

1936 has been called the Golden Year of radio sound effects and drama, for it was on July 18 that CBS inaugurated its experimental workshop with an adaptation of Percival Wilde's one-act play, "The Finger of God." The prime objective of the Workshop was to develop acting, writing, musical and production talent at the same time that new ideas and techniques in radio drama were explored. The Workshop became a regular feature in 1938.

To do anything offbeat in 1936 was to attract a disproportionate amount of press notice, one CBS executive involved in the Workshop recalls skeptically. Ironically, when Robert Landry resurrected the Radio Workshop, for a full year he was confronted by what he calls the myth of the first workshop. CBS execs griped about the new series' lack of pizazz. This alleged pizazz turned out (when Landry investigated) to be mostly copywriters' prefabrications.

There was no Radio Writers Guild when the first Workshop started. One writer got paid a piddling $30 for a ten minute segment. $75-$100 was the the average script fee. (The series' total budget was only $400 a week.) It was a poor network's Philharmonic, *i.e.,* a good cheap way for poor also-ran CBS to get a lot of trade paper chatter. One time at least there was a bitter backlash.

Orson Welles, who used to give the creeps to thousands of young listeners to his radio characterization "The Shadow," gave their parents a real scare with his Halloween spoof, Sunday evening October 31, 1938. Mass hysteria possessed thousands of listeners who refused to believe the interpolations reminding the audience that this was a documentary adaptation of H. G. Wells' fantasy, *The War of the Worlds*. At least a score of adults had to be treated for shock or hysteria. Twenty families from one block in Newark fled a hypothetical gas attack by running out into the street with wet towels and handkerchiefs over their faces. Thousands called radio stations, newspapers, and police for instructions on protecting themselves during the raid. In fact three years later the hoax had much the same impression on some; the bulletins from Pearl Harbor were disbelieved as just another spoof.

Radio drama was meanwhile making more solid, less sensational progress. The BBC's Val Gielgud set up an "Experimental Hour" in 1937 patterned after America's CBS Radio Workshop. Archibald MacLeish's "Fall of the City" was ironically its first production followed by Yeats's "Words Upon the Window Pane" and a diptych of a scene from "Twelfth Night"—in modern and then in Elizabethan English. The late night audience was larger than anticipated, but the series failed because "worthy material" was too hard to come by.

Sandra Michael's *Against the Storm* serial turned new ground in September 1939 by breaking away from the stereotypes of the daytime soap opera. She really was writing an episodic radio novel about the contemporary world and the social, political and economic effects of this realistic world on her characters. In grateful relief the academic community which had become appalled by 77 soapers on the air at one time gave her a Peabody in 1942 for radio's most distinguished dramatic program.

Radio drama was also greatly expanding its audience. In 1939 Paul Robeson sang Earl Robinson and John Latouche's WPA revue sequence "Ballad for Americans" as "The Pursuit of Happiness" premiere directed by Norman Corwin. Davidson Taylor believed the ovation of the studio audience confirmed that what had gone unnoticed in a short-lived WPA revue "articulated something the whole country wanted to have said." "Ballad" became overnight the musical sensation of the season.

Norman Corwin's "We Hold These Truths" is estimated to have reached 60 million listeners, the largest audience a playwright had ever had at a single hearing up to that time, capitalizing as it did over all 4 networks on the patriotic fervor a week after Pearl Harbor. Corwin followed his success by producing the series, "This Is War."

In March 1941, Davidson Taylor, who had already helped radio mature with the CBS Radio Workshop and who would later contribute much to broadcasting by founding the same network's Documentary Unit and be Pat Weaver's public affairs vice-president, tried to define what "good radio" was for *Theatre Arts Monthly*. In the beginning, although radio did not know how to take advantage of its handicaps, "yet from the start it gave rise to certain products which were unique," for example, the ad-lib news broadcast, "oral reporting of events while they were occurring." Programmers soon decided that it was only the very exceptional individual like William L. Shirer who could "cover" Hitler as he walked into the railway car at Compiegne for the armistice. Ad-libbing had to give way to preparation in covering momentous news; it was limited to feature materials. Taylor argued the only way ultimately to be able to recognize quality in radio was to see what could follow from radio's unique qualities. "Good radio," in his view, "vitalizes the isolated recipient, it utilizes sound adroitly, the broadcast starts and stops on schedule, it never flags, it is present for a moment and then it is gone forever, and it reaches huge and democratic audiences." When it adds the seventh capacity—perhaps most important to the artist—to become inspired, "good radio is an art."

Despite some important war-time documentary programs, however, radio drama began to decline during the 40s. Flora Rheta Schreiber analyzes the decline in "Broadcast Poetry: A Lost Art?" (*Hollywood Quarterly*, 1951-52). "Expressions of hope for poetry in broadcasting seem curiously distant, like the echo of an echo of an echo." When the original Columbia Radio Workshop (1936-42), which was in the vanguard of poetic drama, returned to the air between February 2, 1946 and April 27, 1947, script editor Lou Ashworth blamed its second demise on the total absence of first-rate scripts; reading manuscripts for the series became "like sitting at a death watch." Indeed when CBS-TV revived the Workshop on January 14, 1952, Norris Houghton had no definite plans for using either poetry or poetic drama—preferring the off-beat and human interest to the truly tragic.

By contrast in the 30s and early 40s, poets, Miss Schreiber continues, looked to radio to provide a reintegration of drama and poetry, a paradoxical hope, "for radio itself was the offspring of the very technology that had been a contributing factor to the estrangement." This hope by the 50s looked forlorn indeed, at least in America. Archibald MacLeish wrote in January 1952 that "radio offers a stage for poetry, but I doubt that the producers of radio in the United States share that opinion or care that it is held by others. In that sense the hopes I held at the time of *The Fall of the City* have not been realized. I have just finished my third verse play for radio [*The Trojan Horse*]. It was produced (1/14/52) by the BBC on their Home Program, but American production seems to be impossible—at least by one of the broadcasting chains." Who can disagree with Mrs. Schreiber when she asks why an American poet of acknowledged stature should have to "turn to the broadcasting facilities of another country to find his audience?" The average American's imaginative life has been unduly impoverished by a combination of business avarice and academic sloth.

The hope that radio would, *could* bring poet and populace together again rested on the assumption that the folk audience of radio, including many non-readers and non theatre-goers, somehow shared a community of feeling on important issues which the poets could distill and bring into more civilized focus through poetic drama. How much of the failure of this dream is partly due to the educational establishment's apathy and lack of vision about using poetic drama taped from radio in the classroom is hard to determine. Norman Corwin expressed his belief in 1952 that the production of poetic radio plays had declined "because of the disinterest of the producers, combined with the apathy of educators, the audience, and the poets themselves. Writers are using this form very little, if at all, because they are not encouraged to do so. Poetry is still considered a sissy art in this country. Radio has certainly not fulfilled the hope I saw in it. It stood on the brink of the Promised Land, then fled when it saw television coming."

One weakness, moreover, that has inhibited the development of radio drama into a mature medium, is the feeble criticism that has followed performance. In January, 1946 *Variety* published a survey on the status of newspaper radio criticism. Only 324 out of 1700 dailies pretended to have radio editors. *Variety* itself would only qualify 45-50 of these "by the farthest stretch." This corps was even less significant when you deducted the three press associations, two national magazines, and a dozen trade papers. The rest were "mostly office boys or old men" who simply kept the radio logs up to date, sometimes pointing up an unusual program, but mainly processing network publicity releases. *Variety* could only find thirteen radio editors the regularity of whose constructive comment qualified them for the honorific title "critic."

One former radio executive contends that a basic law of American broadcasting is that no broadcaster cares *at all* about programming—the results of the programs are all that concern him; if the very worst anti-social programming will work, fine. If it is so bad it bothers an articulate minority, well, worry until the critic tires, or dump the troublemaking program.

In conclusion, one could argue that the disappointing achievement of radio drama in America was as much a function of educational myopia as of business Philistinism. Fortunately for us, in this land of second chances, scripts by Corwin and MacLeish are still in print. And one school—the University of Detroit—has had the wit to retape a 25th anniversary performance of MacLeish's "Fall of the City." What a challenge for FM equipped colleges! After another quarter of a century let us hope American radio drama will have a more rewarding tradition to chronicle.

By then maybe we'll have a Martin Esslin commissioning 600 BBC plays a year for two million dollars, providing in effect a farm system, as the British do, for our television and theatre. British theatre is the greatest in the world today not a little because BBC nurtured its nation's writers. English professors in the United States would be well advised to import tapes of Esslin's creators and urge their next generation of students to be Ardens, Weskers, Pinters—instead of the fragile Ivy-Tower sneerers of the 20s, 30s, and 40s. Then they might even find radio the civilized pleasure it is in the Commonwealth countries.

Further Reading: A Selected Bibliography

I. AMERICAN LITERATURE AND THE SPANISH CIVIL WAR: A BIBLIOGRAPHICAL REVIEW

by Warren French

Allen Guttmann correctly observes in *The Wound in the Heart: America and the Spanish Civil War* (1962), "Excepting only the Great Depression and the hostilities that began in September of 1939, no public event of the 1930's mattered so much to so many Americans as did the Spanish Civil War." For nearly six pages, his selected bibliography lists novels, plays, short stories, and poems prompted by the War. Although, as he further points out, interest in the conflict remained high enough to boost the number of American books and pamphlets about it from 600 by 1940 to 2,000 by 1962, none of this large number has concentrated on a detailed analysis of the responses of only our imaginative writers. (Guttmann analyzes all kinds of statements about the War; John M. Muste's *Say That We Saw Spain Die: Literary Consequences of the Spanish Civil War* [1966] reviews both British and American creative works.)

Furthermore, only eight of the many productions that Guttmann lists were full-length novels—Upton Sinclair's *No Pasaran!* (1937), John Dos Passos's *Adventures of a Young Man*, Charles Yale Harrison's *Meet Me on the Barricades*, Helen Nicholson's *The Painted Bed*, William Rollins, Jr.'s *The Wall of Men* (all 1938),

Frances Parkinson Keyes's *The Great Tradition* (1939), Michael Blankfort's *The Brave and the Blind* and Ernest Hemingway's *For Whom the Bell Tolls* (both 1940). Even if we add Upton Sinclair's later *Wide Is the Gate* (1943—part of his "Lanny Budd" series describing the adventures through the 1930's and 1940's of an incredible young political trouble-shooter), the total is surprisingly small in view of the enormous American emotional investment in the conflict. Even more curiously, only Hemingway's of all these novels has any continuing reputation as a work of art; and even its title to such distinction is challenged by John M. Muste, who avers that "something like pinnacles" were created out of "the red blood" of the War only in George Orwell's *Homage to Catalonia*, a handful of British poems, and a single Hemingway short story, "Old Man at the Bridge." (We might appropriately notice at this point that despite continued promotional efforts of enthusiasts for James Gould Cozzens's *Guard of Honor* and John Horne Burns's *The Gallery*, Norman Mailer's *The Naked and the Dead* and Joseph Heller's *Catch-22* are the only novels about World War II to have achieved seemingly assured eminence. Blood seems not the life of fictions.)

I doubt that we shall see many more studies of these novels considered solely as souvenirs of this battle. (Those deeply interested in the War will wish also to read Frederick R. Benson's *Writers in Arms: The Literary Impact of the Spanish Civil War* [1967] and Stanley Weintraub's *The Last Great Cause: The Intellectuals and the Spanish Civil War* [1968]; but both are international in scope, say little of the novels mentioned except Hemingway's and Dos Passos's, and neither supplement nor challenge Guttmann's and Muste's conclusions.) Even Guttmann finds these few—especially *For Whom the Bell Tolls*—difficult to place within his definitive arrangement of American pronouncements about the war into examples of a spectrum of positions ranging from the ultra-violet area beyond the far Right to the infra-red reaches beyond the far Left; and Muste finds—as already suggested—little of lasting value in any of these tales which he more debatably assigns to groups determined apparently by the writers' increasing awareness of the seriousness of their subject. Without agreeing always with Guttmann or Muste, I shall try to suggest briefly the reasons that I do go along with their judgments that little of artistic value was likely to emerge from these imaginative responses to the War and to speculate about the application to this matter of Ronald Sukenick's dictum that "the obligation of fiction is to rescue experience from history, from politics, from commerce, from theory, even from language itself—from any system, in fact, that threatens to distort, devitalize, or manipulate experience" *(New Literary History,* Winter, 1975).

There is more than meets the eye to Guttmann's brilliantly orchestrated study: what he tries to establish is the range of American positions toward the War and what emerges from between the lines is that these positions were generally not based—even when taken by Americans actually visiting Spain—upon the political realities of the situation, but rather upon American nativist mythologies of religion.

Beginning with the difficult-to-dispute assumption that Spain suffered as the first battleground between the Fascist and Communist forces that were to struggle subsequently for the control of other European countries, Guttmann establishes that in thoughtful quarters in the United States (actually the majority of Americans were ignorant of the conflict or indifferent to it and violently isolationist in their sentiments), the War was generally viewed as a religious struggle in which one—depending upon his preconceptions—saw the Roman Catholic Church as either the last Christian bulwark against an advancing tide of Communism or else an inquisitorial hierarchy bent upon regaining by the illegal use of violence its slipping grasp on its last European stronghold.

As Guttmann observes, the division of Americans over the Spanish Civil War followed quite rigid lines that changed scarcely at all during the three years of active conflict between July 17, 1936 and April 1, 1939. Except for a tiny handful of occultists and organized Fascist sympathizers, Franco's rebels were supported only by the Roman Catholic hierarchy and those of its congregation it could keep in line. Most other "conservative" groups and publications at first leaned toward Franco as a Communist deterrent, but quickly became uneasy about his methods, especially his pioneering use of the aerial bombardment of civilian populations. The culmination of this policy in the raid on the Basque city of Guernica on April 28, 1937, crystallized American opposition and even "for many Catholics . . . destroyed Franco's claim to moral superiority" (Guttmann, p. 49).

Active support for the Loyalists was confined, however, principally to two groups: the American Communist Party (along with some quarreling Leftist splinter groups) and the liberal intellectual community concentrated—then as now—almost altogether in New England and the major Northeastern cities. The hinterland remained almost monolithically isolationist, opposed to any involvement in European affairs regardless of what political, religious or humanitarian concerns might be involved.

Some figures that Guttmann quotes from the four Gallup polls taken during the War summarize the story: 24 to 34 percent of those queried registered "No opinion." Generally this response came from the unemployed, unskilled workers, and Southerners. (In one poll,

44 percent of the Southerners expressed "no opinion" in contrast to only 20 percent of those queried in the Middle Atlantic states.) The sharpest differences, however, were along religious lines. In one poll, 39 percent of the Catholics were for Franco, but only nine percent of the Protestants and two percent of the Jews. "No American Catholic magazine supported the Republic," Guttmann observes (p. 203), and only the *Catholic Worker* and *Commonweal* (at the expense of a great loss in circulation) failed to support the rebels.

The vast majority of taste-making publications were, of course, at that time still in the hands of the pro-Loyalist Northeastern WASP Establishment (though this term was then unknown). Some four-hundred American writers questioned for the pamphlet *Writers Take Sides* (1938) almost unanimously vehemently supported the Republic, and the only response classified as "pro-Franco"—a rambling tirade by the aging Gertrude Atherton—proves upon disinterested scrutiny to express a then unfashionable "curse on both houses" such as might have been voiced by any of the millions of Americans who protested vigorously any time that President Franklin D. Roosevelt even hinted that there might be reason to modify a Neutrality Act that flatly forbade the shipment of supplies to either side or to neutral countries for transshipment to Spain. As Guttmann points out the only American novelist of "any merit whatsoever" to take Franco's side was the Baroness de Zglinitzki, better known as Helen Nicholson. The attitude that characterized the liberal intellectual community appears best summarized in the statement of literary critic-historian Joseph Warren Beach, which Guttmann in introducing his book quotes from *Writers Take Sides:*

> Since the beginning of the civil war in Spain, I have been for the Loyalist Government, because it is the legal, duly constituted government, because it represents republican and representative institutions as opposed to arbitrary and dictatorial rule, because it represents the economic and cultural interests of the great body of the population, and because it gives the greatest hope for a modern and effective organization of society.

Guttmann believes, however, that the community that shared these honorable sentiments was naively hoodwinked by Communist duplicity. Communist appeals to Americans at the time surprisingly "*avoided* the precedents of the Bolshevik experience" and raised instead battle cries "resonant with the rhetoric of the American revolution," in a "conscious attempt to persuade people that Communism was, indeed, 'twentieth-century Americanism,'" a technique that ultimately led ingenuous liberals to the kind of "excessive disillusionment and skepticism" that characterizes John Dos Passos's *Adventures of a Young Man* (Guttmann, pp. 144-52).

This novel, like *For Whom the Bell Tolls,* is sharply critical of what the author regards as the betrayal of the liberal cause of the Loyalists by Communist units in Spain, especially Barcelona. The difference between the novelists, however, is that Dos Passos's disillusionment in Spain did not lead to his general disillusionment with or enlightenment about the self-seeking of all political activity, but rather to a pathetic drifting through the rest of his life toward Rightist positions as he sought to recover traditional American values and some system in which he could put his faith (a drifting accompanied by a shocking deterioration in the quality of his fiction).

Hemingway was inspired, on the other hand, toward a break with any restrictive systems of thought; and Guttmann—as already noted—is obliged to place *For Whom the Bell Tolls* (which has proved a trial to many categorical critics) outside his generally clearly demarcated categories. In an analysis entitled "Ernest Hemingway's Vision of 'Mechanized Doom,'" Guttmann reads the novel as evidence that for its author, the Spanish Civil War was, "among other things, a struggle waged by men close to the earth and to the values of a primitive society against men who had turned away from the earth, men who had turned to the machine and to the antithetical values of an aggressive and destructive mechanical order" (p. 175). Guttmann finds this perception of the Spanish War "as the opposition of man and machine," not limited to Hemingway, but characteristic of the work of many other writers including even the pro-Franco Helen Nicholson, as well as of a long American tradition deploring technological threats to the American dream of an organic relationship between man and nature.

Guttmann believes Hemingway's picture at the end of the novel of Robert Jordan "crippled and alone, waiting for the onslaught of the newest *conquistadores*" successful at least as a mirror reflecting the United States' image of its "own unquiet desperation" at the impossibility of a primitive vision in a repressive technological mass society. Muste, on the other hand, finds the novel ultimately a failure, because he considers "unsatisfactory" its theme, which he identifies as ostensibly "the oneness of mankind" celebrated in the title, which makes this war "worth fighting and winning." But "when everything is finished," Muste goes on to argue, "the theme of the novel is more like the old Hemingway lesson that it is futile to kick against the pricks" and that "the only consolations that can legitimately be given to Robert Jordan are the purely personal ones" (p. 118). Muste prefers the short story, "Old Man at the Bridge," which he describes as the only one of all Hemingway's writings about this war in which the novelist was "able to objectify his view . . . without violating in any way his own artistic sensibility." The "text" of the story, Muste finds to be that which Hemingway attempted to communicate directly in a speech in his play *The Fifth Column*—"You do it so men will not have to fear ill health or old age." He prefers the short story because since "the text is only implied, the moral does not obtrude" (p. 163).

In view of these judgments it is not surprising to find Muste winding up his inspection tour with the observation that "the literature with which this study has been concerned may well have been the final attempt in British and American literature to comprehend the violent nature of the modern world in terms of a political ideology" (p. 194). (Frederick Benson in *Writers in Arms* reaches the related conclusion that "With the defeat of the Spanish Republic the accompanying disillusionment impelled many writers to reject politics completely.") Muste thinks that the pattern of our literature "for the foreseeable future" will be attempts either —like Stephen Spender's—"to shore personal fragments against public ruins, hoping with fingers crossed that the chaos will not immediately destroy the private order" or else—like T. S. Eliot's— to "attempt to order the human experience in terms of a religious view which makes this world itself ephemeral" (p. 194). Neither alternative makes Muste happy, as is evident from his earlier stricture that while "a larger share of the responsibility must rest with the politicians and businessmen," "the writers and other intellectuals must bear a share of the responsibility for their future to formulate" a credible ideology for Western civilization, "based upon our experience and responsive to the demands of our position in the world," a task which he considers "logically theirs" (p. 193).

Such a "logical" bias makes Muste's pedantic study almost useless as an aid to understanding what happened in our literature under the impact of the disillusioning political blows of the 1930's. He writes in the moralistic "genteel" tradition of the late nineteenth century, which one supposed had been entirely discredited not by World War II, but by World War I and such an epochal work as T. S. Eliot's *The Waste Land*. Muste's view is at the farthest extreme from that presented by Ronald Sukenick in the quotation near the beginning of this review, that "the obligation of fiction is to rescue experience from history, from politics, from commerce, from theory." Muste sees its obligation, quite to the contrary, as that subjection of experience to politics and theory that has not only threatened but achieved the devitalization of experience. Muste's praise for "Old Man at the Bridge" as making points without explicitly stating them indicates his preference for a deviously clever packaging of the same tired old merchandise.

One responds not with agreement but a genuine feeling of warmth for those honest old fabulists who clearly labeled their morals "morals" and spelled them out so that one couldn't mistake them. One also sympathizes, however, when Muste indicates the world-weariness that has characterized the diminishing band of adherents to the "genteel tradition" by his acknowledgement that "it is difficult to blame the intelligentsia for looking outside their society to religion and myth for means of ordering at least their private visions" (p. 193).

A book written say immediately after the Spanish debacle and the publication of *For Whom the Bell Tolls*, which wrote off as a failure the one possible imaginative classic to emerge from the conflict and scolded writers and *other* intellectuals (the term is Muste's and I italicize it to call attention to his concept of the writer) for their failure to come up with a "credible ideology" to forestall the long-prophesied "decline of the West," might be invaluable—however old-fashioned its view—as evidence of a significant part of the intellectual climate of the times; but such a book published in 1966, at the height of President Lyndon Johnson's very troubles with a "credibility gap" in American handling of the Viet Namese adventure, has only the most limited value as an example of the very anachronistic attitudes so much responsible for our unhappy involvement in Southeast Asia. In short, *Say That We Saw Spain Die* adds nothing indispensable to Guttmann's *The Wound in the Heart*. Those concerned about housing a library may be relieved to know that a single book adequately records the generally uncomplicated American literary responses to the Spanish Civil War.

Nor does any supplement seem needed. Although Guttmann's commitment to "Northeastern liberalism" is apparent, he gives judicious consideration and adequate space to all of the positions taken in print toward the conflict during its course. He is not, like Muste, arguing what writers should have done, but rather surveying what they did in a style that as a result of his own vivid intellectual commitment is more lively and readable than that generally found in such useful cataloguings of opinion. If any further consideration of the materials that he deals with is needed, it is not another sifting of the ashes, but a Phoenix-like rising from them to wing—as Guttmann begins to do very cautiously near the end of his book— "Forward from Liberalism."

He uses the quoted words as the title of a chapter that, among other things, touches briefly upon the contribution to the debate over Spain of some anarchist journals, observing that this exchange "went unnoticed in the liberal press," because anarchism "is not a tendency that great numbers of Americans have felt very strongly." He adds, however, that "in a sense this is a great pity, for the anarchists' analyses of the Spanish war were sometimes more informed and cogent than the liberals' naive comments upon Spain's complete religious freedom and dedication to capitalism" (p. 139). Since journals like *Man!* exercised little influence, Guttmann does not linger over this debate. He wrote, however, in the early 1960's when the Kennedy administration occasioned some resurgence of artists' faith in American politics; later he might have felt moved to devote more space to whatever tiny visionary handful regarded collaboration with expedient governments as "capitulation."

In *The Social Novel at the End of an Era*, I have earlier advanced an interpretation of *For Whom the Bell Tolls* that I think worth recalling here. Rather than viewing the novel simply as a presentation of the experience of "man against machine," I see it as a vision of the individual against any organized system that simply exploits machines as efficient vehicles to its own ends.

Many were surprised when Hemingway's novel appeared to find this writer who had in *A Farewell to Arms* voiced a famous mistrust of all abstractions and celebrated the individual who made "a separate peace" apparently making a total about-face by advocating an individual's espousing a cause—even at the cost of his life. Generally these same readers had difficulty rationalizing Hemingway's presentation of the commitment of atrocities by the Loyalist side that he was supporting and his vicious attack on the Communist bureaucrat André Marty, who was also aiding the Republic.

My argument is that both of these difficulties arise from a misreading of the novel by those determined to find in it support for the Loyalist cause, even though this cause had ceased to exist by the time that the novel appeared. This pious misinterpretation has resulted in the novel's being most often regarded as a valedictory for a lost cause, though such a reading runs counter to the implications of the title taken from John Donne's injunction, "Send *not* to ask for whom the bell tolls." Actually, I argue, *For Whom the Bell Tolls* represents not an about-face from *A Farewell to Arms*, but an unprecedented extension of the earlier novel's pattern that like anything unprecedented caught by surprise those whom John Steinbeck once branded "expecters." "Whereas the disillusioned Frederic Henry at last declares 'a separate peace,'" I maintain, "the more sophisticated Robert Jordan attempts to carry on 'a separate war.'" He attempts to fight alongside the Loyalists without becoming more than technically associated with them. Hemingway had not, I conclude, "in the final analysis lost any of the suspicions of high-sounding abstractions that Frederic Henry expresses in *A Farewell to Arms*. He did not insist that the Spanish Republic should have been helped in the sacred name of liberty or justice;

he resorted rather to the individual's primitive fear of being left all alone and he extolled through his portrait of Robert Jordan, the individual who was willing to sacrifice himself rather than permit others to suffer the fate of the abandoned." This is a book "without politics." It is a work that seems to me years before Ronald Sukenick's dictum to fulfill what he considers "the obligation of fiction . . . to rescue experience from history, from politics" and to present an account of that experience that remains vital and unambiguous long after any specific political contexts have disappeared and the seeming ambiguities of the narrative can be perceived as the confusion of readers who expect the novel to brood over the wreckage of the past rather than move beyond it (as Whitman, for example, insisted on doing in an analogous situation in "When Lilacs Last in the Door Yard Bloom'd"). That the only substantial work of seemingly enduring artistic value that uses as a backdrop an episode that roused such fierce political passions as the Spanish Civil War is a novel "without politics" strikes me as an extraordinary clue to clarifying the generally confused attitudes about the relationship between politics and art. (Muste observes that Robert Jordan's war aims "at no time . . . relate specifically to the war in Spain or to the Spanish people" [p. 111], but only as an example of their vagueness.)

During the years since the Spanish Civil War there has been an undeniable decline in interest in imaginative literature. I think that much of this decline can be attributed to the feeling of people like Muste that writers are intellectuals who have failed in their task of creating a "credible ideology." I think that if such ideologies are what readers seek from fictions, their importance in our lives will continue to decline and that the current partiality for nonfiction will increase. I think, however, that fiction has quite another function to serve. If, as Muste theorizes, the imaginative works he studies, "may well have been the final attempt in British and American literature to comprehend the violent nature of the modern world in terms of a political ideology," I think that we should really welcome the end of an ill-advised struggle, even if this event should signal—as, for the time being, it seems to have—a marked decline in the importance to our lives we assign imaginative literature.

As Ronald Sukenick suggests, I think that the "obligation" of fiction is to rescue our individual experience from the distortion, devitalization, and manipulation of ideologies—possibly credible but generally otherwise—to offer, in short, a purely personal consolation to those aware of the need for one and the difficulty of finding it in an increasingly "systematized" world. (I should add that I am quite skeptical about the ability of any intellectual endeavor to

238

produce a "credible ideology," if by *credible* we mean anything like "irrefutably in accordance with some 'natural' system.")

What we learn finally from the literature about the Spanish Civil War is that the place to learn about that war—should we wish to do so—is not from imaginative literature; the only important relationship of this particular episode to such writings is its after-math having inspired possibly a single novel that provides a spring-board for transcending the episode. The real American tragedies of the Spanish conflict are its revelations of the shocking number of people in our complicated and closely-knit world who remained "pre-political"—who had no opinions at all about sharply demar-cated ideological positions (one cannot escape bonds he does not comprehend)—and of the almost total want at that time of artists who were "post-political." Of all those who concerned themselves with the Spanish Civil War, only Hemingway apparently combined a vision adequate to transcend the paralysis of defeat with an ability to project this vision in literary form. Distressingly few others, I should add, possessed the ability to participate under-standingly in his achievement. Even yet most inquirers send to ask for *whom else* the bell tolls. Far from having become a museum piece keeping alive the fading memory of a lost cause, *For Whom the Bell Tolls* remains our still generally underappreciated legacy from this dark time. It should be read like all still meaningful fiction with an eye to what lies ahead, not what lies behind it.

II. PICTURE OF THE DECADE

by Jackson R. Bryer

Study of the 1930's has become fashionable, and books about the decade abound. For a guide through the voluminous literature concerning the Franklin D. Roosevelt administrations, as well as indispensable assistance in beginning any depth study of American literary history, consult Howard Mumford Jones and Richard M. Ludwig, *Guide to American Literature and Its Backgrounds* (Fourth Edition, Revised, 1972). For a detailed checklist of the major books written about and during the 1930's, see Thomas Bonner, Jr., "A Bibliographical Introduction to the American Litera-ture of the 1930's and the Backgrounds," *Bulletin of Bibliography*, April-June, 1974 (Volume 31), pp. 57-66, 70.

Most recent books—many by writers who did not experience the 1930's—stress the Depression and the outbreak of World War II at the expense of other matters that preoccupied those living through the period as escapes from these haunting subjects. The books that give the best sense of the period—and provide still the most readable accounts of it—are Frederick Lewis Allen's *Since Yesterday* (1940), an anecdotal and unscholarly review of popular concerns during the decade, and his *The Big Change* (1952), which places these matters in the larger context of the changes in American culture during the first half of the twentieth century. Allen's reminiscences are usefully supplemented by those of representative Chicagoans who survived the decade in Studs Terkel's *Hard Times: An Oral History of the Great Depression* (1970).

The paste-and-scissors men have also been busy reconstructing montages of the decade from scattered contemporary accounts. By far the most comprehensive of these assemblages is Don Congdon's *The Thirties: A Time to Remember* (1962), which opens with John Steinbeck's "As I Remember the Thirties," which is followed by more than six-hundred pages of articles, editorials, and editorial commentary, presenting every major issue and many passing concerns of the decade from a variety of viewpoints. A similar account from a single source is Cabell Phillips's *From the Crash to the Blitz, 1929-1939* (1969), which is drawn entirely from the *New York Times*.

Still the most vivid of these compilations is *The Aspirin Age— 1919-1941*, edited by Isabel Leighton (1949), "a story of America between two wars, told in terms of the most significant, or typical, or utterly fantastic news events of the gaudy and chaotic years that separated Versailles from Pearl Harbor." Of the twenty-two long, original, chronologically arranged essays by distinguished writers, those dealing with the 1930's are Wallace Stegner on Father Coughlin, Arthur M. Schlesinger, Jr. on "The First Hundred Days of the New Deal," Keith Munro on the Dionne Quintuplets, William McFee on the sinking of the *Morro Castle*, Hodding Carter on Huey Long, Margaret Case Harriman on the royal romance of England's Edward VIII and Mrs. Wallis Simpson, Howard Fast on the Republic Steel strike of 1937, and Charles Jackson on Orson Welles's "Invasion from Mars" radio program.

Dixon Wecter's *The Age of the Great Depression—1929-1941* (1949) is a more conventional history by a single able writer. Wecter's chapter on "Reading, Writing, and Revolution" is supplemented by Leo Gurko's *The Angry Decade* (1947), a primarily "social and literary account" that also contains useful information on political and economic developments and an especially useful bibliography. A longer perspective on the period is provided in Robert Bendiner's *Just Around the Corner: A Highly Selective History of the Thirties* (1968) and *The Strenuous Decade: A Social and Intellectual Record of the 1930's* (1970), edited by Bendiner and Daniel Aaron (author of *Writers on the Left*).

The most comprehensive intellectual history of the decade is Richard H. Pells's *Radical Visions and American Dreams: Culture and Social Thought in the Depression Years* (1973). One of the leading literary intellectuals, Edmund Wilson, has also left his own account of the period in *The American Jitters: A Year of the Slump* (1932) and *The American Earthquake: A Documentary of the Twenties and Thirties* (1964). Another useful supplement to Pell's history is Arthur and Lila Weinberg's *Passport to Utopia: Great Panaceas in American History* (1968), which covers the whole span of our history but is especially useful in the study of the 1930's because of its inclusion of statements of the theories of Upton Sinclair, Huey Long, Father Coughlin, Dr. Francis Townsend, and Father Divine. A specially useful history of one political movement of the period is Sander A. Diamond's *The Nazi Movement in the United States, 1924-41*, described as "definitive" in Leo Ribuffo's useful overview of this and related works in *American Quarterly*, October 1974 (Volume 26), pp. 417-32.

Pictorial histories of the decade are being bounteously provided by Time-Life Books, *American Heritage,* and similar purveyors of simplified history. Volume Four of *This Fabulous Century,* edited by Ezra Bowen (1969) is typical. Somewhat more effective is "The Promise Fulfilled and the Promise Broken," the tenth in a series of thirteen films collectively titled *America,* a very personal history written and narrated for the British Broadcasting Corporation by Alistair Cooke. A most serious and moving photographic history of the Depression years is Dorothea Lange and Paul S. Taylor's *An American Exodus: A Record of Human Erosion in the Thirties* (1969).

III. THE LITERARY CULTURE OF THE 1930's

The earliest study concerned exclusively with the literature of the 1930's—and still one of a very few to be this specifically focused is Halford E. Luccock's *American Mirror—Social, Ethical and Religious Aspects of American Literature 1930-1940* (1940), which is organized around the forms of writing typical of the decade and comments briefly on not only still well-remembered writers, but many whose reputations have faded like J. P. Marquand, Pearl Buck, Albert Halper, Josephine Herbst, Sidney Kingsley, and Muriel Rukeyser. It is uniquely supplemented by Edmund Wilson's *The Shores of Light: A Literary Chronicle of the Twenties and Thirties* (1952), a collection of the outstanding critic's writings during the period. Harvey Swados's *The American Writer and the Great Depression* (1966) seeks to convey the impact of the 1930's on the life and thought of the American people and to present "a cross section of good writing of the period." Another popular collection of similar specimens of the creative writing of the period is *Years of Protest* (1967), edited by Jack Salzman.

Remembered and forgotten radical writers of the period are well represented in *Proletarian Literature in the United States,* edited by Granville Hicks and others (1935) and the later *New Masses: An Anthology of the Rebel Thirties* (1969), edited by Joseph North, one of the contributors to the earlier book. Hicks also provides a Marxist critic's views of these and other writers of the Thirties in *The Great Tradition: An Interpretation of American Literature Since the Civil War* (Revised Edition, 1935). More disinterested scholarly approaches to these writers are Walter Rideout's *The Radical Novel in the United States, 1900-1954* (1956) and Daniel Aaron's *Writers on the Left—Episodes in American Literary Communism* (1961).

FICTION

As is evident even from the above-mentioned studies of radical literature, fiction was the dominant literary genre during the 1930's and studies of the novels of the period far outnumbered general studies or analyses of other genres. Still unsupplanted are three major studies of this fiction that appeared immediately after the end of the decade: Joseph Warren Beach's *American Fiction—1920-1940* (1941), Maxwell Geismar's *Writers in Crisis: The American Novel, 1925-1940* (1942), and Alfred Kazin's *On Native Grounds* (1942), which stresses the impact of the Depression on the writer. (Kazin has since reminisced about his own experiences as a beginning writer during the period in *Starting Out in the Thirties* [1965]).

Most other histories of the novel cover much greater time spans. A useful list of these may be found in Blake Nevius's *The American Novel: Sinclair Lewis to the Present* (Goldentree Bibliographies, 1970); but special attention should be called to two contributions to a multi-volume history of the American literature of the first half of the twentieth century—Frederick J. Hoffman's *The Modern Novel in America, 1900-1950* (1951) and Ray B. West, Jr's *The Short Story in America, 1900-1950* (1952)—because of the distinction of the critics chosen to prepare these retrospective studies. Valuable views of this fiction from a foreign viewpoint are also found in Walter Allen's *Tradition and the Dream: The English and American Novel from the Twenties to Our Time* (1964), by a British critic who has written most perceptively of the whole history of the British and American novel, and Claude-Edmond Magny's

The Age of the American Novel: The Film Aesthetic of Fiction Between the Two Wars, a French study published in 1948, but not translated into English until 1972.

Of extraordinary interest are two collections of principally original essays on two of the most popular subgenres of the period, *Proletarian Writers of the Thirties* and *Tough Guy Writers of the Thirties,* both edited by David Madden (1968). (Madden contributes the essay on James M. Cain to this book.) Walter Wells's *Tycoons and Locusts: A Regional Look at Hollywood Fiction of the 1930's* (1973) is a single critic's study of another subgenre that overlaps those surveyed by Madden. The most intensively focused study of several writers in a subgenre is Warren French's *The Social Novel at the End of an Era* (1966), which discusses Faulkner's *The Hamlet,* Hemingway's *For Whom the Bell Tolls,* Steinbeck's *The Grapes of Wrath* and other related novels published in 1939 and 1940.

Two collections reprint especially important essays on major novelists of the period: *Modern American Fiction: Essays in Criticism,* edited by Walton Litz (1963) and *The Modern American Novel: Essays in Criticism,* edited by Max Westbrook (1966).

So much has been written about individual novelists of the 1930's that only those books most basic to the study of the writers can be mentioned here. Criticism of some of the most significant novelists—Sherwood Anderson, Willa Cather, William Faulkner, F. Scott Fitzgerald, Ernest Hemingway, John Steinbeck, and Thomas Wolfe—is reviewed by authorities on their work in *Sixteen Modern American Authors,* edited by Jackson R. Bryer (1974). These accounts are annually supplemented in review-essays in *American Literary Scholarship.* The invaluable periodical, *Modern Fiction Studies,* has also devoted special issues containing original articles and extensive bibliographies to several of the novelists discussed in this volume: Faulkner (Spring 1967), Fitzgerald (Spring 1961), Hemingway (Autumn 1968), Steinbeck (Spring 1965) and Wolfe (Autumn 1965).

JAMES M. CAIN—The standard study is *James M. Cain* (1970) by David Madden, who has also written about Cain for this book and others.

JOHN DOS PASSOS—Serious study of Dos Passos did not really begin until after his death in 1970. Melvin Landsberg's *Dos Passos' Path to "U.S.A.": A Political Biography, 1912-1936* (1973) begins the account of his life, and Townsend Ludington's *The Fourteenth Chronicle: Letters and Diaries of John Dos Passos* (1973) incorporates these documents into a biographical narrative. *Dos Passos, the Critics, and the Writer's Intention* (1971), edited by Allen Belkind collects seventeen criticisms of his work.

WILLIAM FAULKNER—The official biography is Joseph Blotner's two-volume *Faulkner: A Biobraphy* (1974). Most frequently cited of the many books about Faulkner are Cleanth Brooks's *William Faulkner: The Yoknapatawpha Country* (1963, the first of two projected volumes), Michael Millgate's *The Achievement of William Faulkner* (1966), and the late Olga Vickery's *The Novels of William Faulkner* (Revised Edition, 1964). An indispensable accompaniment to reading Faulkner is Martin J. Dain's collection of photographs *Faulkner's County: Yoknapatawpha* (1964).

F. SCOTT FITZGERALD—Fitzgerald has attracted many biographers but it is unlikely that anyone will add substantially to Arthur Mizener's *The Far Side of Paradise* (1951, revised 1965) and Andrew Turnbull's *Scott Fitzgerald* (1962), although Sheilah Graham's *Beloved Infidel* (1958) is uniquely valuable. These accounts are supplemented by Turnbull's controversial edition of *The Letters of F. Scott Fitzgerald* (1963). The most perceptive criticism remains that of Fitzgerald's "rediscoverer," James E. Miller, Jr., in *F. Scott Fitzgerald: His Art and His Technique* (1964, revised from *The Fictional Technique of Scott Fitzgerald* [1957]). A uniquely valuable compilation of criticisms by Jackson R. Bryer is *The Critical Reputation of F. Scott Fitzgerald: A Bibliographical Essay* (1967), a virtually complete listing of 2,100 items, almost all annotated.

ERNEST HEMINGWAY—Princeton University's Carlos Baker has made his name practically synonymous with Hemingway study. Baker is author of both the fullest account of the novelist's life, *Ernest Hemingway: A Life Story* (1969) and the most frequently cited and revised critical study of the author, *Hemingway: The Writer as Artist* (1952; Fourth Revised Edition, 1972). Baker's principal rival is Philip Young, whose popular *Ernest Hemingway* also appeared in 1952 and was revised in 1966. Both critics have written many shorter works about Hemingway. Many of the most able critics of the novelist gathered at a symposium at Oregon State University in 1973; the papers that they presented are collected in *Hemingway In Our Time*, edited by Richard Astro and Jackson Benson (1974).

HENRY MILLER—Of much written about Miller, only Kingsley Widmer's *Henry Miller* (1963) is an attempt at a dispassionate scholarly assessment. More highly opinionated essays are gathered in *Henry Miller and the Critics*, edited by George Wickes (1963) and *Henry Miller: Three Decades of Criticism*, edited by Edward B. Mitchell (1971).

JOHN STEINBECK—An official biography by Jackson Benson is underway, and Steinbeck's widow, Elaine, is editing his letters for publication in 1975. The basic criticisms remain Peter Lisca's *The Wide World of John Steinbeck* (1958), Warren French's *John Steinbeck* (1961, Revised Edition 1975), and Joseph Fontenrose's *John Steinbeck: An Introduction and Interpretation* (1963). Earlier criticisms are collected in *Steinbeck and His Critics: A Record of Twenty-Five Years*, edited by E. W. Tedlock, Jr., and C. V. Wicker (1957). A guide to other works is Tetsumaro Hayashi's *A New Steinbeck Bibliography* (1973). Professor Hayashi has also edited the very useful *A Study Guide to Steinbeck: A Handbook to His Major Works* (1974) and is founder-editor of the *Steinbeck Quarterly*.

NATHANAEL WEST—The most imaginative and admirable book about West—or virtually any other recent writer—and a model for similar collections is *Nathanael West: The Cheaters and the Cheated*, edited by David Madden (1973) from essays entered in a competition sponsored by the *Southern Review*, accompanied by "A Confluence of Voices" of West and his friends and critics, arranged by Madden. The official biography is *Nathanael West: The Art of His Life* (1970) by Jay Martin, who also edited *Nathanael West: A Collection of Critical Essays* (1971).

THOMAS WOLFE—C. Hugh Holman in *Sixteen Modern American Authors* calls "the three essential collections of factual data" about Wolfe *Thomas Wolfe: A Biography* by his agent Elizabeth Nowell (1960), her edition of *The Letters of Thomas Wolfe* (1956), and Richard S. Kennedy's account of the composition and publication of Wolfe's work, *The Window of Memory: The Literary Career of Thomas Wolfe* (1962). Holman also admires Andrew Turnbull's biography *Thomas Wolfe* (1968), for creating "a convincing and living image of the man," and Louis D. Rubin, Jr.'s *Thomas Wolfe: The Weather of His Youth* (1955). Notable shorter introductions are Holman's *Thomas Wolfe* in the University of Minnesota pamphlet series (1960) and Richard Walser's *Thomas Wolfe: An Introduction and Interpretation* (1961).

RICHARD WRIGHT—The standard biography of this outstanding Black writer is Constance Webb's *Richard Wright: A Biography* (1968), written with his approval and assistance; but a more generally useful account is Michel Fabre's *The Unfinished Quest of Richard Wright* (1973), translated from the French by Isabel Barzun. The most perceptive of a growing number of critical studies of Wright is Keneth Kinnamon's *The Emergence of Richard Wright* (1972). The most valuable of a number of special periodical issues devoted to Wright is a 1969 issue of *CLA Journal* containing a bibliographical essay by Donald B. Gibson (Volume 12, pp. 360-65).

POETRY

Only Amos N. Wilder's *The Spiritual Aspects of the New Poetry* (1940) is focused almost exclusively on the poetry of the 1930's, although Joseph Warren Beach's *Obsessive Images: Symbolism in the Poetry of the 1930's and 1940's* (1960) stresses poets active during the decade. Poet Louise Bogan's *Achievement in American Poetry, 1900-1950* (1951) is part of a distinguished multi-volume series, and Roy Harvey Pearce's *The Continuity of American Poetry* (1961) provides the closest thing to a standard study of the American tradition against which the poetry of the 1930's can be measured. Walter Sutton's *American Free Verse: The Modern Revolution in Poetry* (1973) traces this important movement through its many important manifestations in the United States.

Several books are devoted to the Fugitive and Agrarian movements in the South: John M. Bradbury's *The Fugitives: A Critical Account* (1958), Louise Cowan's *The Fugitive Group: A Literary History* (1959), and John L. Stewart's *The Burden of Time: The Fugitives and Agrarians* (1965).

Under the influence of the New Criticism that flourished from the late 1930's through the 1950's, critics of poetry tended even more noticeably than critics of fiction to write intensive studies of individual artists rather than surveys of schools or movements. *Sixteen Major American Authors* reviews the criticism of five major poets active during the decade—T. S. Eliot (by Richard Ludwig), Robert Frost (by Reginald Cook), Ezra Pound (by John Espey), Wallace Stevens (by Joseph Riddel), and William Carlos Williams (by Linda W. Wagner).

ARCHIBALD MACLEISH—There has been no study to supplement Signi Falk's pioneering *Archibald MacLeish* (1966), except Grover Smith's pamphlet of the same title published in the Minnesota

series on American authors in 1971. MacLeish is also the
subject of a special 1975 issue of *Pembroke Magazine,* edited
by the irrepressible Norman Macleod.

EZRA POUND—The long controversy over this irascible visionary has
precipitated a disproportionate number of writings about him.
Most to be recommended are those by Hugh Kenner, *The
Poetry of Ezra Pound* (1951) and the monumental *The Pound
Era* (1972), which John Espey describes as "Kenner's major
attempt to recreate the literary and personal atmosphere of
the decades dominated by Pound as poet, impresario, and
teacher."

WALLACE STEVENS—There is no biography of this very retiring man
who greatly disliked being "studied," and only a selection of
his letters were edited for publication in 1966 by his daughter
Holley. Samuel French Morse's "long-awaited critical biography," *Wallace Stevens: Poetry as Life* (1970), is described by
Joseph Riddle as "neither a biography nor a significant piece
of criticism." Riddel explains that his own *The Clairvoyant
Eye: The Poetry and Poetics of Wallace Stevens* (1965) is the
most comprehensive of many interpretive books "if only because it presumes to explore the entire body of poetry as well
as the theory of poetry upon which the canon is erected."

DRAMA

Writers about the theatre of the Thirties have concentrated almost
entirely upon the Federal Theatre Project and various left wing
groups. Accounts of the Federal experiment began as early as 1937
with Willson Whitman's polemical *Bread and Circuses: A Study
of the Federal Theatre,* which was followed by Hallie Flannagan's
Arena (1940), recollections of the director of the venture, and
Clarence J. Wittle's *Some Social Trends in the WPA Drama*
(1939). Definitive studies, however, have appeared only recently
in Jane D. Matthews' *The Federal Theatre, 1935-1939* (1971) and
Jerre Mangione's *The Dream and the Deal: The Federal Writers'
Project, 1935-1943* (1973).

Accounts of radical theatre begin even earlier in 1934 with
Virgil Geddes's call for action, *Left Turn for American Drama* and
Ben Blake's *The Awakening of the American Theatre* (1935). These
early studies ended with Joseph Mersand's twenty-page "Modern
Chapbook," *The Drama of Social Significance, 1930-1940* (1940).
The era of appraisal began with Harold Clurman's publication of

his recollections of one of the most important projects of the Thirties, *The Fervent Years: The Story of The Group Theater and the Thirties* (1957). There followed key comprehensive studies— Morgan Y. Himmelstein's *Drama Was a Weapon: The Left Wing Theatre in New York, 1929-1941* (1963) and Gerald Rabkin's *Drama and Commitment: Politics in the American Theatre of the Thirties* (1964). The study still continues with Sam Smiley's *The Drama of Attack: Didactic Plays of the American Depression* (1972).

A contrasting commercial venture is recalled in Roy S. Waldau's *Vintage Years of the Theatre Guild, 1928-1939* (1972), while the period is placed into perspective in Alan S. Downer's *Fifty Years of American Drama, 1900-1950* (1951), and seen from a traditional conservative point of view in Arthur Hobson Quinn's *A History of the American Drama from the Civil War to the Present Day* (Revised Edition, 1955).

The situation in drama is quite different from that in fiction and poetry in that there are many more studies of the genre before World War II than of individual playwrights except Eugene O'Neill. The distinct bias for playwrights with liberal and radical political commitments is obvious not only in general studies, but also in the much greater attention to Lillian Hellman, Clifford Odets, and Robert Sherwood than other popular dramatists of the decade.

LILLIAN HELLMAN—The long neglect of Miss Hellman ended when her autobiography, *An Unfinished Woman, A Memoir* (1969) was closely followed by Richard Moody's *Lillian Hellman, Playwright*, and Lorena Ross Holmin's *The Dramatic Works of Lillian Hellman* (1973).

CLIFFORD ODETS—Four full-length studies of Odets appeared during the first decade of increasing activism since the 1930's: R. Baird Shuman's *Clifford Odets* (1962), Edward Murray's *Clifford Odets: The Thirties and After* (1968), Michael Mendelsohn's *Clifford Odets, Humane Dramatist* (1969), and Gerald Weales's *Clifford Odets, Playwright* (1971). Mendelsohn's account is based on the critic's interviews with the playwright.

EUGENE O'NEILL—John Henry Raleigh writes in *Sixteen Modern American Authors* that "it seems not unlikely that we shall finally know more about O'Neill than any other American writer," as a result of such mammoth studies as Arthur and Barbara Gelb's *O'Neill* (1962, Revised Edition 1973) and

Lewis Sheaffer's two-volume *O'Neill: Son and Playwright* (1968 and 1973). The most recent comprehensive critical study is Travis Bogard's *Contour in Time: The Plays of Eugene O'Neill* (1972), and the most complete critical bibliography is Jordan Y. Miller's *Eugene O'Neill and the American Critic* (1962, Revised Edition 1973).

The only book about Maxwell Anderson is Mabel Driscoll Bailey's *Maxwell Anderson: The Playwright as Prophet* (1957); and Howard R. Floan's *William Saroyan* (1966), the only book about the writer, devotes little space to his plays. One tribute that should be cited to a playwright of the 1930's is John Mason Brown's two-volume *The Worlds of Robert E. Sherwood* (1965 and 1970, the second volume cut short by Brown's death) a comprehensive account of the complex career of a dedicated man whose plays are also studied in Walter Meserve's *Robert E. Sherwood, Reluctant Moralist* (1970).

CRITICISM

The elusive history of the rise of the influential New Criticism has not been tracked down, but the movement is studied along with others of significance in William Van O'Connor's *An Age of Criticism: 1900-1950* (1952). Two principal disseminators of New Critical doctrines, Cleanth Brooks and William K. Wimsatt, Jr., also wrote *Literary Criticism: A Short History* (1957). Still worth seeking out as the most compact guide to these doctrines is W. R. Elton's *Guide to the New Criticism* (1953). Other contributors to the movement and important books about it are listed in Jones and Ludwig's *Guide to American Literature and Its Backgrounds*.

About the Contributors

JACKSON R. BRYER (Bibliography) is Professor of English at the University of Maryland. A graduate of Amherst, he received his doctorate from the University of Wisconsin—Madison. He is the author of *The Critical Reputation of F. Scott Fitzgerald* (1967) and editor of *Sixteen Modern American Authors* (1974), *Dear Scott—Dear Max: The Fitzgerald-Perkins Correspondence* (1971), and other works about Fitzgerald, as well as numerous bibliographical checklists. He contributed articles on the Rodgers-Hammerstein musicals to *The Forties* and on Eugene O'Neill's *Long Day's Journey into Night* to *The Fifties*.

PASCAL COVICI, JR. (John Steinbeck) is Professor of English at Southern Methodist University. All of his degrees are from Harvard. He is the author of *Mark Twain's Humor: The Image of a World* (1962) and editor of the revised edition of *The Portable Steinbeck* (1971). He also wrote on John Steinbeck for *The Fifties*.

WILLIAM FREEDMAN (Henry Roth) is Professor of English at the University of Haifa, Israel. A graduate of Rutgers, he received his Ph.D. from the University of Chicago, where he served on the editorial staff of the *Chicago Review*. Although his dissertation was on *Tristram Shandy*, he has published

249

many articles on twentieth-century American writers, including analyses of Lionel Trilling's novel *The Middle of the Journey* for *The Forties* and Bernard Malamud's fiction for *The Fifties*.

SHELDON NORMAN GREBSTEIN (Hemingway) is Professor of English and Dean of the College of Arts and Sciences of the State University of New York at Binghamton. A graduate of the University of Southern California, he received his doctorate from Michigan State. He has contributed *Sinclair Lewis* (1962) and *John O'Hara* (1966) to the Twayne United States Authors Series and has also published *Hemingway's Craft* (1973) and edited *Monkey Trial* (1960), *Perspectives in Contemporary Criticism* (1968), and *Studies in "For Whom the Bell Tolls"* (1971). He is at work on a book on Jewish-American fiction, also the subject of a series of lectures he has taped. He has written on Nelson Algren for *The Forties* and Hemingway's *The Old Man and the Sea* for *The Fifties*.

ROBERT J. GRIFFIN (Clifford Odets) is Executive Secretary of the University of California—Berkeley Faculty Association. A graduate of George Washington University, he received his doctorate in eighteenth-century literature from Berkeley and has taught at Yale. He has written many articles on eighteenth-century British and modern American literature and has edited *Twentieth Century Interpretations of Sinclair Lewis's "Arrowsmith"* (1968). He contributed an article on Eudora Welty to *The Forties*.

MAX HALPEREN (Ezra Pound) is Professor of English at North Carolina State University. A graduate of the City College of New York, he received his doctorate from Florida State University. He has also written about Pound for *The Twenties* and other publications, and he is Managing Editor of *Southern Poetry Review*.

PATRICK D. HAZARD (Radio Drama) is Professor of English and former Chairman of the Department at Beaver College, Pennsylvania. A graduate of the University of Detroit, he received his doctorate from Western Reserve. Best known for his enthusiastic work on the "newer media," film programs at national professional conventions, and imaginative promotion of Third World Poetry festivals, he has published *A Documentary History of Broadcasting* (1963), *Hawaii* (1964),

Language and Literacy Today (1965), and *TV As Art* (1966), as well as many articles, including a survey of television drama for *The Fifties.*

FREDERICK J. HOFFMAN (Henry Miller), who died suddenly in 1967, was Distinguished Professor of English at the University of Wisconsin—Milwaukee, following appointments at the University of Wisconsin—Madison and the University of California—Riverside. One of the most prolific and respected of American critics, the most important of his many books are *Freudianism and the Literary Mind, The Little Magazine, The Twenties, The Modern Novel in America,* and *The Mortal No.* He published books also on William Faulkner, Conrad Aiken, Samuel Beckett, and Southern fiction; and he had begun an article re-assessing Paul Bowles for *The Forties.*

BLYDEN JACKSON (Richard Wright) is Professor of English and Associate Dean of the Graduate School at the University of North Carolina—Chapel Hill, following appointments as Chairman of the English Department and Dean of the Graduate School at Southern University. A graduate of Wilberforce University, he received his doctorate from the University of Michigan. He has served as Chairman of the College Section of the National Council of Teachers of English and President of the College Language Association. He has co-edited with Louis D. Rubin, Jr., *Black Poetry in America* (1974) and has written many essays on Black writers, including those on Langston Hughes and Jean Toomer in *The Twenties.*

DAN JAFFE (Archibald MacLeish) is Associate Professor of English and Poet in Residence at the University of Missouri—Kansas City. A graduate of Rutgers and the University of Michigan, he has also been a fellow of the Breadloaf Writers' Conference. Most active as a poet, his major work is *Dan Freeman* (1967), the story through a skein of narrative poems of the man honored as the first homesteader. Jaffe is also Editor-in-Chief of Bookmark Press, which published his *The First Tuesday in November* (1971). He has written plays and the libretto for a "jazz opera," as well as many book reviews and essays for all of the "decades" books—on Don Marquis for *The Twenties,* the poetry of World War II for *The Forties,* and Theodore Roethke for *The Fifties.*

JAMES JUSTUS (William Saroyan) is Professor of English at Indiana University. A graduate of the University of Tennessee, he received his doctorate from the University of Washington. He is co-editor of a textbook and is completing a book about Robert Penn Warren, about whom he has written several articles including one for *The Forties*.

SY KAHN (Kenneth Fearing) is Chairman of the Department of Drama and Director of the Pacific Playhouse at the University of the Pacific. A graduate of the University of Pennsylvania, he received his doctorate from the University of Wisconsin—Madison. He has been a Fulbright lecturer in Greece, Poland, and at the University of Vienna and, for several years, has taken his Pacific Players on Christmas holiday tours of Europe. He has published several volumes of poetry: *Our Separate Darkness* (1963), *Triptych* (1964), *A Later Sun* and *The Fight Is with Phantoms* (both 1966), and *Another Time* (1968). His many articles on poetry and drama include contributions to all of the "decades" books—on Glenway Wescott in *The Twenties*, Eugene O'Neill's *The Iceman Cometh* in *The Forties*, and Archibald MacLeish's *J. B.* in *The Fifties*.

DAVID MADDEN (James M. Cain) is Writer-in-Residence at Louisiana State University. A graduate of the University of Tennessee and San Francisco State College, he has worked also at the Yale Drama School. He has published several novels—*Cassandra Singing* (1969), *Brothers in Confidence* (1972) and *Bijou* (1974)—and a collection of short stories, *The Shadow Knows* (1970). He has contributed *Wright Morris* (1964) and *James M. Cain* (1970) to the Twayne United States Authors Series. Some of his most exciting books are the remarkably imaginative ones that he has edited: *Proletarian Writers of the Thirties* and *Tough Guy Writers of the Thirties* (both 1968), *American Dreams, American Nightmares* (1969), *Rediscoveries* (1971, in which other writers celebrate negelected works), *Nathanael West: The Cheaters and the Cheated* (1973), and *Remembering James Agee* (1974). He has also been Assistant Editor of *Kenyon Review* and Associate Editor of *Film Heritage*.

JORDAN Y. MILLER (Maxwell Anderson) is Professor of English and Chairman of the Department at the University of Rhode Island. A graduate of Yale, he received his doctorate from Columbia. He has been a Fulbright lecturer at the University of Bombay. His publications include the valuable textbook, *American Dramatic Literature* (1961), *Eugene O'Neill and the American Critic* (1962, Revised 1973), *Playwright's Progress: O'Neill and the Critics* (1965), and *Twentieth Century Interpretations of "A Streetcar Named Desire"* (1971). He has contributed essays also to all of the "decades" books—on both Expressionism and Eugene O'Neill to *The Twenties*, on the Drama of World War II to *The Forties*, and on Tennessee Williams' cryptic *Camino Real* to *The Fifties*.

GUY OWEN (Southern Poetry) is Professor of English at North Carolina State University and Founder/Editor of *Southern Poetry Review*. He received all of his degrees through the doctorate from the University of North Carolina—Chapel Hill, and he has been a fellow of Yaddo and the Breadloaf Writers' Conference. He has published four critically acclaimed novels —*Season of Fear* (1960), *The Ballad of the Flim-Flam Man* (1965, basis of a memorable movie starring George C. Scott), *Journey for Joedel* (1970), and *The Flim-Flam Man and the Apprentice Grifter* (1972). He has also published two collections of poems—*Cape Fear Country* (1958) and *The White Stallion and Other Poems* (1969) and edited *Modern American Poetry; Essays in Criticism* (1972). He has also contributed an essay on Robert Frost to *The Twenties*.

DAVID G. PUGH (Proletarian Fiction) teaches English and Communications at Western Michigan University. A graduate of Drury College, he has worked at the University of Chicago and the University of Iowa. He has written for all of the "decades" books—on Sinclair Lewis's *Babbitt* for *The Twenties*, on Frederic Wakeman's best-selling *The Hucksters* for *The Forties* and on Elizabeth Spencer's *The Voice at the Back Door* for *The Fifties*.

GERALD RABKIN (Federal Theatre) is Professor of English at Livingston College of Rutgers University. A graduate of Brooklyn College, he received his doctorate in American dramatic literature from Ohio State University. He is the author of *Drama and Commitment: Politics in the American Theatre of the 1930s* and contributed an essay on Thornton Wilder's *The Skin of Our Teeth* to *The Forties*.

GENE RUOFF (New Criticism) is Associate Professor of English at the University of Illinois at Chicago Circle. A graduate of Centre College, he became a Woodrow Wilson Fellow and received his doctorate in British Romantic literature from the University of Wisconsin—Madison. Although he has written most often about Wordsworth, he has—partly because of his Kentucky origins—a strong interest in Southern American literature and he has contributed essays to all of the "decades" books—on Faulkner to *The Twenties,* on Truman Capote to *The Forties,* and on James Agee's *A Death in the Family* to *The Fifties.*

DONALD SHEEHAN (Wallace Stevens) teaches at Franconia College, New Hampshire. A graduate of the University of Florida, he received his doctorate from the University of Wisconsin—Madison and has taught at the University of Chicago. He was managing editor of *Wisconsin Studies in Contemporary Literature.* With David Keller, he has published a group of poems, *Starting-Point* (Francesca Press, 1966), and he has also contributed essays on Wallace Stevens to *The Forties* and *The Fifties.*

JONAS SPATZ (F. Scott Fitzgerald) is Professor of English at the University of Missouri—Kansas City. A graduate of Brooklyn College, he received his doctorate from Indiana University, where his specialization in American literature led to his book *Hollywood in Fiction* (1969). He has since become principally interested in nineteenth-century British literature, but he has contributed essays on Ring Lardner to *The Twenties* and Theodore Dreiser's *The Bulwark* to *The Forties.*

RICHARD WALSER (Thomas Wolfe) became Emeritus Professor of English after a quarter century of distinguished teaching at North Carolina State University. A graduate of the University of North Carolina—Chapel Hill, he was a Guggenheim Fellow in 1957-58. He has been a prolific publisher of perceptive studies of works about North Carolina authors, including *The Enigma of Thomas Wolfe* (1953), *Thomas Wolfe: An Introduction and Interpretation* (1961), *Literary North Carolina* (1970), and *Tarheel Laughter* (1974).

ELEANOR RACKOW WIDMER (John Dos Passos) is a novelist who has taught at the University of California—San Diego. After work at Columbia, she received her doctorate from the University of Washington. She has published *Mister Jack,* a novella, and *Is It an Owl?,* a children's story, and co-edited two anthologies, *Literary Censorship* and *Freedom and Cul-*

ture. She has written for all the "decades" books—on Edith Wharton for *The Twenties,* on Malcolm Lowry for *The Forties,* and on Mary McCarthy for *The Fifties.*

KINGSLEY WIDMER (Nathanael West) is Professor of English at San Diego State University. A graduate of the University of Minnesota, he received his doctorate from the University of Washington and has been a visiting professor at the University of California—Berkeley, Simon Fraser University, and the State University of New York at Buffalo. He has also been a Fulbright lecturer at the University of Tel Aviv and Nice. One of the most prolific and provocative writers about "Modernist" literature, he has published *The Art of Perversity: The Shorter Fiction of D. H. Lawrence* (1962), *Henry Miller* (1963), *The Literary Rebel* (1965), *The Ways of Nihilism: A Study of Herman Melville's Short Novels* (1970), and *The End of Culture: Essays on Sensibility in Contemporary Society* (1975). He has also written articles for the *Village Voice* and many literary and sociological journals on the deterioration of our socio-political culture, including major keynote essays in each of the other "decades" books—on the Boom and Bust in *The Twenties,* on the literary impact of the atomic bomb in *The Forties,* and on the short-lived culture of the Beat Generation in *The Fifties.*

Index

257